Women and Gender in Ancient India

A Study of Texts and Inscriptions

Women and Gender in Ancient India

A Study of Texts and Inscriptions

Vijaya Laxmi Singh

Aryan Books International
New Delhi

Dedicated to

My Grandmother,
Mother &
Mother-in-Law

WOMEN AND GENDER IN ANCIENT INDIA
A Study of Texts and Inscriptions

ISBN: 978-81-7305-517-1

Published in **2015** by
Aryan Books International
Pooja Apartments, 4B, Ansari Road, New Delhi-110 002 (India)
Tel.: 23287589, 23255799; Fax: 91-11-23270385
E-mail: aryanbooks@gmail.com
www.aryanbooks.co.in

Designed and Printed in India by
ABI Prints & Publishing Co., New Delhi.

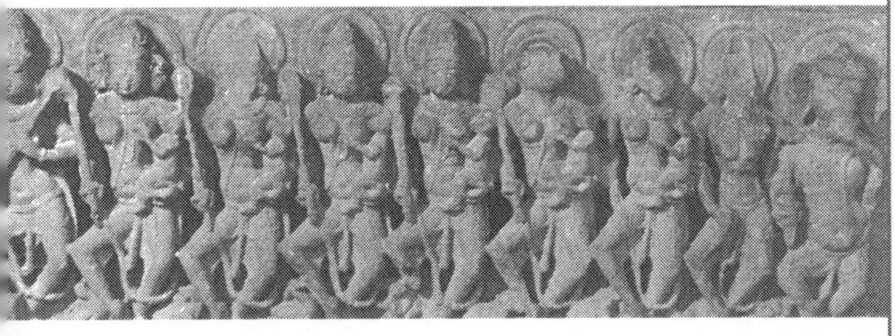

Prologue

This book is based upon the textual and epigraphic materials of early India. The book is based on selected sources. Sources show deviation from both the conjecture made in the post-Altekerian tradition that originated in colonial period but has ample influence on the writings of post-colonial times as well as projection of women in epigraphic records. The results may not be conventional because even though subordination of women is a common feature of almost all stages of history and is prevalent everywhere in the world, the extent and form of that subordination has been conditioned by the social and cultural environment in which women have been placed. Even today, women are often forced to choose between the demanding career clock and ever-ticking biological clock.

To understand the position of women in early India, we have to study women in their wider context. The first chapter is the introductory chapter which deals with two aspects: one entitled 'Historiographical

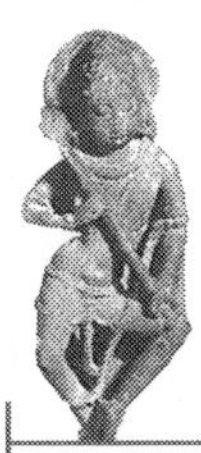

Trends and Perspectives in Indian and Non-Indian Sources for Early Historical Societies' and the second entitled 'Ancient India and the Women Question: Brief Survey from the Earliest Period to Pre-Maurya Period'.

There is a spate of studies on the gender question, some on Buddhist literature. In the second chapter we have tried to explore the women's space in Budhhist society. There is a general belief that history of women in Buddhism is a linear narrative of progress from oppression to liberation. But this is not true as patriarchal value system, often bordering on misogyny, has been quite pronounced in Buddhism. Within this ambit we have to define the place of women and construction of gender in androcentric tradition. Buddhism is paradoxically neither sexist nor as egalitarian as is commonly thought. We notice two kinds of approaches in Buddhist texts; the Buddhist bias against women and attempts to overcome this bias (the canonical texts) and second the active role of Buddhist women to counter the stereotype of women as passive cultural subjects (*Therigatha*).

In the third chapter (i) 'Gender Differentiation and Contentious Feminine Voice of Sita in the *Ramayana*' reflects the condition of India during 4th cent. BC-4th cent. AD. The sex appropriate ideals prominent throughout the *Ramayana* are reflections of the patriarchal values that structured ancient Indian society. We consider the *Ramayana* as post-Mauryan. The centre of attention in Valmiki's composition is literature, whether mythical or real story, it is a reflection of the thoughts prevailing during the Kushana-Gupta period. (ii) *Devi Mahatmya* (*Markandeya Purana*) and mythical and theological traditions of goddess worship in early India is based on the original text *Devi Mahatmya* translated by V.S. Agrawala and its scholarly analysis by Coburn. The purpose of this study is not to deal with religious texts per se, but to consider literary characters presented to us as human, taking part in ordinary human pursuits, albeit in a somewhat extraordinary manner at times, and to discover in them greater or less degree of divine identity or at least evidence of their being special foci of their divine predilection. We find in the lives of these epic women characters, a frequent, sometimes constant intervention of the divine, often at the cost of pain and shame, at other times bringing comfort, reassurance and ultimate glory.

The connections suggested between goddesses and women in Indian society have been questioned. The distinction is made between feminization of certain attributes—righteousness, justice, wealth, earning—

or more accurately their embodiment in the female form, and the elevation of strong and aberrant women with these attributes to divinity. The goddess is a product of the first process, not the second. The implication of this distinction lies in this: that the symbolic valuation of the form is not a reflection of the actual material and the historical condition in which they take shape. A necessary co-relation between powerful goddesses and empowered women would imply simplistic theories of role models and uni-gender projection.

The fourth chapter 'Gendered Identity: The Case of Queen Didda of Historical Kashmir' deals with Kalhana's text *Rajatarangini* where he highlights the power and agency of women in royal court culture in two essential ways—as sovereign rulers in their own right and as powers behind the throne. Power is wrested and executed by them in what is essentially a patriarchal edifice, thus causing a certain amount of tension and ambiguity, not only in specific phases of Kashmir's history but also in Kalhana's portrayal of them. On the other hand, the text makes it very clear that the queen had a very definite political role to play—whether as a part of policy-dictated matrimonial alliances or as a popular choice of wielding power. In this sense, the notion that 'the kingship or the state was associated with the control of women and was an instrument of their subjugation' does not hold true for women in *Rajatarangini.* The question which arises here is that 'Is the force of patrilineal ideology and norms overrated?' 'Have we imputed greater hegemony to patrilineal orthodoxy than is warranted?' Continuous research and close scrutiny of source material is needed to bring real people in the past alive and to arrive at a fresh understanding of the history of women in early Kashmir.

The fifth chapter 'Gender in Inscriptions' discusses women in various inscriptions. The period from the third century BC to the early centuries of Christian era was very important from the point of gendered history of Buddhist/Jaina sites in north India, the testimony of which is seen in the epigraphic data. Hundreds of inscriptions are found at the sites of Mathura, Sanchi, Bharhut.

One of the significant aspects of the societies of Mathura, Sanchi and Bharhut is represented by religious donations of female donors. These donors are also of two categories: (i) queens and women of royal family, (ii) ordinary women. Donations from queens and women of royal family are of course known from the early phases of a few Buddhist sites.

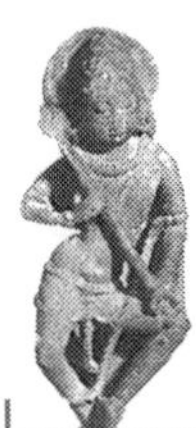

The role of women in the political history of ancient India is confined to royal families and the participation of common women like common men in the state administration has never been dealt with in contemporary history. Thus, the role of common women cannot be ascertained for want of literary or other data though women in the Saka-Kushana period are noticed making small donations for religious causes (Buddhist, Jaina and Brahmanical) as discussed above. Moreover, the Brahmanical social structure little encouraged public life for women. Owing to the lack of sources and the little impact of the common man on the political history in monarchical times, we may conclude that the role of common women cannot be systematically analysed for want of data. But we have ample proof of royal women playing vital role in the state affairs as instruments of political alliance, Queen mothers influencing decisions and acquiring crowns for their sons, Regent Queens (in the event of the death of their king husbands, when their sons were minors), Queen consorts influencing the king at the helm of political affairs and in Kashmir, Queen ruling the state. The approach in traditional historiography is textual and it almost totally excludes epigraphical records. To make real women visible on historical stage, the epigraphic records need to be collected and classified.

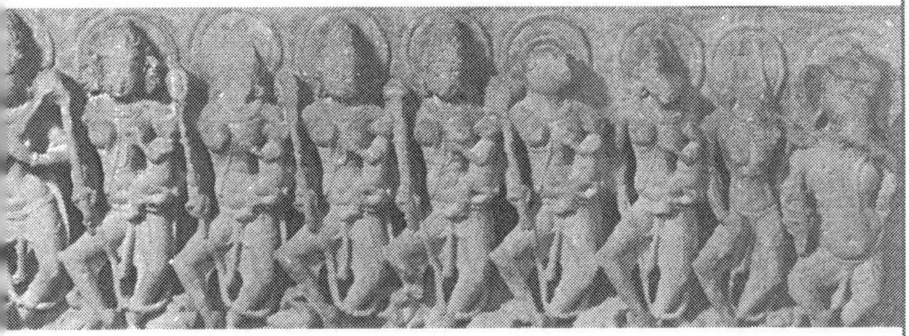

Contents

Prologue *v*

Acknowledgements *xi*

List of Abbreviations *xiii*

List of Illustrations *xv*

I. Women and Gender in History **1**

A. Historiographical Trends and Perspectives in Indian and Non-Indian Sources for Early Historical Societies 1

B. Ancient India and the Women Question: Brief Survey from the Earliest Period to Pre-Maurya Period 14

II. Buddhist Perspective of Women **27**

A. Visibility of Egalitarian Concepts of Buddhism in the Images of Women in the Androcentric Literature (*Therigatha*) 28

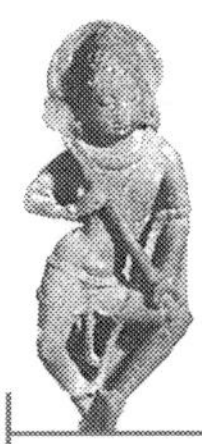

B. Misogynous Literature 42

III. Images of Women in Sanskrit Texts **57**

A. Gender Differentiation and Contentious Feminine Voice of Sita in the *Ramayana* 57

B. *Devi Mahatmya* (*Markandeya Purana*) and Mythical and Theological Tradition of Goddess Worship in Early India 65

IV. Gendered Identity: The Case of Queen Didda of Historical Kashmir **87**

A. Introduction 87

B. Didda as Queen Consort, Regent Queen and the Ruling Queen 92

C. Conclusion 100

V. Gender in Inscriptions **111**

A. Women and Gender in Inscriptions 112

B. Conclusion 135

Epilogue 143

Glossary 145

Bibliography 157

Index 167

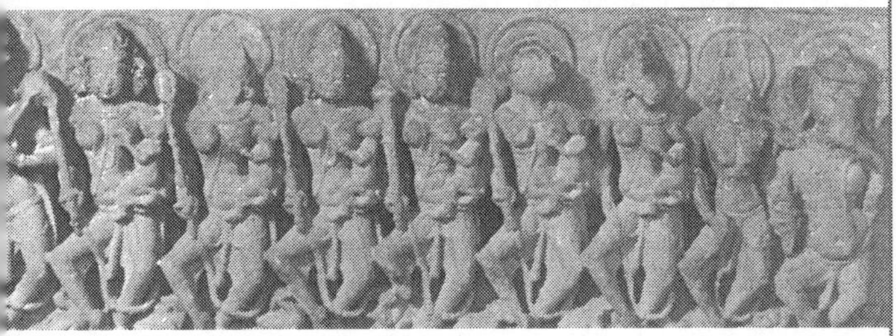

Acknowledgements

In writing this book I have received kind and generous support from a large number of friends and colleagues. I wish to express my thanks to my teacher Prof. B.D. Chattopadhyaya for continuously inspiring me to work. I thank my colleagues and friends from Delhi University and JNU, and Dr. P.K. Shukla (rtd.) from Indian Council of Historical Research,

I am grateful to Prof. R.P. Poddar, Bhandarkar Oriental Research Institute, Poona; Dr. Jaya Verma, Sri Bhim Rao Ambedkar College; Prof. C. Mora and Ms. Benedicta Baluchi from Pavia University, Italy, who have responded to my queries and helped me in various ways in the completion of this work.

I am happy to record great sense of appreciation for UGC to render financial support for the project which is modified in the form of book. I gratefully acknowledge the works of Dr. Manish Karmwar and

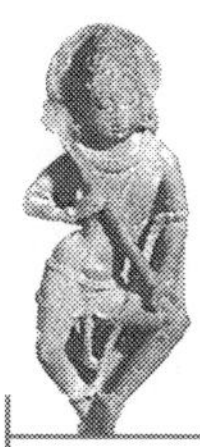

Ms. Santoshi Kumari as my project fellows. I thank my colleagues from Sri Aurobindo College (Eve.) for administrative help.

I also wish to thank librarian and staff of Central Library and South Campus Library of Delhi University, Jawaharlal Nehru University, Indian Council of Historical Research, National Museum, Archaeological Survey of India, Indira Gandhi National Centre for the Arts, American Institute for Indian Studies, Mathura Museum, Punjab University (Chandigarh), Lucknow University, Bhandarkar Oriental Research Institute (Poona), Indian Institute of Advanced Study (Shimla) and Patna University; for providing valuable material and extending their kind coperation. I am indebted to *Social Science Probings* for publishing my research paper 'Visibility of Egalitarian Concepts of Buddhism in the Images of Women in the Therigatha', which is part of my book.

My greatest gratitude as always goes to my husband Ajay and my son Utkarsh and my father-in law K.S. Thakur who continue to provide endless support. In writing this volume I have drawn widely and deeply from the published research of other scholars. I wish to acknowledge the contributions of all those listed in my Bibliography. Though I may not agree to their view point, this work would not have been possible without their scholarship.

It is my privilege to dedicate this work to my Grandmother, Mother and Mother-in-Law who are not with me but their blessings always encourage me to keep going.

Vijaya Laxmi Singh

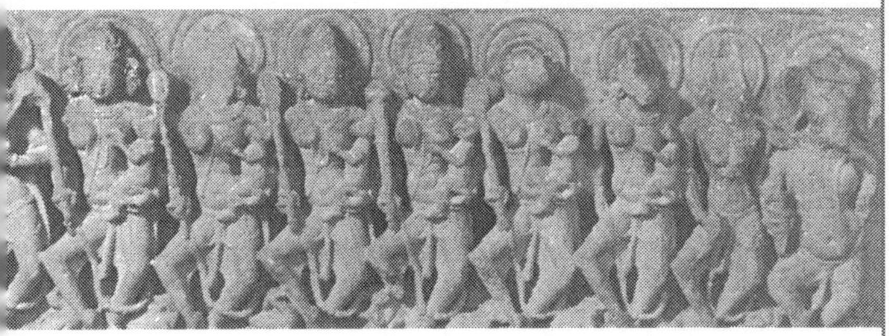

List of Abbreviations

ABORI	*Annals of the Bhandarkar Oriental Research Institute*, Poona
AN	*Anguttara Nikaya*
ARASI	*Annual Report of the Archaeological Survey of India*
CII	*Corpus Inscriptionum Indicarum*
EI	*Epigraphia Indica*
IA	*Indian Antiquary*, Bombay
IC	*Indian Culture*, Calcutta
IHQ	*Indian Historical Quarterly*, Calcutta
JASB	*Journal of the Asiatic Society of Bengal*, Calcutta
JBORS	*Journal of the Bihar & Research Society*, Patna
JBRAS	*Journal of the Bombay Branch of the Royal Asiatic Society*
JBRS	*Journal of the Bihar Research Society*, Patna
JRAS	*Journal of the Royal Asiatic Society*, London
MN	*Majjhima Nikaya*

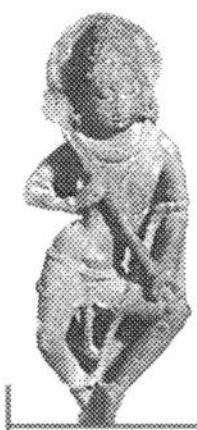

PTS — Pali Text Society, London
RT — *Rajatarangini*
SBB — *Sacred Books of the Buddhists*, London
SBE — *Sacred Books of the East*, Oxford
VIN — *Vinaya Texts*

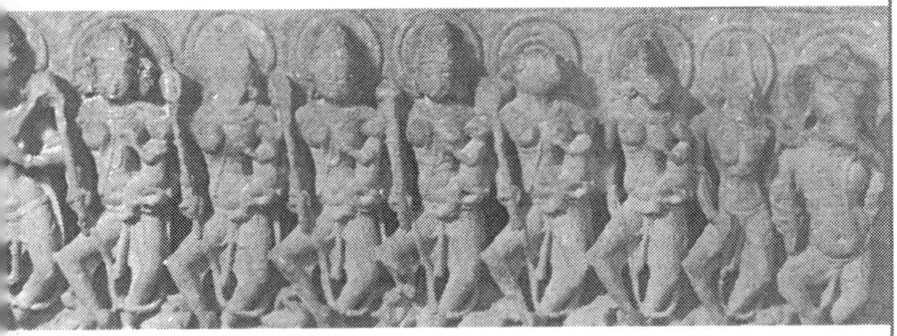

List of Illustrations

Page No.

MAPS

1. Spread of Buddhism in North India. 49
2. Places of Goddess worship in early North India. 80
3. Edicts of Ashoka. 134
4. Areas of Study of Inscriptions. 135

FIGURES

1. Mathura woman, Kushana Period. 12
2. Standing female figure, Arjun Pura, Mathura. 13
3. Seven Matrikas, Mathura. 67
4. Goat-headed Jaina Mother Goddess, Mathura. 68
5. Sachia Mata at Osian Temple, 8th-9th century AD (central shrine). 72

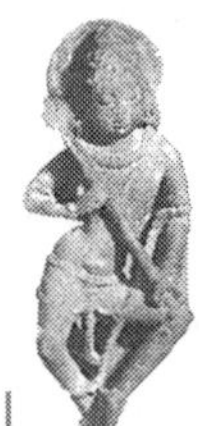

6. One of the nine forms of Devi at Osian. 72
7. One of the nine forms of Devi at Osian. 73
8. One of the nine forms of Devi at Osian. 73
9. Medieval Durga Mandir at Jodhpur. 74
10. Osian Temple also known as Sachia Mata Temple, Osian village, Jodhpur. 75
11. Entrance of Osian Temple, Osian village, Jodhpur. 76
12. Shiva and Parvati with bull. 78
13. Coins of Didda Rani, Ruler of Kashmir. 92
14. Vasantasena: Scenes of a courtesan's house, Kushana, 2nd century AD, Mathura. 118
15. Coins, Chandragupta-Kumaradevi type. 121

Chapter I

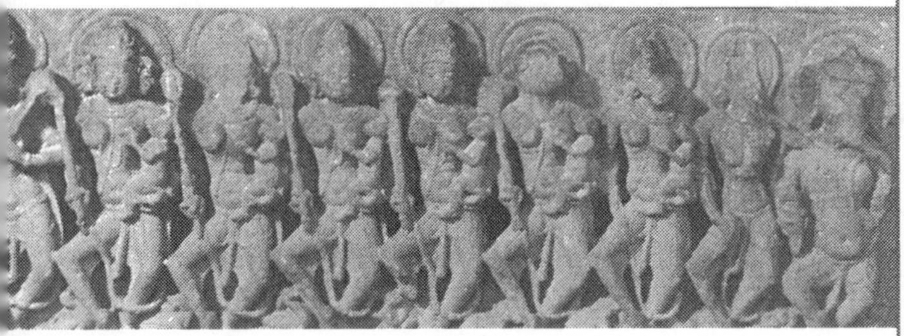

Women and Gender in History

A. HISTORIOGRAPHICAL TRENDS AND PERSPECTIVES IN INDIAN AND NON-INDIAN SOURCES FOR EARLY HISTORICAL SOCIETIES

Views on women have been expressed in many different cultures and can be traced back as far as the ancient civilizations of Greece and China. Christine de Pisan's Book *The City of the Ladies,* published in Italy in 1405, foreshadowed many of the ideas of modern feminism in recording the deeds of famous women of the past and advocating women's right to education and political influence. Women, as silent sufferers, made tremendous contribution to society in the past, which remained unrecognized and therefore, history is considered 'his' achievement and 'hers' has been completely blacked out. Though feminism in India has emerged as one of the most creative and challenging disciplines; in both literature and social sciences, to the extent that feminist discourses define women as being problematic. However, these discourses too ironically

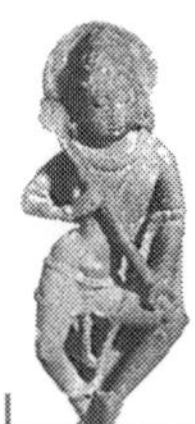

exempt the man from being determined by gender relations. As Jane Flax[1] puts it, "From the perspective of social relations, men and women are both prisoners of gender, although in highly differentiated but interrelated ways".

Women's history began as a revisionist methodology; it started with a story that had already been written, and found to be incomplete. Historians documenting women's history said: "Where are the women?", then found them, wrote about them and convicted a few people who wrote general history to add a few women. Then they found out more about women, started thinking and talking about gender and convinced some generalists to stir a little when they added women, which resulted in separate sections out of the boxes usually labelled "women and the family", a linkage many criticized. Then because they were used to being revisionist, women's historians revised themselves and became extremely self-critical, asking "who are the women?" and "are they really women?" and sometimes "Is there really sex (the difference not the act)?"[2] Writing of the experiences and aspirations of the Ist World War women's movement, Olive Schreiner's comments raise questions for the modern reader: "You will look back at us with astonishment! You will wonder at passionate struggles that accomplished so little, at the, to you, obvious paths to attain our ends which we did not take; at the intolerable evils before which it will seem to you we sat down passive; at the great truths staring us in the face, which we failed to see; at the truths we grasp at; but could never quite get our fingers round."[3]

Women in much of the world lose out by being women. Their human powers of choice and sociability are frequently thwarted by societies in which they must live as the adjuncts and servants of others, and in which their sociability is deformed by fear and hierarchy. But they are bearers of human capabilities, basic powers of choice that make a moral claim for opportunities to be realized and to flourish. In the 19th century European feminist's consciousness began spreading during and after the French Revolution, and by the end of the century feminist ideas were being expressed by radicals in England, France and Germany. By the mid-19th century women's issue had taken centre stage for Russian reformers and anarchists; while in India wrongs being done to women began to be deplored by social reformers mainly in Bengal and Maharashtra. The women's movement of the 60s and 70s in the Western world had a fundamental impact on the education of women at higher levels.[4] The connection of academic world to the social movement meant that the setting up and teaching of such courses was a profoundly political act. Theoretical analysis was seen as being intimately connected to social change, which was broadly defined as the recognition and analysis of women's oppression, and therefore the knowledge of how to end their subordination in patriarchal and capitalist societies. There has been debate over whether women's studies is an extention of women's movement, if it is now structurally distinct from that movement (and some would maintain ideologically).[5]

In the last thirty years, there has been an explosion of studies on women's history. Historians have searched for new sources that revealed the historical experience of, and used traditional sources in innovative ways. They analyze the distinctive experiences of individuals and groups, and relate these histories to political, ideological and economic developments.

Interest in women's history has resulted from several different academic and political movements. Beginning in the 1930s, many historians turned their attention from the traditional subjects of historical inquiry such as public and political developments, diplomatic changes, military events and major intellectual movements to investigating the lives of more ordinary people. Instead of focusing simply on great dramatic changes such as the French and the Industrial Revolutions, these social historians are investigating things that have changed much more slowly, or in fact largely stayed the same for centuries, such as people's diet and underlying beliefs about the world. In the words of French Annales School's historians, leaders in this new approach, they were interested in *longue duree*, in economic and intellectual institutions and structures which have shaped people's lives over a long period of time. Building on this during the 1960s, some younger historians consciously developed what they termed as the new social history, which differed somewhat methodologically and ideologically from older social history. In terms of methodology, new social history often borrowed techniques developed in other social sciences, such as quantitative analysis from economics or the interpretation of symbols from anthropology. In terms of ideology, new social history was shaped by civil rights, anti-war, student and national liberation movements of the 1960s, to be more overtly political, using

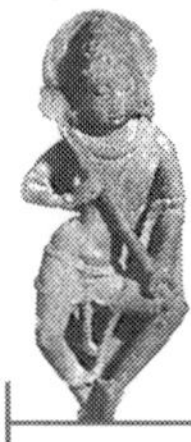

historical investigation of past incidents of racial, class, or religious oppression in support of demand for change in the present institutions and power structures.

The political movements in 1960s also reinvigorated the feminist movements as women involved in the civil rights and anti-war causes discovered that even their most revolutionary colleagues did not treat them as equals or considered their ideas or contributions as valuable as those of men. The feminist movement which began in the sixties—often termed 'the second wave' to set it apart from the first wave of feminism that began in the 19th century included a wide range of political beliefs, with various groups working for a broad spectrum of goals, one of which was to understand more about the lives of women in the past. This paralleled a similar rise of interest in women's history which accompanied the first wave of feminism, from which emerged studies that are still influential.

Women's history began in some ways as a subfield of social history, but over the last 30 years it has widened to include investigations of intellectual, political, economic, and even military and diplomatic history. Historians of women have demonstrated that there is really no historical change that does not affect the lives of women in some way, though often very differently than it affects the lives of men of the same class or social group.[6]

The studies and ever increasing ongoing research on women have resulted in some conclusions, each of which reinforces the need for still more research of all types. The first is that historical experience of early modern women was much less uniform than we realised several decades ago. Women's experience differed not only according to the categories that we had set out based on male experience, social class, geographical location, rural or urban setting but also as per categories that had previously not been taken into account—marital status, health and number of children. Historians are, thus, much less comfortable talking about the status of women in general without qualifying exactly what type of women, or in what type of sources; we can draw conclusions about, for example, the legal status of women in theoretical treatises, or the role of widows in a particular craft guild, but a statement about the rise and fall of women is too vague.[7]

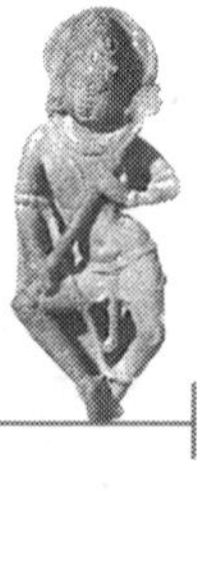

A second and related conclusion is that the role of gender in determining the historical experiences of men and women varied over time, and from group to group. For some people, such as the very poor, social class was probably more important than gender, though this 'equality of misery' was certainly not much consolation to women experiencing it. For the nobility and urban bourgeoisie however, the early modern period appears to have been a time when in words of Rosemary Radford Ruether, "the perception of women as marginalized by gender became stronger than the perception in women as divided by class." How much this perception reflected reality and how it shaped reality are not being investigated for many areas of Europe. In India, since the mid-70s a lot has been discussed and written about women's history. But there are very disparate and fragmented accounts of conditions of women's lives and their roles and status, ranging from ancient to contemporary situations. While some writers have idealized the position of women in different times and places, others have focussed upon their continuous exploitation and oppression. Generalization on women's position has always appeared an impossible task, specially for historians and sociologists. D.D. Kosambi[8] states, "There is no caste or class differentiation within tribes. Agriculture was then the monopoly of women. Women were the first potters and weavers. Weaving was speciality of women, though male sheer might weave a hymn, as if it was a patterned garment of the loom. Women were the rulers and the system of matriarchy prevailed before 400 BC in different parts of the continent. During the early Vedic period the women in India enjoyed almost an equal status with men in different spheres of life. Vedic studies were then not the prerogative of men. Girls and boys were required to undergo 'upanayana' ceremonies in order to undertake Vedic studies". Nationalist historian Altekar states, "One of the best ways to understand the spirit of civilization and to appreciate its excellence and realize its limitations is to study the history of the position and status of women in it." The marriage laws and the customs enable us to realize whether men regarded women as market commodities or war prizes or whether they realized that the wife is after all husband's valued partner whose cooperation is indispensable for the happiness and success of family life.[9] However, Romila Thapar points out, "within the Indian subcontinent there have been infinite variations on the status of women diverging according to cultural milieu, family

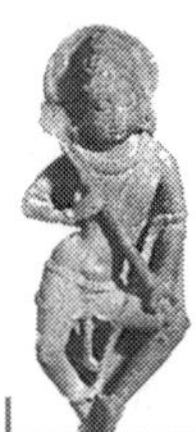

structure, class, caste, property rights and morals[10]." M.N. Srinivas[11] also emphasizes the existence of considerable variation among regions, between rural and urban areas, among classes and finally among different religions, ethnic and caste groups. While in certain contexts the Indian subcontinent is a single cultural region, in many others it is heuristically more rewarding to look upon it as a congeries of micro regions, differences between which are crucial. Besides the methodology in taking an overview of women's history, scholars confront the problem of sources. We come across complaints of paucity of literature available as a source, and the unevenness of the sources, which are traceable in the way of comprehensive and systematic endeavour to present an interpretive history of women.

Feminism in the West emerged as a powerful challenge to existing power structures and gender equations at the level of family, the economy and polity. When used in Western context, the word 'feminism' evokes many positive associations of nearly two centuries or more of struggle by courageous women who braved social attacks, ridicule, ostracism and male wrath in order to press women's claim for equality at home, in the workplace, in education, politics, religion, and culture. In helping to achieve certain equality for women, and by expanding the space for their aspirations, feminists in Western societies pushed their societies to become more democratic.[12] However, the word 'feminism' evokes no such political connotation in India. This is not because the ideas of women's right and dignity are alien to our society. Far from it, we have a much longer history of individual women's assertiveness in India and a well-established tradition of making space for women whose aspirations take them in different directions.

The position and status of women has frequently been employed as a popular barometer for measuring civilizational progress. Not surprisingly the 'women question', as it was usually, though rather inelegantly referred to, figured prominently in the nationalist imperialist debate regarding India's 'fitness' for self-government. The British used the particular form which gender inequality took in India as a vehicle for proving their cultural superiority, as a demonstration of their concern.

Women and gender issues need to be recognized and addressed in early historical studies owing to their importance as well as their bearing on our understanding of contemporary society. Women have emerged as a force in history. Historians of women may differ from one another in the writings which have appeared, but writing about women in history has had its impact on the broader discipline. Recently, there has been some effort towards developing methodologies and studying the texts, inscriptions and other archaeological artefacts. I propose to extend this work, especially in the context of early India.

"Women's history has a dual goal: to restore women to history and to restore our history to women."[13] Human identity determined only in specific places at specific times can be the object of study within a historical perspective. Similarly, understanding of women's issues necessitates understanding the dimensions of her social and cultural construction from a historical point of view. Women's history began in some ways as a subfield of social history, but over the last 40 years it has widened to include investigations of intellectual, political, economic, and even military and diplomatic history. Historians of women have demonstrated that there is really no historical change that does not affect the lives of women in some way, though often very differently than it affects the lives of men of the same class or social group.[14]

Subordination of women is a common feature of almost all stages of history and is prevalent everywhere in the world, only the extent and form of that subordination has been conditioned by the social and cultural environment in which women have been placed. To understand the position of women in early India, we have to study women in their wider context.

Interest in status of women in classical antiquity extends back to the 19th century when women as a conceptual category, isolated from the rest of history, became the focus of scientific and positivist inquiry. The scholars of 19th century examined not only images of women found in poetic texts but also studied their social positions in numerous judicial, philosophical and historical texts from their antiquity. The treatises of this period on ancient women *Das Mutterrecht*, written by Johan Bachofen (1967) (English trans. *Myth Religion and Mother's Right*, tr. R. Manheim, N.J. Princeton) discusses articulated stages of cultural development in which women reacted to an original communal society in which individual family ties and property rights were not sufficiently delimited. This approach has put women in the bracket of a separate cultural category.

Sarah Pomeroy's *Goddesses, Whores, Wives and Slaves* (New York,1975) set out to recover the lives of ancient women even in the face of acute challenges posed by the primary sources, most of which were written by men for a male audience. She observed that literary sources such as plays and epics do not bear a close correspondence to everyday life, although they may shed light on how ancient cultures conceptualized women. Rather, other types of texts, history, biographies, letters, legal works as well as visual material and papyri can more accurately illuminate the daily lives of ancient women, particularly the elite. *Reflections on Women in Antiquity,* ed. by Helene P. Foley, New York, 1981, represented the first collection of essays on women in the ancient world. Mary Lefkowitz and Maureen Fant's *Women's Life in Greece and Rome: A Source Book in Translation* (2nd edn., Baltimore, MD, 1992) is a comparative study of women from Greece and Rome. Averil Cameron and Amelie Kuhrt's *Images of Women in Anquity,* 1993, 2nd edn., Detroit, ML, had a comparative purpose, providing material on women from many different ancient societies including Greece, Rome, Near East and historical periods ranging from the classical world to early Christian era and Jewish thought and the medieval era. E. Fanthom, H. Foley, N. Kampen, S. Pomeroy and H. Shapiro (eds.), *Women in Classical World* (New York, 1994), is a collection of most important primary sources on ancient women and places them in their social and historical context. It shows how the study of women in antiquity has evolved from a fringe movement in the 1970s to its position with academy, as a subject of scholarly inquiry and pedagogy. A more recent publication *Sexuality and Gender in the Classical World: Reading and Sources* Laura K. Mc Clure (ed.), Blackwell (UK, London, 2002), reflects on the lives of ancient women and the social and political forces that shaped them.

Women in ancient India have also been the focus of scholarly attention since the early 20th century. Both Indian and Western scholars undertook the study of status of women from different perspectives. Brahmanical normative texts of early historical India have positioned women within the household, as a daughter, wife, mother and in other capacities. Women in these works constitute a practically undifferentiated group within a fixed set of norms and duties. In the works of A.S. Altekar, *Position of Women in Hindu Civilization* (1938, 1959); Pinkham, *Women in Sacred Scriptures of Hinduism* (1941); Indra, *The Status of Women in*

Hindu India (1940) many of the specific features of a patriarchal society were taken for granted. They have used the sources uncritically. National historian A.S. Altekar's focus on a limited set of concerns: property rights, marriageable age, enforced widowhood, the participation of women in rituals and so on are mainly or exclusively applicable to the upper caste Hindu women. I.B. Horner in his book *Women in Primitive Buddhism* (Delhi, 1930), studied Buddhist sources for an in-depth study of women, wherein he deals with people, places and events with their narrative style. Horner was the first scholar who attempted to analyse the role of women outside the kinship network. Motichandra, in his study *World of Courtesans* (1973) has listed references to courtesans which may provide a good source material for meaningful analysis on my subject. Sukumari Bhattacharji, in her publication *Women and Society in Ancient India* (Calcutta, 1994), focuses on the economic relations woven around prostitution, including relation to the state, provision for taxing prostitutes, and somewhat unique financial status of prostitutes in comparison to other women. D.D. Kosambi's work *Myth and Reality* (1962), contains incidental references to women. By and large, women remained peripheral to his main concern. R.S. Sharma in his book *Perspectives in Social and Economic History of Early India* (Delhi, 1983), did not turn to women in a structural way, but he has been somewhat exceptional in using brahmanical texts to provide systematic information and analyses on a number of crucial linkages relating to women, which are commonly overlooked. Suvira Jaisawal, in *Women in Early India: Problems and Perspectives* (1981), discusses the possible connection between women's status and their involvement in production within the framework of what she perceives as an emerging class divided society and postulates links between the kinship structure and the mode of production. Chitralekha Gupta's article (1988) 'Rural Urban Dichotomy in the Concept and Status of Women: An Examination (From Mauryan to Gupta Period)' in Kumkum Roy (ed.), *Women in Early Indian Societies* (2001), opens up the possibility of investigating women's relationship to the economy from a distinctive perspective. In other articles like "Gender Relations during First Millenium: An Overview" in B.D. Chattopadhyaya (ed.), *A Social History of Early India, Project of History of Indian Science, Philosophy and Culture* (PHISPC), 2009, Uma Chakraborty and Kumkum Roy in their various articles[15] generally discuss women in brahmanical patriarchal society, exposing the traditional historians' works, which have tried to elevate women's position in early India. Taking a cue from Gerda Lerner, Uma Chakravarty talks of an alternative paradigm prevailing in the name of Altekar... "There is an urgent need to move forward and rewrite history, a history that does justice to women by examining social processes and the structures they create, thus crucially shaping and conditioning the relations between men and women. Just as Altekar displaced James Mill in his work, it is time we realized that despite Altekar's substancial contribution we must lay his ghost aside and begin afresh ("Beyond the Altekarian Paradigm: Towards a New Understanding of Gender Relations in the Early Indian History", *Social Scientist*, Vol. 16, No. 8, 1988, pp. 51-52). Vijaya Ramaswamy's *Walking Naked Women, Society and Spirituality in Ancient India* talks of women and spirituality in its diverse manifestations in the Sangam Age.

The studies on women and ever expanding ongoing research have resulted in some conclusions, each of which reinforces the need for still more research. Historical experience of early historical women was much less uniform than we realised several decades ago. Women's experience varied growth not only against the parameters set to measure male experience like social class, geographical location, rural and urban setting but also their marital status, health, number of children, etc. Historians are thus much less comfortable talking about the status of women in general without qualifying exactly what type of women, or in what type of circumstances. We can draw conclusions about, for example, the legal status of women in theoretical treatises, or the role of widows in a particular craft guild, but a general statement about women would be too vague. The role of gender in determining the historical experiences of men and women varied over time, and from group to group. For some people, such as the very poor, social class was probably more important than gender, though this 'equality of misery' was certainly not much consolation to women experiencing it. Since the mid-70s in India, a lot has been discussed and written about "women's history". But there are very disparate and fragmented accounts of conditions of women's lives and their roles and status, ranging from ancient to contemporary situations. While some writers have idealized the positions of women in different times and places, others have focussed upon their continuous exploitation and oppression. Generalization on women's position has always appeared an impossible task, specially for historians and sociologists. While in certain contexts, the Indian subcontinent is a single cultural region, in many others it is heuristically more rewarding to look upon it as congeries of micro regions, differences between which are crucial. Given the near invisibility of women in economic histories, there has been an understandable preoccupation with documenting women's presence in a range of activities besides economic. We have to identify and explore whether participation in productive and other activities translated into economic and social power or not. The other issue which has to be explored is the sexual division of labour. While division of labour is nearly universal, its specific form and content is subject to historical variations in different contexts. Any further study would be based on commitment to the idea that the question of women's authority in the ancient India of a specified period can and should be approached from a number of different angles.

Besides the methodology in taking an overview of women's history, scholars confront the problem of sources. We come across complaints of paucity of literature available as a source, and the unevenness of the available sources, in presenting a comprehensive and systematic work on the history of women. But research has to progress despite all limitations. My basic sources for north India will be *Arthashastra, Manusmriti, Dharmashastras, Kamasutra, Therigatha* and several other inscriptions. Secondary sources mentioned above and the bibliography shall help me in theorizing my work.

The work on gender issues in cultures known primarily through texts—specially institutional, not private—is problematized by androcentrism in their content and function as a foundation and support for an elaborate, well organized and institutionalized religious system.[16] While women's role in religio-philosophical thought formulation and ritual practice is undercut and their experience of and response to such activities unrecorded, unequal socio-religious roles and inter-personal relations of men and women and underlying notions of masculinity and feminity are defined by religious texts and communicated through prescribed religious behaviour, i.e. ritual practices.[17] One of the most complicated problems in understanding gender relations in early India is posed by the near ubiquitous goddesses or if one prefers, multiple manifestations of the great goddess. The wealth of evidence pointing to the existence and popularity of the goddess, both iconographic and textual, is immense.

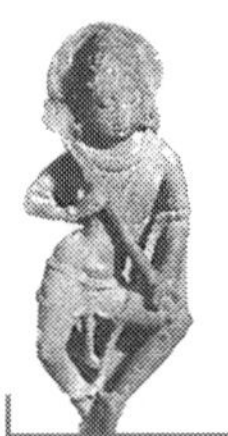

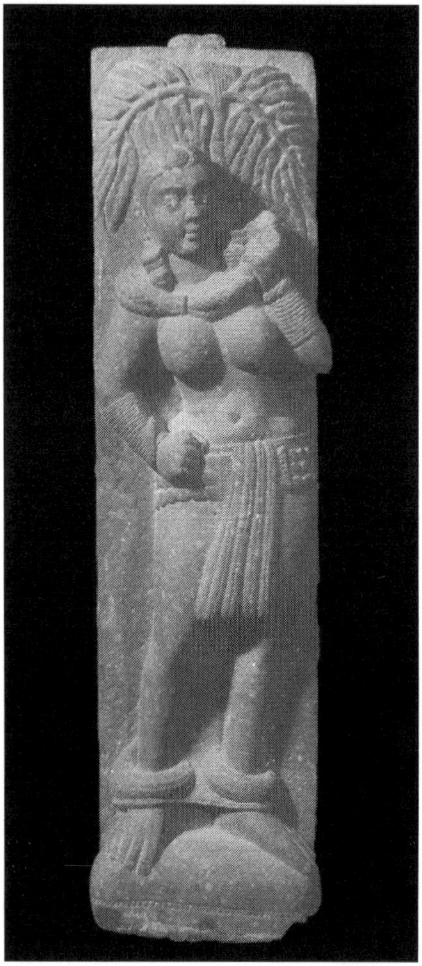

Fig. 1. Mathura woman, Kushana Period.

Thus her presence and importance is established without doubt. What have proved more problematic are attempts to interpret the data in social or historical terms. While histories of specific cults have been traced, problems surface in an attempt to translate and or equate the divine situation with the human. Clearly, the relationship between the two tends to be complex.

The approach in traditional historiography is textual and it almost totally excludes epigraphical records. To make real women visible on historical stage, the epigraphic records need to be collected and classified. Women in epigraphical records are free from male bias and are closer to historical realities than the idealized or condemned women in historical literature. The early Indian literature, be it Dharmashastra tradition of orthodox brahmanism or heterodox faiths or even the epic variety, is of normative nature in respect of women. What inscriptions offer us are variations of or even deviations from the norm. The inscriptional evidence dating from the 3rd century BC onwards shows that most of the ruling dynasties made grants to religious institutions. There has also been a complex relationship between gender and religion. K.M. Shrimali points out in his article, "How not to be a Vamana Traversing Gender Constructions of the Domains of Divinities", in Kirit K. Shah ed. *History and Gender: Some Explorations*, Delhi, 2005, that the religious system and symbolic structures therein participate in the construction of gender roles (Figs. 1 & 2).[18] It is hoped that the recognition of their existence will provide an understanding of the complex two-way relationship whereby religious meanings and symbols are gendered, and gender relations are expressed through religious symbolism. All the above-mentioned themes are interwoven.

Patronage to religious institutions is obviously linked to the notion of an expression of women's and men's social, political and economic identities.

We have to explore the articulation of self-perception by women about their social self and examine the way patriarchy in India functioned in relation to women and the public space it offered to them for expressing their religious fervour and articulating their self-image in the process. Kumkum Roy's "Women and Men Donors at Sanchi: A Study of Inscriptional Evidence" (in L.K. Tripathi (ed.) *Position and Status of Women in Ancient India*, Vol. I) and *Upinder Singh's Sanchi:* "The History of Patronage of an Ancient Buddhist Establishment" (*IESHR*, Vol. XXXIII, no. I Jan-March, 1996), are studies of the inscriptions from Sanchi and have rightly recognized the historical value of those inscriptions which represent a deliberate attempt to record the donors identified with their native place, position in kinship structure, occupation and relationship with Buddhism. Kirit K. Shah's (2001) *Problem of Identity: Women in Early Indian Inscriptions*, OUP, Delhi, through a study of limited number of inscriptions, aims to remove androcentric bias from historiography on early Indian women and works towards making them visible. My own preliminary works "Situating Women Donor's in Early Historical Urban Mathura" (pub. in *Proceedings of Indian History Congress*, 2002) and "Repositioning Women in Ancient India in the Context of Amaravati Inscriptions" (*Proceedings of Indian History Congress*, 2003) indicate that the historical realities are complex and multidimensional where women have played visible roles.

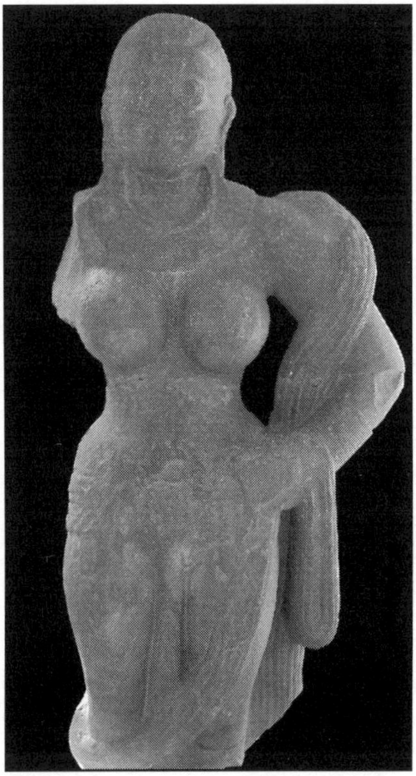

Fig. 2. Standing female figure, Arjun Pura, Mathura.

The traditional writings on the position of women are entirely based on brahmanical sources which show bias towards men. We must use the brahmanical works when we analyze Indian history but we do not know the extent to which they actually describe reality because, they are more interested in prescribing an ideal. Whenever possible their statements must be cross-checked with other types of evidences (such as inscriptions), which however, are not always available. It should also be borne in mind that according to most cultural historians, these texts are affecting historical reality to various degrees with the passage of time. Secondly, we have to work cautiously, without exaggerating the space available to women in history. Close scrutiny of source material is needed to bring real people in the past alive and to arrive at a fresh understanding of the history of women in early India.

By exploring women's role in ancient civilizations, one can gain an insight into social patterns that structure women's lives today. For example, the development of social attitude and behaviour in many ancient civilizations, often patriarchal, formed the basis for women's modern roles in those cultures.

We have contradictory mentalities and attitudes towards women in ancient texts to enable us to argue in favour of both the higher and lower status of women.

B. ANCIENT INDIA AND THE WOMEN QUESTION: BRIEF SURVEY FROM THE EARLIEST PERIOD TO PRE-MAURYA PERIOD

The traditional writing on the position of women is entirely based on brahmanical sources which show bias towards men. We must use the brahmanical works when we analyze Indian history but we do not know the extent to which they actually describe reality because they are more interested in prescribing an ideal. Whenever possible, their statements must be cross-checked with other types of evidences (such as inscriptions), which however, are not always available. It should also be borne in mind that according to the most cultural historians, these texts are affecting historical reality to various degrees with the passage of time.[19] The analyses of the position of women in India has been coloured by the fact that almost all the works have been written by scholars who would fall within the nationalist school of history writing at the time of colonial imperial period when Hindu social institutions were subjected to fierce criticism by newly Western educated people. Contemporary evils reflecting the low position of women were responsible for the Hindu sense of inferiority in relation to their ruling masters. As a result, the Hindu scholars argued that the evils were only temporary aberration and could easily be eliminated. The general thrust of the work has, therefore, been to demonstrate that the status of women was very high in Vedic period, and there was a general decline afterwards, reaching rock bottom with the coming of invaders, especially Muslims, who abducted the Hindu women and violated them, and these circumstances resulted in the development of such evils as purdah, sati and female infanticide.[20]

Subordination of women is a common feature of almost all stages of history and is prevalent everywhere in the world, only the extent and form of that subordination has been conditioned by the social and cultural environment in which women have been placed. Archaic Roman law granted to the husband the power over the life and limbs of the wife, and for many centuries matrons with several children continued to be under the tutelage of their male relations. In ancient Palestine, the women were a piece of property to be bought and sold. In studies of women in early India any scientific analyses of society should be both materialistic and historical. It should begin not only with what people think about what they do but with (as far as we can tell) what they actually do; and an understanding of the past cannot be gained by simple derivations from data about societies existing in a later period. The first point means that any literary evidence has to be used with extreme caution. The second means that evidence gathered by anthropologists from currently existing "tribal" (hunting-gathering or horticultural) societies cannot be simply applied to characterize hunting-gathering societies existing thousands of years ago. The total social and environmental context, the availability of tools and weapons, the impact of external state societies is completely different. Thus, for example, the fact that many tribal societies today show various forms of patriarchy/ patriliny/ matriliny, etc. does not mean that these social forms existed in the pre-state period of, say 4000 BC, and the existence of what looks like "matriarchal" features in some societies around 1500 BC also cannot be assumed to characterize a 'stage in history' or apply to a genuinely pre-state period. We cannot simply assume that any social features are "remnants" of the past. Therefore, the evidence used to assess the question of exploitation, patriarchy and violence is primarily archaeological and secondarily historical (use of written materials available from the early state period onwards) and not anthropological.

We do not have archaeological evidence for gender differentiation before about 30,000 BC (that is, of seeing 'males' and 'females' as

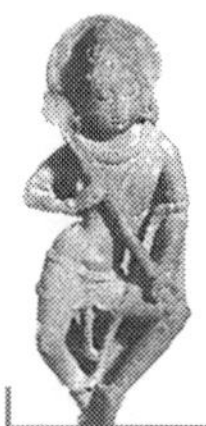

somehow different social beings), although there is evidence of human cultural activity for about 100,000 years. In other words, the existence of a primordial but human, pre-gender society (in which, while biological males and females existed, they were not differentiated sociologically through a division of labour or in terms of cultural conceptualization) is at least possible. Evidence from cave paintings of Mesolithic period in central India suggests that in the hunting-gathering stage, there was no rigid sexual division of labour, i.e. men hunt and women gather. It is likely that women participated in hunting right from the all important task of gathering, which in any case accounted for a major source of food in tropical climate. Women played an equal role in the hunting-gathering economy. Based on the modern anthropological data on the tribal societies, it has been postulated that the most egalitarian societies are to be found among hunting-gathering tribes which are characterized by interdependency.[21] Here the relative status of men and women can at best be characterized as "separate but equal".[22] It was further enhanced by the importance attached to the reproductive role of women. Pregnant women, women in their nurturing roles as mothers, and women portrayed in the act of childbirth are sometimes depicted in the paintings, besides the mother goddess. It has been argued that the first form of religious expression for men and women is the psychological bond between mother and child, and that the life-giving mother appeared to have power over 'life and death.' Thus, men and women, observing this dramatic and mysterious power of the female turned to the veneration of the mother goddess.[23] Female reproductive power in such a hunting and gathering society was regarded as valuable because the very survival of continuity is dependent upon it. Prehistoric paintings at Kathotia, Bhimbetka and Kharwai treat female sexuality as one aspect of female existence. Thus, women as reproducers are as evident as women participating productive activities in the hunting-gathering economy.[24] Society in this phase has been characterized by one scholar as *matristic*—one in which women were not subjected to the authority of men, or of other women.[25] From about 35,000 BC, there is evidence of gender conceptualization – e.g. in Cro-Magnon cave paintings in France (which show in detail flowering, fertility, seasons of plants and animals and later depictions of pregnant women), in widespread female figurines or "mother-goddess" figures which appear all over the world specially in the pre-State and early State period. However, there is no evidence that this gender differentiation, the difference in conceptualization of women and men, was associated with either male domination (patriarchy) or female domination (matriarchy). In other words, we should reject both radical feminist notions of male domination associated with hunting as the earliest form of exploitation and violence and the traditional Marxist notion of an early stage of matriarchy. The unique aspect of humankind is that women in prehistory believed that conception and generation of foetus did not limit her in her actions. She continued to work within the commune, and according to the cave art, even participated in hunts and fishing. In 1973, a new find was announced to the world by Richard E. Leakey. He discovered that there is a distinct possibility that the first human being on earth was in truth a woman. In 1974, Donald C. Johanson announced to the world his discovery of the 3.18 million old hominid skeleton, popularly known as 'Lucy'. Leakay observed that both the sexes worked in harmony. There is no indication that the tasks, occupations or physical requirements were differentiated, separated or limited on the basis of sex or sexuality and its various functions and conditions. Equality was the rule. Women assumed a central pivotal position in prehistoric age by producing life. Because of their regenerating ability, they were believed to be closer to the deities of the earth, who expressed their love for humankind by generating crops, roots, grains, nuts, animals, birds and fish.

Settled agricultural societies appear from about 10,000-8000 BC, but there is not much evidence that this first production of a "surplus" led to violence, class exploitation and patriarchal domination until after a long period. On the contrary, archaeological excavations at such sites as Huyuk in Turkey show a relatively peaceful society, with no economic differentiation between households, with goddesses, and women playing the role of priestesses, but with no evidence of women domination (matriarchy). In other words, the production of a surplus or potential surplus may have made private appropriation (exploitation, patriarchy etc.) possible but not necessary; there is evidence, on the contrary, of thousands of years of quite peaceful early agricultural societies. It is believed that in such societies, women played major economic role. She was a inventor of textile loom and potter's wheel, besides being a developer of chemistry and discoverer of yeast, which is so critical to beer and bread-making.

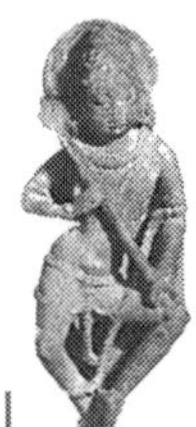

An understanding of how Harappan society was organized internally in terms of its economy and polity is still inconclusive as the archaeological data is not yet complemented by written evidence. Also the society is not analyzed from gender point of view. It is, thus, not possible to elaborate upon questions of gender. However, Uma Chakravarti[26] points out that the existence of numerous mother goddess icons and the bronze statue of the dancing girl could be interpreted as the continued importance of women's special relationship with reproduction and may also be seen as an acceptance of their sexuality. However, the evidence is not enough to indicate whether the sexuality was already under some kind of control, whether by men or certain category of women.

Evidence of patriarchal domination over women does appear in the period after the rise of the first states in Mesopotamia and Egypt, as shown in the excellent study by Gerda Lerner.[27] Her work is both theoretically and methodologically useful for historians in outlining the historical process of the creation of patriarchy in the Mesopotamian region. Lerner describes her growing awareness of the fact that crucial to the organization of early Mesopotamian society was the total control of women's sexuality by men of the dominant class. From this time after about 3000 BC, we can trace male domination as rulers; "male control as head of the family", slavery in which women are of special importance as slaves; and legal systems that legitimize the patriarchal control of men over wives and children, patriarchal and patrilocal marriage as well as crucial distinctions between wife, mistress and prostitute—all backed up by the organized violence of the State. (And all existing at a time when mother goddesses continued to have great importance, though we can also trace the gradual suppression of these traditions by patriarchal religion). She found puzzling evidences wherein women seemed to have greatly differing status, some holding high positions and enjoying economic independence but whose sexuality was controlled by men. This led her to recognize that there was a need to look beyond economic questions and focus on the control over women's sexuality and manner in which reproduction was organized and thus, to look for the causes and effects of the sexual control.[28] Numerous Mesopotamian clay inscriptions have been deciphered, which make better interpretation and analyses of evidence. Lerner's stimulating study of the creation of patriarchy would suggest that some form of community or clan control over women and their sexuality were aspects of social organization in the archaic state and may have existed in the Harappan culture too.

Uma Chakravarti further contrasts the Harappan culture with the Rig Vedic period which is characterised by the lack of information on material culture in general but particularly on anything that may have had a bearing on women.[29] The *Rig Veda* itself, however, does throw some light on the ideology of the early Aryans. Rig Vedic society witnessed a continuing struggle between the Aryans and the "indigenous" tribes who were viewed with particular hostility by the Aryans for their dark skins, and their racial 'inferiority'. As the Aryans succeeded in establishing their control over certain areas, most of the men either fled or were killed; the conquerors then enslaved the women of the subjugated peoples. Thus, the first large group to be enslaved in early Indian history were women as there were more frequent references to *dasis* than *dasas*.[30] The evidence of *Rig Veda* is in consonance with Lerner's argument that all early conquering tribes killed the defeated men and enslaved the women, at least in the first stage of conquest.[31] Rig Vedic evidence reflects an essential stratification within women, between women of the conquering tribes and women of the subjugated people. Their roles and their place in society were very different. But still, Altekar feels that the position of women in Vedic Age was much better than what is ordinarily expected to have been. There are undoubtedly a few indications that show that brides were sometimes sold in marriage or even carried away by force. But better conscience of society had already begun to assert itself, and condemn these practices as unholy and unworthy.[32] The *Rig Veda* describes the Aryan women ruling over bipeds and quadrupeds, i.e. slaves and cattle.[33] References to *dasas* as object of *dana* (gifts) make it evident that the recipients were always men; often the *rajanya*, as the captors, gift them to priests. The possession of women slaves was clearly a major element in the primitive accumulation of wealth. The famous hymn about gambling in the *Rig Veda* (X.34) shows that sometimes habitual gamblers would put their wives at stake to their opponents; even though the advice given to the gambler in this hymn shows that social conscience had already begun to disapprove of this practice.

In the Vedic model, institution of marriage is the defining structure for women. Although it is clear throughout the dharma literature that women are thought to be thoroughly bodily beings with sweeping sexual

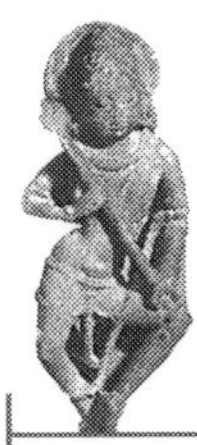

and amoral inclinations,[34] this sexuality can be controlled, primarily through the institution of marriage. When tamed by marriage, a woman's erotic tendencies are domesticated, stabilizing her as a threat to the social and moral order. Thus, marriage becomes a context in which rati or sexual pleasure can be expressed and where the goal of praja or offspring can be pursued.[35] Women and wives then stay within the constraints of marriage for these two pursuits become honoured by the men of their families.[36]

Altekar is of the opinion that the general freedom and better status which women enjoyed in the Vedic Age were largely due to men being engrossed in the work of conquest and consolidation. Women used to take an active part in agriculture, and manufacturing of cloth, bows, arrows and other war material. They were, thus, useful members of society, and could not be, therefore, treated with an air of patronage and contempt. Altekar suggests that the Aryan conquest of indigenous population and its loose incorporation as members of a separate *varna* had given rise to a huge population of semi-servile status. Under such a situation, Aryan women ceased to be productive members of the society and thus, lost the stem of the society. The introduction of non-Aryan wife into the Aryan household is the key to the gradual deterioration of the position of women. "The non-Aryan wife, with her ignorance of Sanskrit language and Hindu religion, could obviously not enjoy the same privileges as the Aryan consort. Association with her must have tended to affect the purity of speech of the Aryan co-wife as well. This must have naturally led to grave mistakes and anomalies in the performance of the rituals, which must have shocked the orthodox priests. Eventually, it was felt that the object could be gained by declaring the whole class of women to be ineligible for Vedic studies and religious duties.[37] This origin of obnoxious practices and beliefs of the early periods goes back to the Aryans, adopted the agricultural mode of life and became settled. The bulk of productive labour fell on the menfolk and the women were relegated to the domestic chores. Also, after society was split into classes, the upper stratum withdrew from manual labour and women of affluent section were relieved from their share by the advent of the new class of slaves from the conquered people. Women were then confined within the four walls. The ethos percolated to the lower rung of society. Women then became redundant in productive labour, except in their functions as mothers and housekeepers. Economically, women became liability and a breadwinner lorded over her.

The Rig Vedic corpus too suggests that the status of women was higher than it was in later centuries. For example, daughters as well as sons were given the education of the time; both memorized the hymns and were instructed in their meanings. One text says: "an unmarried young learned daughter should to be married to a bridegroom who like her is learned." In the hymns, female as well as male seers (*rishis*) appear, and are equal and better in ascetic exercises. The texts are often cast in the form of dialogues in which females as well as males have speaking roles, which led to the speculation that some hymns were actually composed by women. Also, women were not barred from public speaking, as is shown by the hymn that exhorts the newly married wife: "you should address the assembly (*vidatha*, a type of popular meeting) as a commander."

Girls were permitted to move about freely in public, attend the festive gatherings called *samanas* in search of husbands and lovers and sometimes spent the night abroad. Marriage, although expected to be universal (as occasionally it was not), took place when the bride was fully mature and usually to the man of her choice, although her father and specially her mother had a veto. The presence and participation of wife, as donor, at the sacrifice, was the requirement of various rituals. Daughters could, at a pitch, take the place of sons and women could inherit property. Widows were mentioned and even remarried; the contemporary evidence of the later custom of widow immolation is dubious at best.

Nevertheless, the purpose of marriage for women was the birth of sons, so as to perform funeral rites and sacrifices for their progenitors; wives were subordinate to their husbands and women were also depicted as sexual temptresses, diverting men from their ascetic and moral duties. The standard litany of misogynist abuse was present too, even the *Rig Veda*, which says, "there can be no friendship with women, as they have the hearts of wolves and jackals".

It should also be stressed that there is no evidence that private property and ownership of land or "other means of production" precedes the formation of these states; there is no evidence of separate "landholding" or "slaveholding" class whose power is based on the control of property. In other words, instead of "Engles model" (which presumes the primitive

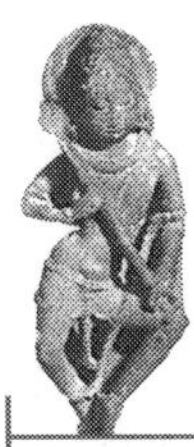

communism/slavery/feudalism/capitalism/socialism version of the "stages of history"), the evidence seems to fit a model which proposes an "Asiatic mode of production" as the first type of exploitative society in which the earliest states were ruled by a "State Class" (the Priest-Kings of the Mesopotamian city-states, the Egyptian Pharaohs) who extracted surplus from the peasantry still immersed in collective kinship (lineage) relations of production. Only later and gradually did classes of merchants and independent landholders appear. The Engels model, and the general historical description in the *Origin of the Family, Private Property and the State*, does fit well the states he described—the Greek looting, and Roman States, as well as many aspects of the Magadha-Maurya states in India, all of which arose in the middle of the first millennium BC. But these were what anthropologists call "the secondary states", arising over 2000 years after the historic first states of Egypt, Mesopotamia and the Indus Valley, and influenced by the socio-historical processes initiated with these first states. It appears that rather than looting and violence creating exploitation and patriarchy from the time of the first rise of the agricultural surplus, the role of the State itself in organizing and legitimizing violence appears to be central. It appears that all forms of domination—looting, economic exploitation and patriarchy—began not immediately or automatically but only after a historically long period.

It is clear from the historical records that the "dialectics of sex" is crucial. From the very first written records in the period of rise of first states, we have evidence of the centrality of male-female relations of sexual domination, of the definition of women as good/bad wife/mistress/prostitute, in terms of a state regulated sexual relationship to men. In this sense, the insights of radical feminism have to be incorporated into any analysis.

There are some special problems. As the ancient Indian texts lack definite chronology, one constantly works with suspicion. The break between theory and practice, and the related truism that what prevails in the society does not generally confirm to the norms set forth in the texts, is perhaps even more applicable to these contexts. For instance, in the study of Sanskrit texts, one must work with many texts within a single period, without a corresponding sense of their relative dating. The historical difficulty of dating some of the important texts like the *Vedas*, epics, the *Manusmriti*, the *Dharmasutras*, various *Dharmashastras* and many other texts is well known. In addition, because of this lack of genuinely historiographical material in the early texts, we have not been able to glean much useful information on women. Because of these limitations, scholars working on socio-historical problems, specially in the case of women in ancient India, work against great odds. Aside from these general technical issues, one deals with the ancient texts concerned with the sociological issues like the position, authority or autonomy of women, such topics within the perview of *Dharmasutras/ Dharmashastras*, and perhaps also the epics. Amazingly, in these very texts, we tend to encounter a single, uniform ideology about women. It is well known that "the power of patriarchy" the world over was not genuinely challenged till the feminist movement came on the scene. But what is difficult to understand is that in India, almost all the *Dharmashastra* texts that deal directly with society, and therefore with women, seem to depict one kind of social ideology in presenting the picture of women. For instance, while one need not accept the totally glorified picture of women in the Vedic period, by the same token it is difficult to believe that she had fallen to such a pathetic state without a voice of her own, as we see in *Smritis*. Women composed hymns in the Vedic period, they were philosophers in the Upaniṣadic times, also there were women poets, writers and *sanyasins*. Therefore, it is bit surprising to see that there is not a single woman writer of a *Dharmashastra* text.

While this age seems to be heavily weighted against women in a socio-historical context, facts are not just black or white. There can be many grey areas in between, and it may be in these grey areas that we have our only clue to such multiple voices. For instance, we are very familiar with the statement of Manu that a woman does not merit freedom (*na stri svatantryamarhati*). There are other statements in the *Manusmriti*, which are not so condemnatory towards women. We find another saying, also well known, that only such a society can thrive in which women are respected (*yatra naryastupujyante ramante tatra devatah*)[38]. Then again we are told by Manu that a mother is more worthy of respect than a thousand *acharyas*, or teachers.[39] Manu also gives a woman full right over her *stridhana*. He even mentions that, rather than be married to a man having no good qualities, a daughter should not be given in marriage at all.[40] He, then, has a whole set of verses in the fifth and ninth chapters that look upon women as deprived. What is one to make all these conflicting

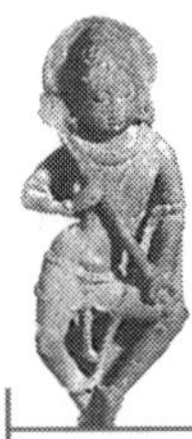

statements in the same book? Are these all written by the same Manu or by a number of people and compiled by one Manu much in the manner of Patañjali's *Yogasūtras* ? It is difficult to believe that one and the same Manu could have had such different views, both of an extreme nature, on women. The contradictory statements of Manu hint at the different possible perceptions of women prevalent in the society, as well as the attempt to paint all those images with a single colour in keeping with a single ideology, mentioned earlier.

When we discuss the history of early India, it becomes difficult for us to do a period-by-period survey because the data available to us is too scanty for the purpose. Further, we do not know the precise dates of any of our authorities. For example, the *Mahabharata* and *Manusmriti* contain ideas popular in epochs, which were separated from each other by more than half a millennium.

NOTES AND REFERENCES

1. Jane Flax, "Postmodernism and Gender Relations in Feminist Theory", *Signs*, University of Chicago Press (Chicago) 12.4, 1987, p. 629.
2. Merry Wiesner- Hanks, "Women's History and World History Course", *Radical History Review*, winter, 2005, Vol. 9, p. 136.
3. Olive Schreiner, "Women and Labour", in Fisher and Unwin's *South Africa*, 1911, p. 29.
4. Lees Sue, "Feminist Politics and Women Studies: Struggle not Incorporation" in Jane Aaron and Sylviya Walby (eds.), *Out of Margins: Women Studies in the Nineties*, London, 1991.
5. Susan Sheridan, "Feminist Knowledge, Women's Liberation and Women's Studies" in Sneja Gunew (ed.) *Feminist Knowledge: Critique and Construct*, London,1990. For this debate see J. Radford, "History of Women's Liberation in Britain: A Reflective Personal History", in Gabriele Griffin's *Marianne Hestine;* Shirin Rai and Sasha Roseneil (eds.), *Stirring It: Challenges From Feminism*, London, 1994; R. Morley and Val Walsh (eds.), *Feminist Academics: Creative Agent For Change*, London, 1995; Warwick, Alex and Rosemary Auchmuty; "Women Studies as Feminist Activism" in Gabriele Griffin (ed.) *Feminist Activism in the 1990s*, London,1995; Charles N. and Felicia Hughes Freeland (eds.),*Practicing Feminism Identity Difference Power*, London, 1996 and also Robbinson Victoria and Diane Richardson's, *Introducing Women's Studies: Feminist Theory and Practice*, London, 1997.
6. Merry E. Wiesers, *Women and Gender in Early Modern Europe*, 2nd edn., London, 2000, pp. 1-3.

7. *Ibid.*, p. 7.
8. D.D. Kosambi, "Historical Perspective of Women", in H.C. Upadhyaya (ed.), *Status of Women in India*, Delhi, 1991.
9. A.S. Altekar, *The Position of Women in Hindu Civilization,* Delhi, 1987, p. 1.
10. Romila Thapar, "Looking Back in History", in Devaki Jain (ed.), *Indian Women*, New Delhi, Publication Division, Ministry of Information and Broadcasting, Govt. of India, 1975, p. 6.
11. M.N. Srinivas, *The Changing Position of Indian Women,* Bombay, 1978, p. 7.
12. Madhu Kishwar, "A Horror of Ism: Why I Do Not Call Myself a Feminist" in Maitreye Chaudhuri (ed.), *Feminism in India*, Delhi, 2004.
13. Joan Kelley, *Women, History and Theory, The Essays of Joan Kelley*, London, 1984, p. 1.
14. Merry E. Wiesers, *Women and Gender in Early Modern Europe,* 2nd edn., London, 2000.
15. Referred to time and again in my thesis.
16. S.W. Jamisom, *Encyclopedia of Religion and Ethics*, 1996, pp. 4-5.
17. *Ibid.*, p. 214.
18. See the iconic representations from Mathura explaining gender representation in its society, Figs. 1 & 2.
19. A.L. Basham, *The Wonder That Was India,* New York, 1959, p. 1.
20. Uma Chakravarti, "Beyond the Altekarian Paradigm: Towards a New Understanding of Gender Relations in Early Indian History", p. 77, in Kumkum Roy (ed.) *Women in Early Indian Societies*, Delhi, rept., 2001.
21. Gerda Lerner, *The Creation of Patriarchy*, Delhi, 1986, p. 29.
22. Uma Chakravarti, "Conceptualizing Brahmanical Patriarchy in Early India: Gender, Caste, Class And State", *Economic and Political Weekly,* April 3, 1993.
23. Gerda Lerner, *The Creation of Patriarchy*, Delhi, 1986, p. 39.
24. Uma Chakravarti, "Conceptualizing Brahmanical Patriarchy in Early India: Gender, Caste, Class and State", *Economic and Political Weekly,* April 3, 1993.
25. A. Neumayer, *Pre-historic Rock Paintings in Central India*, 1983, p. 21.
26. Uma Chakravarti, "Conceptualizing Brahmanical Patriarchy in Early India: Gender, Caste, Class And State", *Economic and Political Weekly,* April 3, 1993.
27. Gerda Lerner, *The Creation of Patriarchy*, Delhi, 1986, p. 29.
28. Gerda Lerner, *The Creation of Patriarchy*, Delhi, 1986, p. 8.
29. Uma Chakravarti, "Conceptualizing Brahmanical Patriarchy in Early India: Gender, Caste, Class And State", *Economic and Political Weekly,* April 3, 1993.
30. Uma Chakravarti, "Of Dasas and Karmkaras: Service Labour in Ancient India", in Usha Patnaik and Manjari Dingwancy (eds.), *Chains of Servitude: Bondage and Slavery in India*, Delhi, 1985, pp. 35-75.
31. Gerda Lerner, *The Creation of Patriarchy*, p. 78ff.
32. A.S. Altekar, *The Position of Women in Hindu Civilization*, Delhi, 1987 (rept.), p. 337.

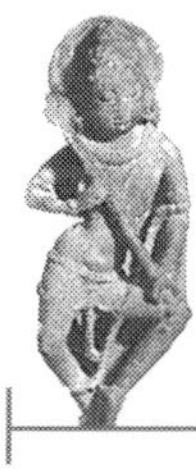

33. *Rig Veda*, IX: 85.43.
34. *Manu*, 2.213; 9.5, 7, 12.
35. Manu, 3.45; 5.153; 9.26, 27, 45.
36. *Manu*, 3.55.
37. A.S. Altekar, *The Position of Women in Hindu Civilization*, Delhi, 1987 (rept.), p. 345.
38. *Manu*, 3.56.
39. *Manu*, 2.145.
40. *Manu*, 9.89.

Chapter II

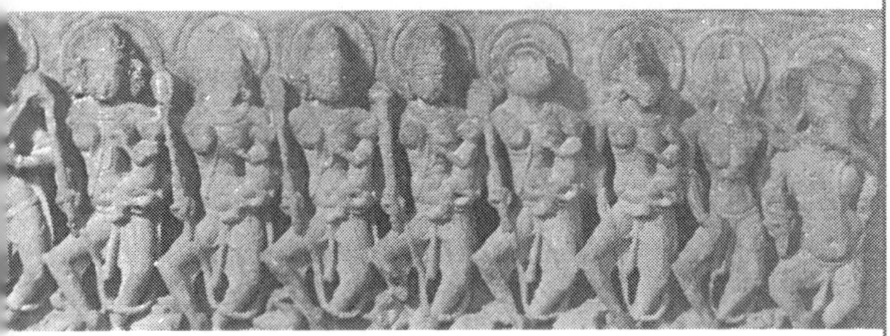

Buddhist Perspective of Women

There is a spate of studies on the gender question but not much in Buddhist literature. There is a general belief that history of women in Buddhism is a linear narrative of progress from oppression to liberation. But this is not true as patriarchal value system often bordering on misogyny has been quite pronounced in Buddhism. Within this ambit we have to define the place of women and construction of gender in androcentric tradition. We appreciate the view of Bernard Faure that Buddhism is paradoxically neither sexist nor as egalitarian as is commonly thought.[1]

We notice two kinds of approaches in Buddhist texts; the active role of Buddhist women to counter the stereotype of women as passive cultural subjects (*Therigatha*) and second the Buddhist bias against women and the attempts to overcome this bias (The Canonical texts).

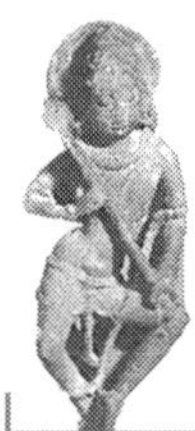

A. VISIBILITY OF EGALITARIAN CONCEPTS OF BUDDHISM IN THE IMAGES OF WOMEN IN THE ANDROCENTRIC LITERATURE (*THERIGATHA*)

The gender study perspective claims quite reasonably that a recounted past which ignores data about the female half of the population cannot be accurate. They have been excluded as actors and authors from featuring as they should have in history. Romila Thapar observes, "Gender studies have not been just the accumulation of more data on the history of women but gathering the views and activities of women and observing how these conditioned society. Particular social forms became patterns of control over women, and resistance to these is significant to social history. Earlier, popular belief held that Gargi asking philosophical questions, or the official recording of the donations of Ashoka's queen, Kauravaki, were proof of women generally being held in respect. But when such references were placed alongside the evidence of a subordinate status, the assessment required reconsideration. Historically, women were as central to the creation of communities and identities as were men."[2] This observation needs to be taken into account. In this context, I am selecting the text *Therigatha* for discussion. My analyses and reconstruction of images of women will be purely based on this text and I am leaving scope for comparison with other Buddhist texts which may be done later.

Buddhists advocated both that there is some problem with women and also that women are just as capable of achieving the goals of Buddhism as men. The well-known story of Buddha's reluctant permission to found the *bhikkhunis*' (nuns') order contrasts significantly and starkly with lesser known record of early *bhikkhunis'* success, as recorded in the *Therigatha* (the collection of the "Verses of the Elder Nuns"). My aim in this chapter is to explore the contradiction between the egalitarian concepts of Buddhism and its patriarchal history. Various authors have emphasized the fundamental ambivalence of the Buddha as a religious reformer, who while opening his community to women, singularly diminished the boldness of his move by relegating them to a subaltern position. Perhaps this ambivalence reflects socio-historical conditions and in particular the antagonism that existed among various clerical factions. Eight strict rules may have been an attempt by early Buddhists to stay in line with common practice of the time. In an attempt to reconcile with this concept of ambivalence, women gradually became equal to men as they reached higher stages in Buddhism. This ideal is expressed in the *Therigatha* where women are said to have become *arhats* (priests). In the *Therigatha*, there are many stories of women for whom Buddhism was deeply liberating and satisfying. These women manifest that women are highly capable of achieving goals of Buddhism. The 1990s witnessed a re-examination of classic Buddhist text, the *Therigatha*. This is a unique document ascribed to *theris*, literally elderly women, respected *bhikkhunis* within the Buddhist traditions. Ever since its discovery in the 19th century, the text has been the subject of debate regarding the extent to which it permits travel to women's voices. Neumann, one of the earliest translators of the text (in German)[3], was of the opinion that although the verses were ascribed to women, their real authors were men. Another historian of Buddhism and gender points out, "most of the arguments in favour of early Buddhist egalitarianism rest on rare documents such as the *Therigatha*, a text allegedly recording 'triumph songs' of women". We have no evidence that these verses were actually composed by women to whom they were attributed, for the text was compiled, edited and annotated by a monk, Dhammapada.[4] Rhys Davids[5], a woman scholar, who produced the first English translation in 1909 energetically refuted Neumann pointing to differences in style and content between the *Thera* and *Therigatha*, apart from highlighting the obvious bias in attributing every literary composition to men.[6] Blackstone observes, "The *Therigatha* is an exciting and provocative text. As far as I know it is the only canonical text in the world's religions that is attributed to female authorship and that focuses exclusively on women's religious experiences".[7] She draws attention to subtle variations in the ways in which men and women were thought to have conceptualized their experiences in *Thera* and *Therigatha* respectively. Thus, for women attainment of *nibbana* was often represented as conquest, the result of strenuous endeavour, whereas the process was represented as being relatively smooth for men. Blackstone explains this diversity by suggesting that the texts were expected to function as manual for aspirants to *nibbana*. She also highlights the relatively impersonal tone adopted in the works attributed to men; those ascribed to women, on the other hand, are characterized by a greater sense of involvement, including mention of past experiences, often located in a vividly detailed social context. These differences, as she acknowledges, are subtle and not always obvious. In other words, while

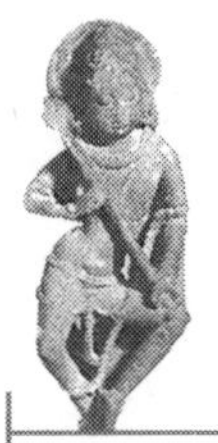

pointing out that gender identities were significant, Blackstone is sensitive to the shared spiritual and worldly domains of monks and nuns.

The *Therigatha,* as available at present, is the product of a long and complicated history. Many of the ascribed authors were recognized as contemporaries of the Buddha, and some of the *gathas* have had a respectable antiquity, others were probably incorporated at a later date. The logic of the compilation as well as addition of biographical notes to the verses provide some insight into the processes which went into the making of the text. Blackstone's analysis opens up possibilities of moving beyond literal readings, or even listening to what apparently seem to be women's unmediated voices, to viewing the text as providing a more complicated representation of gender relations[8].The *Therigatha* has been hailed as a text containing women's voices. These are not male fantasies or projections about women. So, it is worth bearing in mind that while we can pull out images of women (and men) from both *gathas* and commentary, these are images which were drawn and assembled from diverse traditions and incorporated within the canonical framework.

In the *Therigatha,* the gatha attributed to Bhadda Kundalakesi [9] and Punna[10] is illustrative of this. Bhadda is one of the few women represented as experimenting with alternative traditions and practices before adopting Buddhism. Her history, as collated in the commentary, is an amalgamation of folk tales. She was born into a rich family, but fell in love with a robber and married him. The robber wanted to make off with her jewels, but she foiled this attempt by simply pushing him over a precipice and he was killed. Unable to return home after this, she took to a life of wandering, and became a famous debater, who literally staked her claim by planting a branch outside the city gates, inviting the challengers to pull it down. She was ultimately outtalked by the eminent monk Sariputra.[11] Bhadda's verses have been handed down to us in *Therigatha*[12] as she summarizes her life, "that she travelled before in a single cloth, with shaven head, covered in dust, and saw *bhikkhus* revering Buddha. She too humbly bowed down before Him. The Buddha called and ordained her. Then she travelled for fifty years in Anga, Magadha, Vajji, Kasi and Kosala, living on the alms of the land and propagated Buddhism."

On the other hand, Punna[13] figures as a slave woman who goes to draw water from the river even in the extreme weathers as she is afraid of being beaten by her mistress (*ayyanam dandabhayabhita*). Her *gatha*

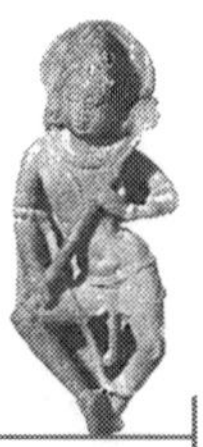

is constructed as a dialogue with a brahmana who comes every morning to perform ablutions. He shivers as he takes a dip in the river to wash away his sins. Punna tries to dissuade him by using commonsensical arguments. She wonders whether the fish and tortoise are redeemed, for example, or whether the water will not wash away his merits as well.

She said,

> Drawn of water I go down to the stream
> Even in winter in fear of blows,
> Harassed by fear of blame from mistress
> Brahmana what fearest thou that ever thus
> Thou goest to the river?
> Why with shivering limbs (thou) suffer bitter cold

Upon hearing the reply of the brahmana that he was trying to wash off his sins and accumulate merit, Punna replied,

> Nay, now, who hath told the this that water baptism
> From evil karma can free thee?
> Why, then the fishes and the tortoises
> And all that haunt the water
> Straight to heaven will go?
> But the water would bear away thy merit
> Leaving the stripped and bare
> To battle and shiver here
> That even that leave thou undone,
> and save thy skin from frost.[14]

Ultimately the brahmana is convinced, and declares that until now he was merely a *brahmabandhu* and has only now become a true brahmana. Punna demolishes the claims of the brahmanas as a caste to inherit superiority and monopoly over knowledge. She had been a domestic slave but her master was so pleased by this that he freed her, and on her request he also entered the *samgha*.

Just as there were two foremost disciples in the order of monks, namely Sariputta and Moggallana, likewise the Buddha named two women as foremost amongst *bhikkhunis*, namely Uppalavanna and Khema. The name Khema[15] means well-settled or composed or secure and is a synonym for *Nibbana*. Khema belonged to a royal family from the land of Magadha and she became one of the chief consorts of King Bimbisara.

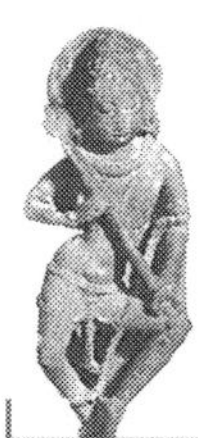

According to the legend, on her visit to the *Vihara*, she was instructed by Buddha himself and she immediately attained arhatship. Thereafter, she became known for her great insight and was ranked high by the Exalted One himself and given a seat in a conclave of Aryans at the Jeta Grove Vihara[16]. Later, Khema taught her companion, Vijaya the norms of the *samgha* so as to agitate her mind concerning rebirth and make her seek comfort in the *samgha.*[17]

Patacara was the beautiful daughter of a very wealthy merchant of Savatthi. She married against her parents' wishes and later lost her husband and sons and parents. She joined the Buddhist *samgha* to reduce her grief. Buddha said about Patacara that she was the foremost "Keeper of the Vinaya" amongst the *bhikkhunis.* She was deeply versed in human sufferings. Patacara was, thus, the female counterpart of the bhikkhu Upali. That she had chosen the "Rules of Conduct" as her central discipline is easy to understand, because the results of her former indulgences had become bitterly obvious to her. She learned in the *samgha,* that an intensive study of the rules was necessary and purifying, and brought with it the security and safety of self-discipline; she learned not to become complacent through well-being or anxious and confused through suffering. Through her experiences she had gained a deep understanding of the human predicament and could be of great assistance to her fellow *bhikkhunis.*

She was a great comfort to those who came to her in difficulties. Bhikkhuni Chanda said that Patacara showed her the right path of compassion and helped her achieve emancipation. Another *bhikkhuni,* Uttara II, reported how Patacara spoke to the group of *bhikkhunis* about conduct and discipline:

> Having established mind,
> One-pointed, well-developed,
> Investigate formations
> As other, not as self.[18]

Uttara took Patacara's words to heart and said:

> When I heard these words, —
> Patacara's advice,
> After washing my feet —
> I sat down alone.[19]

Thus, this *bhikkhuni* too was able to attain the three *vijja*, true knowledge and *nibbana*. In the "Verses of the Elder Nuns" we have a record of Patacara's instructions to the nuns and their resultant gains:

Having taken flails,
Young men thresh the corn.
Thus wives and children feed;
So young men win their wealth.
So likewise as to Buddha's Teachings,
From doing which there's no remorse.
Quickly cleanse your feet
And sit you down alone.
Devote yourselves to calm of mind,
And thus do Buddha's Teachings.
When they heard these words —
Patacara's instructions,
Having washed their feet,
They sat down, each one alone,
Devoted themselves to calm of mind.
And thus followed the Buddha's Teachings.
In the night's first watch
Past births were remembered;
In the middle watch of the night
The eye divine was purified;
In the night's last watch
They rent asunder the mass of gloom.
Having risen, they bowed at her feet,
Her instructions having done;
We shall live revering you
Like the thirty gods to Indra,
Undefeated in war.
We are with triple knowledge true
And gone are all the taints.[20]

Patacara was responsible for bringing 500 women to the order. The number of women recorded to have left the worldly life under Mahapajapati may be recorded as six.[21] Women in trouble are not recorded to have gone to Mahapajapati, but to Patacara, because she was a great

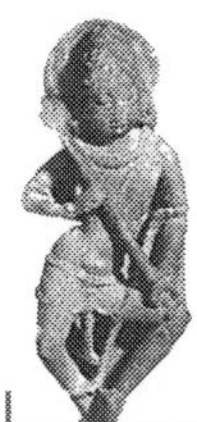

teacher. The three women Mahapajapati, Patacara and Dhammadina[22] (Dhammadina was instrumental in leading two women to arhatship, one of them was Mahapajapati's nurse[23]) specially stand out as preachers and by converting women to Buddhist religious order they showed them the way to happiness.The most significant aspect here is that conversion of women by women is part of the weighty contribution that they made to the Buddhist religion. As teachers, they exhibited a variety of attracting forces, based upon their individual characters and histories. But irrespective of whichever aspect of the system made a greater appeal to each one of them and through her to her listeners, whether it was impermanence including the transitory nature of self, the surrender to spiritual calm, which is the carrying out of Buddha's will, etc., fundamentally they all taught the same thing.[24]

I.B. Horner suggests "that a woman could be represented as making such an utterance is a proof that the old life of Hinduism in which women were regarded merely as child-bearers and commodities was if not suffering a decline, at least not passing entirely unquestioned. It is not unnatural that this appeal should emanate from a woman, for they were always there in the background. However slight their effect on a religion might appear to be externally, internally they had great influence, moulding it because they were in it, actively interested and in reality colouring any opinions held by their menfolk".[25]

According to the *Therigatha*, Buddha often taught both *bhikkhunis* and laywomen, directly and appropriately, with great compassion and skill. He praised them lavishly for high achievements and for generosity. Literature provides two lifestyles available to Buddhist women of this period, that of a nun and that of a laywoman. The *Therigatha* seems to be a record that women themselves kept, which was somehow included in the *Pali canon* when men collected and edited the scriptures. Without this text, our picture of early Buddhism would be much more limited for the *bhikkhunis* stories do not figure predominantly in the numerous records kept by men. Clearly, women were not prohibited from joining the Buddhist order as equal to men in their achievements and understanding of the dharma. "That their legends have not been discussed or highlighted in the texts shows more of an influence of patriarchy on the scholars who wrote them than the Buddha's actual teachings".[26] Without *Therigatha*, we would not have known *bhikkhunis*' order, mainly as something about which even Buddha was quite ambivalent, at best. The records that men kept deal far more with laywomen than with *bhikkhunis.*

Laywomen, as we may have already seen, are negatively portrayed sometimes as wives who try to regain their husbands or otherwise present obstacle to men. The stories of these women were of no interest to either the monks or the nuns and their voices were probably irretrievably lost. But another class of laywomen also figures prominently in the men's record. These are pious laywomen donors who came off best in the early Buddhist literature as a whole. As Nancy Falk has pointed out, "the grand heroine of Buddhist story telling is not the nun's order's founder Prajapati, as one might expect, but Vishakha, a prominent merchant's daughter and wife who belonged to the early community and who never took the *bhikkhuni's* vow"[27] Her story presents two common themes in Buddhist literature—the importance of lay donors to the religion and the tendency of androcentric record keepers[28] to prefer such women to female world renouncers, to *bhikkhunis.*

Therigatha discusses three types of women. The first type being those who thought that life in *samgha* might provide a comfortable milieu for many women after the trials and tribulations they had suffered in the world, in no other sense was it to be regarded as a relaxation. The second type were the women who regarded entry into the order as a blessing.[29] They thought of it as securing the means of self-realization and larger and fuller field of mental activity, more vital than that of domestic circle. These women were never filled with missionary zeal or drawn on by any theories concerning the advantage of a community over a home life. They were animated solely by the desire for a real search for enlightenment, for it was the religious life as such that they recognized to be their genuine vocation. They did not seek it as an escape from an existence which they could no longer endure, but knew it to be the life that they would prefer above all others to lead, the life for which, as they would express it, they were destined. No emotion centering in the past drove them forth from the home to the homeless way, but the religious call, clarion with the hope of winning a treasure more glorious than any to be gained in the turmoil of worldly life. The price religious life demands is renunciation, but renunciation is looked upon as privilege where freedom, insight, peace are to be the gains. The third type of women who came to the *samgha* because of the urge for Dhamma. Sumedha, with her aversion

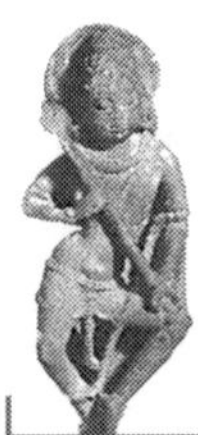

from pleasures of senses but a definite devotion to religion, may be looked upon as a bridge between the above two kinds of women.

Sumedha entered the order against her parents' wishes. They could not deter her when she put forward the alternative of dying. Sumedha was an independent girl who declared, "my duty lies not in the life of the house". She refused the royal suitor they brought to her, cut off her hair and practiced meditation. Later, she became famous and learned and she was able to convert her parents, her suitor and his retinue.[30] Here the choice between renunciation and marriage is constituted as a dramatic conflict.

Some of the earliest expressions of women's perception of the limitations of the roles allotted to them by patriarchal society are available to us in the poems left behind by the *bhikkhunis* in the text. They make it clear that the search for identity outside domesticity in the case of women goes back to the sixth century BC. This is not a product of Western influence as the centre of feminism like to pose—but a very indigenous and ancient search for a self-identity outside of patriarchal structures.[31]

There were women who were frustrated in the traditional role as a wife and saw themselves as escaping from the trapped role assigned to them. We have examples of women celebrating their liberation from drudgery of the pestle and mortar. Sumangala's mother records her feelings in the following verse:

> "O Woman, Well set free!
> How free I am
> How thoroughly free of kitchen drudgery".[32]

Therigatha serves as invaluable counterbalance to convention. The theme of freedom, both spiritual and social, dominates the poem. These poems contrast significantly to culturally dominant stereotype about women as subservient to men and dependent upon them. As Mutta states:

> I am free, totally free
> In freedom from those three hideous shapes
> My grind stones, my pestle and my hunch backed husband
> I am free from birth and death.[33]

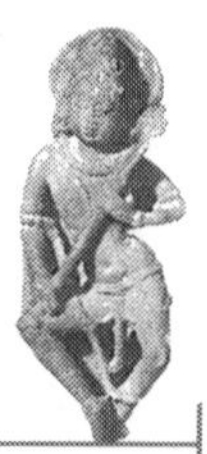

Uma Chakravarti[34] states that emancipation by *bhikkhunis* was perceived as space or opportunity for developing and concentrating, it was only as *bhikkhunis* that women, in the age of Buddha, found any liberation from the conferred roles assigned to them by their society.

Quest for knowledge led these women to follow Buddhism. Bhadda Kundalakesha[35], after failing in her unfortunate love affair with a thief of brahmana caste and later failing to find her intellectual equals, joined the Jaina sect. Outwitting the Jainas in debate and finding that she could learn nothing more from them, she left them and sought to satisfy her intellectual carvings by debating with the Buddhists. Another woman, Nanduttara[36], who was born in a brahmana family, after having led a varied religious career, eventually found an outlet for intellectual need in Buddhism, after participating in a debate with Maha-Moggalana. On his advice, she entered the *samgha* of almswomen.

The story of Bhaddha Kapilani is told in *Theragatha* by her husband and in *Therigatha* by herself. Kassapa, her husband, had decided to take care of his parents till they were alive and declared that he would renounce the world after their death. When his parents died, both Kassapa and Bhadda, after consulting each other, cut off each other's hair, put on robes, took begging bowls and parted ways from each other. Both became arhats and important leaders in Buddha's community. Bhadda was ranked first among those who remembered past lives by the Buddha. In her verses in the *Therigatha*, she celebrates both her own achievements and his, as well as their shared vision:

> We both have seen, both he and I, the woe
> And pity of the world, and have gone forth.
> We both are arhants with selves well tamed.
> Cool are we both, Ours is Nibbana now.[37]

Clearly men and women can cooperate with each other in the world of renunciation and achievement of liberation and peace. Rita Gross states that the existence of *Therigatha* with its systematic portraits of women who took Buddhism's message fully to heart and achieved its goal of peace and release, stands as a challenge to all Buddhists of all times who would prefer women to do less.[38]

Horner[39] points out 'the *Therigatha* as compared with the *Theragatha*, portrays an apparent insensibility to nature. In the former, few references are made to it, while in the latter, there are many. But this was not because women were normally less impressionable to natural phenomena than

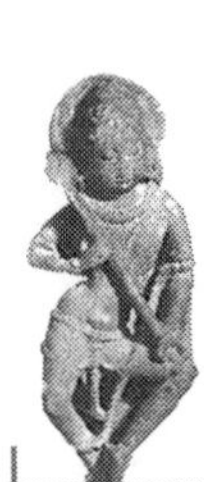

men, for we hear now and again of a woman who loved nature[40], but it was because in meditation they concentrated more intensely then men, and shut away all distracting sites and sounds by an effort of the will, determined to surrender the bonds that dragged them backward to hither shore".[41] In order to reach the goal, these women managed to restrain the senses, and for this reason the moment of attainment and its expression are free from all sensory images.

There were 23 royal entrants, of whom three were particularly famous in the order, these were Mahaprajapati, the reputed founder of the *samgha* of almswomen, Khemma and Kissa Gautami, another kinswoman of Gautama, who became chief among those who wear the rough robes (*lukhacivardhara*). Here I accept Margery Wolf's argument which she gave in the context of Chinese Buddhist women that women could wield power in ways that were not recognized in a patriarchal gender ideology.[42]

Thirteen women came from the merchant families, out of which Dhammadina became one of the greatest preachers and was regarded as Dhammakathika. Patacara became the greatest teacher and was well versed in *Vinaya*.

At least 18 almswomen mentioned in the *Therigatha* belonged to brahmana families. The most eminent were Bhadda of the Kapilas, Nandutara, Sakula and Sundari. The reason may be the lack of dogma and strictness in Hinduism, which made it easy for its women members to equip themselves with fresh religious ideas, and thus, it is not surprising that the priestly caste yielded a large number of recruits to the new teaching order.

There were four women from other castes and at least eleven entrants whose castes are not mentioned. There was, moreover, the category of the courtesans who were four in number[43], Vimala, Addhikasi, Abhaya's mother, and the most famous, Ambapali, who realized the worthlessness and foulness of the body. The *samgha* of the almswomen yielded an accessible and honourable alternative to all those who wanted to relinquish the line of business they had been pursuing. But once they were admitted, they had to confirm to strict moral rules.

Entry into the order was in no way dependent on social status, and by the sixth century BC the importance attached to the notion of release had filtered through all strata of society and was not the monopoly, like

Plato's philosophy, of a leisured class, but was something which could be understood, striven for and held by high and low alike.[44]

The women were in the category of married, widowed and unmarried. Permission of husband or parents was sought in the case of married women. It is a general scholarly belief that in ancient India, it was unthinkable that patriarchal gender hierarchy could be ignored and that women could live the homeless life without conventional social ties. Whether it was the dominance of patriarchy[45] or if it was to find out whether the aspirants were really free from home ties and could be spared for arhatship[46] that led the Buddhist *samgha* to check with the family members, is a thoughtful question.

I agree with Kumkum Roy's observation[47] that the images of women in *Therigatha* strike us as somewhat different, this may be because the text was directed less towards monks (for whom references to the horrors of the female body may have sufficed) but more towards laymen and women, including potential believers. To be successful with such an audience, monopoly of the stereotype probably had to be broken and replaced with the variety of the individuality, which characterizes the *Therigatha*. Precisely because the majority of Buddhist historical sources demean, silence and erase women, whatever meagre references we do find become very important.

Allan Sponberg emphasizes that misogyny was not the fate of Buddhism. Women played an important role in early Buddhist community, not only as donors, but also as practitioners and teachers. Despite their institutional inferiority, they were recognized as having a spiritual status equal to men. The *Therigatha* is read as a poetic tribute to the spiritual achievements of some of these women, who reached awakening and became saints or arhats. Such is the case of Khema, the consort of King Bimbisara, who obtained deliverance long before her virtuous husband[48]. Yet even if one granted such egalitarian beginnings, it remains to explain the trend reversal and the progressive hardening of Buddhist community towards its female constituents. The *Therigatha* provided us with an account of the way women perceived the unequal relations between men and women and sought to achieve an identity outside of domestic role.

Until the *Therigatha* was discussed, the story or history of women in Buddhism has been represented in a relatively linear fashion: a shift from oppression to freedom, a teleological narrative of progress and liberation (from so-called Hinayana to Mahayana or again from an elitist ideology to a more open and democratic one). However, Rita M. Gross[49] warns that though the stories of the women narrated in the *Therigatha* are highly useful, their utility is also limited. These women are heroines, but they are also tokens in an androcentric and patriarchal past. We need to know about and celebrate our heroines and role models, but on the other hand it is important not to overcompensate by making more of them than is justified.

Uma Chakravarti's contention that some of the earliest expressions of women's perception of the limitations of the roles allotted to them by a patriarchal society are available to us in the poems left behind by the *bhikkhunis* in the corpus called *Therigatha*. They make it clear that the search for identity outside domesticity in the case of women goes back to the sixth century BC. It is not a product of Western influence as the critics of Western influence like to posit—but a very indigenous and ancient search for self-identity outside of patriarchal structures. In these poems, women spoke of the joy at leaving behind the drudgery of the kitchen, and the brutality of the husbands. They also spoke of the space they found for themselves as they entered the *samgha* and practised self-awareness".[50]

Rita Gross's observation,

> When the roles and images of women throughout Buddhist history are studied as part of feminine revalorization of Buddhism, the quest for an accurate past intertwines with the quest for a usable past, and each enhances the other. An accurate record connected for the omissions of androcentricism demonstrates two things very clearly. It demonstrates that women have participated in the Buddhist discourses in varied and significant ways, and their roles and images have been discussed relatively frequently in Buddhist texts. On the other hand, looking specifically at women's roles and images throughout Buddhist history also demonstrates quite clearly the patriarchal inadequacies of the past

........fits in here. The history of Buddhist community and monastic life reveals different attitudes at different time periods and the impress of contemporary social values.

While reviewing Rita M. Gross's book, Ian Astely points out,

> In an androcentric patriarchal society, it must have been indeed a tricky situation whereby on the one hand, *bhikkhus* and *bhikkhunis* had to maintain

> sufficient distance from each other to avoid the question of impropriety, and on the other the samgha had to deal with the social unacceptability (indeed unimaginability) of an autonomous group of women not under the direct regulation and control of some male authority. By being formally associated with the monks, the *bhikkhunis* were able to enjoy the benefits of leaving the household life without incurring immediate harm. Whilst it is understandable to abhor the attitude and behaviour of the society towards women, which necessitated such a protection, but it is misplaced to criticize the samgha for adopting this particular policy.[51]

But here I have tried to explore the contradiction between the egalitarian concepts of Buddhism and its patriarchal history, seeking both to explain that contradiction historically and to rectify that situation in a future manifestation and form of Buddhism. Such reconstructions take us beyond the current institutional form of Buddhism as well as its conceptual structure.

Even Uma agrees that "entry into the samgha did provide women with an important resource through which they succeeded partially in escaping patriarchal structures".[52] Otherwise also a woman entering the Buddhist *samgha* was required to take the following oath, "I go forth to a homeless life, following lord Sakyamuni. I abandon the superficial characteristics of a householder".[53]

Many scholars are of the opinion that Buddha considered women's position to be inferior to that of men and was reluctant to take women into *samgha.* Admitting women to the sacred and venerating society of *samgha* would corrupt its sanctity and destroy the Buddhist order is a patriarchal viewpoint. Bartholomeusz suggestion that "the dialogue with Buddha suggests that he may be reluctant to establish the bhikshuni samgha, but he nonetheless regarded it as an essential support of the religion"[54] seems to be correct. Chapla Verma[55] points to the social constraints and practical needs of the *samgha,* if Buddha did[56], in fact, discourage women from joining the *samgha,* to be more important than the inferiority of women to men. The reluctance of Buddha in taking women into the *samgha* probably reflected social concerns that their entry may endanger the family unit or that life in and for monastic order would simply become more complicated if women joined it. Secondly, decisions regarding the admission of women to the Buddhist *samgha* were thought to belong to the realm of social concerns that needed to be taken into consideration. Apprehension that the *samgha* might get a bad name if a monk and nun got involved with each other might have been the main concern that prompted later Buddhist leaders to impose such stringent rules. Lastly, in a patriarchal society, where monks who dominated the power structure were more in number, these rules would work more against women than against men.

Most of our understanding about the Buddhist attitude toward women is based on the functioning of the *samgha* and its members, not society at large. But society may have played a vital role in influencing the decisions of the Buddhist *samgha*. Androcentric society in which patriarchal norms were dominant, regarded men as normal and women as exceptional when they deviated from the prescribed social norms.

B. MISOGYNOUS LITERATURE

We notice two kinds of anti-feminism in Buddhism: first is the early monastic attitude, which stipulates that 'a Bodhisattva should wander alone like a rhinoceros'. The fact of lonely women being easy targets for rape made it difficult for female ascetics to follow this principle. Secondly, Buddhism, while trying to strike roots in patriarchal societies, tends to adopt local gender prejudices, reducing Buddhist *samgha* to patriarchal institutions. This explains the *samgha* being suspicious of women in general; the gender bias in eight rules rendering nuns subordinate to monks, irrespective of seniority, thus making *samgha* 'a bastion of male priviledge'.

Jataka stories, images and ideals, which were written long after Buddha's time, portray women negatively, which has effectively damaged the image and position of women in Buddhism. *Jataka kathas* show marked disdain for women. However, there is no evidence that this denigration of women was propounded or countenanced by Buddha himself. *Jataka* stories, images and ideals became vehicles of misogynist views. They presented themselves as ultimate examples of virulent attitude. Such an attitude is reflected through innumerable episodes like a bodhisattva taking pride in being called a woman-hater (*anitthigandha*)[57], seducing the bride of a king to prove a point[58], a generous king giving away his wife to a man to enjoy for seven days[59], a king telling a woman, with whom he has had casual sex, to bring the child to him only if she gives birth to a male child[60], etc.

Jataka tales tell about women: "They are like unto robbers with braided locks, like a poisoned drink, like merchants that sing their own praises, crooked like a deer's horn, evil-tounged like snakes, like a pit that is covered over, insatiate as hell, as hard to satisfy as she-ogre, like the all-rapacious Yama, all devouring like a flame, sweeping all before it as a river, like the wind going where it lists, undiscriminating like mount Neru, fruiting perennially like a poison tree."[61]

Polygamy was in vogue in the vast majority of the royal houses during this period as revealed by the *Jataka* texts. The *Chullasuttasoma Jataka*[62] speaks of the king who had seven hundred wives, while another refers to one claiming as many as 84,000 queens. Though the figures mentioned in these texts are overtly exaggerated, it is revealed that Bimbisara, Prasenajit, Udayana and Ajatsatru were all polygamists.

Kathahahari-Jataka tells the story of a king who refuses to recognize his son. The mother throws the child into the air, praying that if he be not the king's son, he may be killed by his fall. The child rests in mid-air and the king recognizes him as his son and makes his mother his chief queen, who happened to be the daughter of a slave by birth.

Anadabhuda Jataka, a story about the innate wickedness of a woman, tells of a girl, who from infancy grew up without seeing any man till her marriage. The story, then, revolves around her intrigue and liaison with a lover and the deceits she practises upon her husband. Therefore it has been said –

"A sex composed of wickedness and guise unknowable, uncertain as the path of fishes in the water, womankind told truth for falsehood. Falsehood for the truth! As greedily as cows seek pastures new, woman unsated years for mate on mate and stand unstable, cruel as the snake, women know all things, nothing from them is hid!"[63]

Asamanta Jataka is a similar story about the wickedness of women. It tells about the endeavour of a woman to kill her virtuous son to facilitate an intrigue with a youth. The narration describes her lust as

> In the lust unbridled, like devouring fire,
> are women frantic in the rage
> The sex renouncing, fain would I retire
> To find peace in a hermitage.[64]

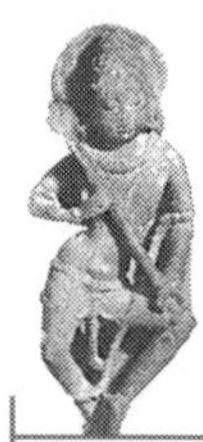

This story offers clear proof of inherent misogyny as expressed in the nobleman's poem about the girl, his lust and his control over her whole life.

Jataka stories summarize eight reasons why a woman despises her husband: poverty, sickness, old age, habitual drunckeness, recklessness, dullness, overwork and the lack of a sense of obligation.[65] But the *Jataka* narratives, which vouchsafe the low standards of morality of women, have to be carefully scrutinized, as they are primarily intended to caution the *bhikksus* against the danger of falling from the ideal of celibacy.

The Buddhist misogyny finds its best expression in the domain of defilement related to female body functions, evoking male repulsion towards female menstrual blood and its putrefying power.[66] Faure points out, 'the rhetoric of equality' in Buddhism tends to solve the problem by denying it. The concepts of non-duality, non-differentiation between men and women from the standpoint of the ultimate truth and such other postulates did not go far to undermine the structure of domination.[67] Faure admits that Buddhism may have contributed to the relative improvement of the feminine condition, yet he laments that it also maintained a situation of relative inequality that it could have more radically questioned. This, in my opinion, is a subjective statement and much depends on how one looks at the problem in its historical context. Faure complains, "Buddha rejected the caste system, brahmanical rituals, animal sacrifice etc. and yet, he by his initial hesitation to admit women into *samgha*, endorsed the dominant ideology at times a little more than was needed." What he overlooked was the gender inequality embedded into the structure of brahmanical social order at that time, condemning women to perpetual subordination of men. Men had power over women and monopolized all the roles and pursuits that society most valued and rewarded, such as religious leadership and economic power.[68] Despite this inequality in status there was some space for women for economic activities.

Buddha's counsel to the daughters of Gahapati Uggaha was not only to guard and protect the material property of their future husbands and to manage deftly and sensitively the household staff but to learn their husbands' craft as well: "We will be skilled and diligent at the domestic crafts of our husbands, whether they be of wool or of cotton, focussing on understanding the techniques therein, in order to do it or to get it done".[69] In another passage, a wife tells a sick husband that having learnt his craft well, she will be able to support herself and her family handsomely on his check pattern should die.[70]

This movement towards the individual handling and disposal of wealth by women is seen nowhere better than in the great number of individual women donors to the *samgha*, who on their own gave not only monumental quantities of food, medicine and robes but land and lodgings as well. The greatest woman donor was Vishakha, also called Migaramata because she was instrumental in the conversion to Buddhism of her father-in-law, Migara. She fed hundreds of monks each day, and her construction and gift of the monastery, Migaramatupasada provided Buddhist renuncients with lodging and retreat.[71]

The *Vinaya Vatthu*[72] records the somewhat later tradition that Vishakha paid for the building with her own ornaments, that is out of her *stridhana/itthidhana.* The courtesan (*ganika*), Ambapali frequently gave large meals to groups of Buddhist monks and signed over a residence at her Magoorove (Ambpativana) to the *samgha* for their use[73]. Motichandra notes "It is significant that though the *ganikas* were not free persons legally, yet they had full authority over the assets which consisted of jewellery, income from salary and the gifts received from their lovers".[74]

The daughter of the king of the Koliyans became the foremost woman[75] to give good alms food (*agga panita dayikanam*) and Buddha's aunt who raises him, Maapajapati, became a conspicuous donor of robes, though she was most known to the *Pali canon* for trying to give them to individual monks, including Buddha, rather than to the *samgha* as a whole.[76]

Much of the feminist work on Buddhism has been concerned with "singing the praises of exceptional women" or chronicling the indignities suffered by women. This approach, however, is increasingly criticized as being blind to cultural and historical contexts and inequalities other than those related to gender, and so as being complicit in perpetuating the image of women as passive victims. A more nuanced reading would acknowledge that while some women were passive victims, others were not. The responsible historian needs to attend to both sides. All models, whatever their initial validity, become counterproductive when they are determined by an ideological or political agenda and are flawed from an historians' viewpoint.

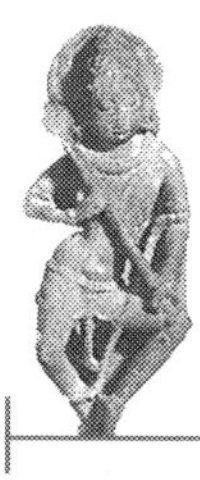

Like most clerical discourses, Buddhism is indeed relentlessly mysogynist, but as far as misogynist discourses go, it is one of the most flexible and open to multiplicity and contradiction.[77]

In early Buddhism, for instance, genders were not fixed, but fluctuating, and cases of trans-sexualism seemed a common occurrence. Buddhist attitude towards women was a pact of monastic attitudes towards society and laypeople. We find two types of anti-feminism in Buddhism. First, the early axiom on monastic attitude, which posits that "a bodhisattva should wander alone like a rhinoceros". In principle, the female ascties were accepted, but in practice, it was difficult for them to follow this ideal. Lonely women tend to get raped, and the Vinayas report how after such a case, Buddha is said to have prohibited women from wandering alone in the forest. The second type results from the fact that when Buddhism became more worldly, it began to accept the social prejudices of the patriarchal societies in which it was trying to take root.[78]

The gendered approach to Buddhist history is not simply to try to retrieve or rediscover a feminine world ("her/story"), one that would stand next to the male world as another self-contained territory, but to review how feminized the dominant male world already is—to deconstruct it from within and to see the fault lines in its discourse.[79]

It is enough to retrieve women as a separate object of study, to see that they had their own history within an outside Buddhism; the point is rather to see how the history and doctrines of Buddhism were changed because of its relationship with women, and to examine how gender gives meaning to the organization and perception of historical knowledge.[80]

Buddhism provided alternative to women's family role in the form of Buddhist *samgha*. Women's monasticism was most often women's closest approximation to the self-determination and prestige normally accorded to men. However, this was not without its problems as women's order fared far less well than men's monasticism. Women as nuns received less economic support and prestige and less access to the highest quality of teaching and practising environment. Women, who could be cited as role models, were not very many as compared to their male counterparts. They were largly exceptions to the norm for their gender. They could be called tokens. More importantly, they were largely unsupported by the institutional fabric of their society and their religion.[81]

In a seminal article entitled 'The Case of Vanishing Nun", Nancy Falk argued that the eight strict rules, through their structural and economic effects, actually brought the decline of female order in South Asia. By implying that only monks deserved honours and offerings, they deprived the female *samgha* of donation necessary to its development and at the same time prevented nuns from playing an active role in the Buddhist community.[82]

At the beginning of the eighth centuries, the Chinese monk Yijing, returning from India, contrasted the lowly status of Indian nuns to that of Chinese nuns. According to him, the former received very little support from society and many convents could not even feed their members.[83] The epigraphic and sculptural evidences found at Sanchi and elsewhere however, suggest quite a different picture.

According to Gregory Schopen, even though the emergence of the Mahayana in the fourth or fifth century CE seems to have coincided with a marked decline in the role of women in Indian Buddhism, until that time, "nuns, indeed women as a whole appear to have been very numerous, very active and as a consequence, influential in the actual Buddhist communities of early India". Jonathan Walter argues from similar epigraphic evidence that nuns continued to play significant religious, political and economic roles in Indian Buddhism right up to medieval period.[84]

He questions the simplistic notion that "one half of the Buddhist samgha could have simply disappeared and sees this as exemplifying the general neglect that Buddhist women have suffered in modern studies". For him the eventual disappearance becomes part of a larger and still largely unexplained phenomenon: the demise of Buddhism in India.

Although the actual impact of the eight rules for the female clergy is difficult to acertain, it remains that they wanted a fundamental asymmetry between nuns and monks.

As Liz Welson remarks, however, it is crucial to understand that rules, apparently aimed against the female renouncer, contained buried tributes to her disruptive power.[85]

In as much as they represent an attempt by monks to check the increasing antimony of the nuns, they suggest that, contrary to Yijing's perception, the female order was thriving. Trying to downplay their negative character, Falk herself admits that they did not compromise the essential, a practice leading to spiritual freedom, even to the implication that nuns were more protected than monks against corruption because they could not receive generous donations sounds rather paradoxical. Schopen has shown, for instance, that nuns could be an object of real violence on the part of monks who, at times went as far as destroying the stupas worshipped by these nuns and assimilated their devotion to heretical practices[86]. Nuns, however, were far from passive and they could at times be combative. A good example of nuns' combativeness can be found in a *Vinaya* talk illustrating their acrimonious relationship with Jain neighbours. Of course, the purpose of this story is to justify yet another rule for nuns, namely that nuns should never use quarrelsome language with anybody, but it could be heard as a vivid echo of the "voice" of these women.[87]

The stringent limitations imposed on women's ordination most notably the required presence of ten fully ordained monks and nuns paradoxically forced female religiosity to find other ways to express itself. The sociological reality of nunhood was also much more diverse and complex than what official sources (Vinayas) would let us believe and despite the emphasis on proper ordination, the line between laity and clergy was sometimes blurred. Even as the female order began to decline in South and South East Asia, other women continued to play important role, as is shown by generous donations made by pious laywomen.[88] Thus, the case of "vanishing nuns" might simply reflect a shift from one type of female religiosity to another rather than a total eclipse of women. This is why, while acknowledging the strong desire of contemporary Theravada nuns to restore orthodox ordination and condemning the strong resistance of patriarchal societies against such claims for a higher status, it is important to keep in perspective and to look beyond the recurrent debate about "official" nuns.[89]

In Indian mythology, the representation of women as evil is continued, but we have a more complex form of the myth of Eve. The dominant and invincible goddess is Devi, who slays the gargantuan buffalo in the Puranas. As the Hindu Goddess Kali, she is fearsome and loathsome, depicted as an old hag with skull lader necklace, gluttonously drinking the blood of her victims.[90]

She functions more powerfully than an Eve, like mother of the human race. As Devi, she is the primeval force of the consumer, the material

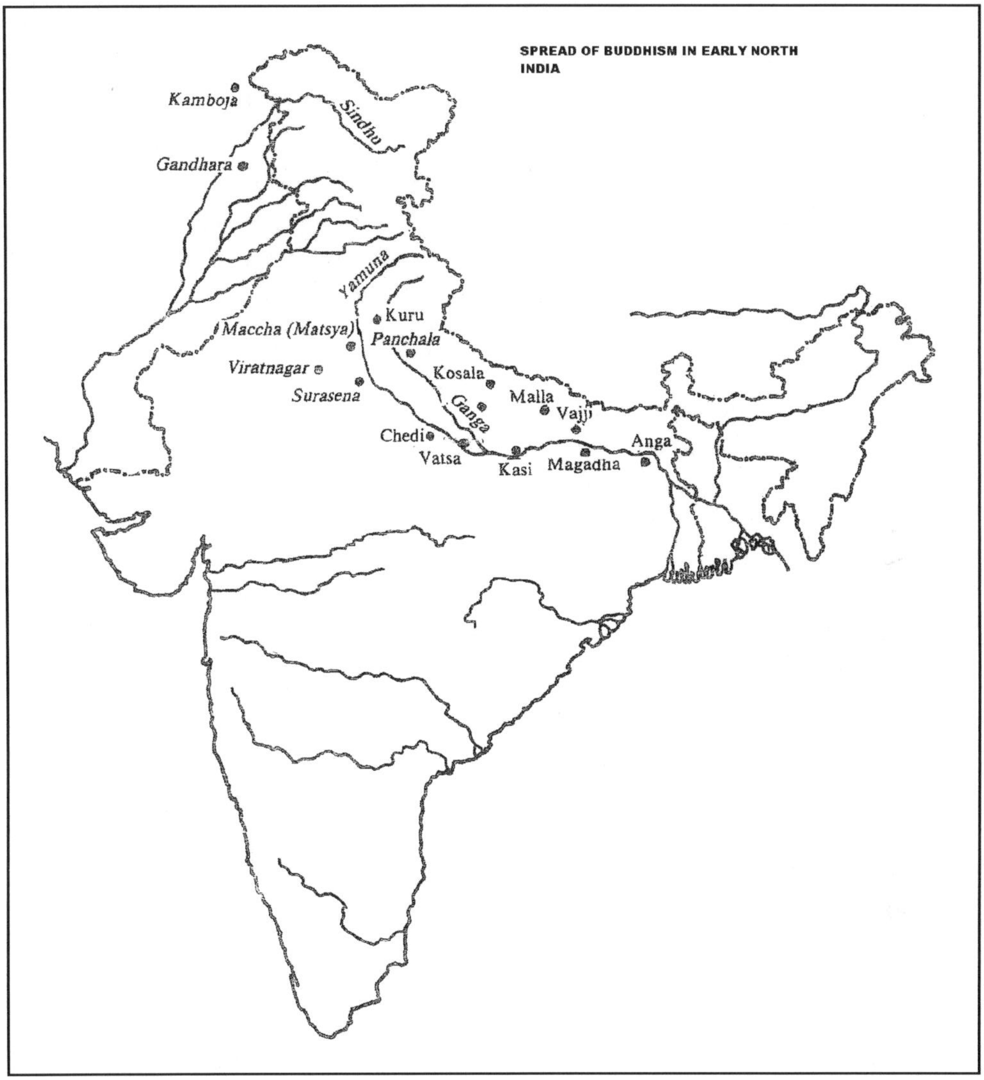

Map 1. Spread of Buddhism in North India.

power which has a dualistic dimension of demomic and creative proportion. As the power of the universe, she can either bestow life or annihilate it. She can also be the life-giving force of fecundity as a positive energy.[91]

Buddhism inherited the Indian mythological structure in which tension existed between the material aspect and the destructive aspect, explicitly illustrated by Kali. Whereas Kali represents both the maternal and destructive forces of the cosmos, the Buddhist representation of women as evil is one traditional attitude, and the women as mother is another. The two representations are not combined in one image as in the case of Kali. In sharp contract to the traditional attitude of positive feelings towards women as being an embodiment of maternal love, they were portrayed as purely sensual with uncontrollable desires in a number of early sectarian Buddhist texts. "Monks, I known of no other song form, sound, scent savour and touch by which a woman's heart is so enslaved, as it is by a form sound scent, savour and touch of a man. Monks, woman's heart is obsessed with these things".[92]

Buddhist Indian texts generally believed that a woman's sexual drive was stronger than a man's. Women were believed to be the recipients of a portion of Brahmanic god Indra's excess energy or sexuality. Buddhist literature frequenty incorporated this belief in some of its mysogynist literature. The early Buddhist texts such as *Jatakas* (birth) tales of Buddha incorporated many strident misogynist remarks from the orthodox tradition of brahmana ascetics. *Jatakas* have portrayed women negatively.

The misogynist literature of the Mahayana Buddhism was based, in part, upon the mythological context of India in which woman was an embodiment of physical and ultimate sexual power in the universe. Diana Paul argues, "The one sided portrayal of woman in these literature is by no means the predominant attitude towards women in Buddhist literature. The extreme prejudice against women in these texts illustrates the reactionary biases of only one portion of the Buddhist population, a segment of the monastic community. Then rejection of the household life represented in part the rejection of women".[93]

As a result of the threat that woman represented to the stability of the monastic community, disciplinary rules emphasizing the avoidance of women at all costs become the standard for chastity as is evident in this dialogue between the Buddha and his favourite disciple Ananda.[94]

A – How are we to conduct ourselves, Lord with regard to womankind ?

B – As not seeing them Ananda

A – But if we should see them, what are we to do?

B – Not talking Ananda

A – But if they should speak to us, lord what are we to do?

B – Keep wide awake, Ananda

The contact with women was further complicated by the fact that monks had to beg for alms from house to house as a part of their daily routine. Since housewives should be the principal alms-giver, the monks were dependent upon them, yet afraid of the order's punitive action for misconduct.[95]

Psychologically, there would be a reinforcement of a low self-image for those monks, who hated the women, upon whom they were economically dependent. The monks' feelings of being manipulated and dependent would result in self-hatred projected upon women. An antagonistic attitude towards women inevitably resulted, with the evil nature of women dramatically emphasized in some early Theravadin literature such as *Jatakas*.

The texts that are taken today as the earliest sources of the Buddhist thoughts were compiled at least two hundred years after the Buddha's *parinirvana* and represent a reinterpretation of Buddha's teachings in the light of social developments through those two centuries. Those texts were written by men, so the rules came to be framed from the male perspective. It is necessary to highlight the meagre literature available about the female voices of that era which may lead towards accuracy in reconstruction of Buddha's teachings and their implications. By this, without accepting the exegetical texts uncritically, we reanalyze the texts from gender point of view by considering the voices and images of the nuns in the *samgha* and also of the laywomen of that period who committed themselves to Buddhism and played an important role as donors.[96]

I end this chapter by accepting Rita Gross's view, "Since history is always a selection from the past, it can only be more or less accurate and complete. What is selected and what is omitted, the reason for not including or excluding certain data, always coincides with certain uses of the past. Feminist history is concerned both with the uses to which an androcentric past has been put and what would constitute usable past for women. The uses to which one would want to put the past reflects one's current value."[97]

NOTES AND REFERENCES

1. Bernard Faure, *The Power of Denial – Buddhism Purity and Gender,* New Jersey, 2003. He has studied the place of women in Buddhism, with special reference to Japan.

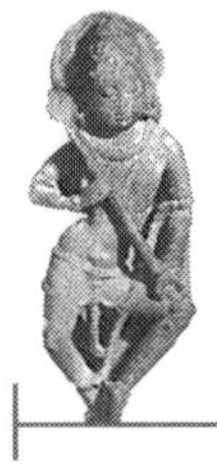

2. Romila Thapar, "Decolonizing the Past, Historical Writing in the Time of Sachin-and Beyond", in *Political and Economic Weekly,* April 2, 2005, p. 1446. See chapter V for detailed description of Kauravaki, the Queen of Ashoka.
3. K.E Neumann, *Die Lieder der Monche and Nonnen Gotama Buddhos,* Berlin, 1899.
4. Bernard Faure, *The Power of Denial – Buddhism, Purity and Gender,* New Jersey, 2003, p. 57.
5. C.A.F. Rhys Davids, *Psalms of the Early Buddhists,* (Tr.), Pali Text Society, London, (1st edn.1909, 1913), 1964.
6. Kumkum Roy, "Of Theras and Theris: Vision of Liberation in Early Buddhist Tradition", in Vijaya Ramaswamy (ed.), *Reserarching Indian Women,* Delhi, 2003, pp. 76-95.
7. Kathryn Blackstone, *Women in the Footsteps of Buddha: The Struggle for Liberation in the Therigatha,* Curzon Surrey, 1998.
8. Kumkum Roy, "Recent Writings on Gender Relations in Early India", in Kirit K. Shah (ed.), *History and Gender: Some Explorations,* Delhi, 2005, pp. 79-80.
9. C.A.F. Rhys Davids, *Therigatha (Psalms of the Sisters),* (tr.), p. xlvi.
10. *Ibid.*
11. The *gathas* ascribed to her mention her wandering as a Jaina ascetic, shaven, dirty, and with a single cloth, through the realms of Anga, Magadha, Vajji, Kasi and Kosala, i.e. present day Bihar and Eastern Uttar Pradesh. See Map no. 1 for Spread of Buddhism in north India.
12. C.A.F. Rhys Davids, *Therigatha (Psalms of the Sisters),* tr, pp. 107-11.
13. *Ibid.,* p. lxv.
14. *Ibid.,* tr. pp. 116-19.
15. *Ibid.,* p. lii.
16. C.A.F. Rhys Davids and K.R. Norman, *Poems of the Early Buddhist Nuns,* 1989, p. 67.
17. See Commentary on Therigatha, lvii, also I. B. Horner, *Women in Primitive Buddhism,* reprint, Delhi, 1975, p. 205.
18. C.A.F. Rhys Davids, *Therigatha, (Psalms of the Sisters),* (tr,), p. 177.
19. *Ibid.,* p. 178.
20. *Ibid.,* pp. 117-21.
21. *Therigatha,* ii, iii, xxxiii, lvi, lxx, lxxi.
22. *Therigatha,* xii.
23. *Therigatha,* xxxiv.
24. See a Commentary on Therigatha, I; also I.B. Horner, *Women in Primitive Buddhism,* p. 205.
25. I.B. Horner, "Women under Primitive Buddhism", p. 99, in Kumkum Roy (ed.), *Women in Early Indian Societies,* Delhi, 2003.
26. Chapla Verma, "The Wildering Gloom: Women's Place in Buddhist History", in Mandakranta Bose (ed.), *Faces of Feminine in Ancient, Medieval and Modern India,* Delhi, 2000, p. 83.

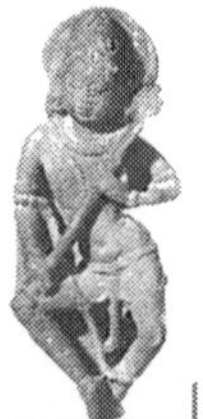

27. Nancy Auer Falk, "The Case of Vanishing Nuns: The Fruits of Ambivalence in Ancient Indian Buddhism" in Nancy Auer Falk and Rita M. Gross (eds.), in *Unspoken Worlds: Women's Religious Lives,* C.A. Wadsworth, 1989, p. 162-63.
28. Androcentricism is a mode of consciousness, a thought form, a method of gathering information and classifying women's place in the (male dominated) scheme of things. Most Western scholarship on Buddhism is quite androcentric and often agrees with the biases of Buddhist records, to the point of further ignoring the few records about women or even ridiculing the women in them. For example, H. Kern, *Manual of Indian Buddhism*, Delhi, 1974 (reprint of 1893), p. 31, tells the story of the founding of the nuns' order, presenting the Buddha as "fully aware of the dangerous consequences attending on the admission of women". He delights in following this allegation with assertions that the nuns immediately engaged in scandalous behaviour. He does not discuss their achievements. See Rita M. Gross, *Buddhism after Patriarchy: A Feminine History Analysis and Reconstruction of Buddhism*, New York, 1993, pp. 18, 22 and 50.
29. At least 18 cases are discussed in *Therigatha,* I, pp. ii, iii, xvi, xvii, xxiv, xxv, xxxi, xxxiv, xxxv, xxxvi, xliv, liii, liv, lviii, lxii, lxvii.
30. *Therigatha,* p. lxxiii.
31. Uma Chakravarti, *Gendering Caste through a Feminist Lens,* Calcutta, 2003, pp. 94-95.
32. C.A.F. Rhys Davids, *Therigatha* (*Psalms of the Sisters*), (tr.), p. 25.
33. *Ibid.*
34. Uma Chakravarti and Kumkum Roy, "Breaking out of Invisibility: Rewriting the History of Women in Ancient India" in *Retrieving Women's History,* p. 331.
35. *Therigatha,* p. xlvi.
36. *Therigatha,* p. xlii.
37. C.A.F. Rhys Davids, *Therigatha,* (*Psalms of the Sisters*), (tr.), p. 34.
38. Rita M. Gross, *Buddhism after Patriarchy: A Feminist History Analyses and Reconstruction of Buddhism,* New York, 1993, p. 54.
39. I.B. Horner, *Women in Primitive Buddhism,* Delhi, 1975, p. 209.
40. Commentary on *Therigatha,* p. xii.
41. *Therigatha,* p. lvi.
42. Margery Wolf, " Women in Chinese Society", referred in Bernard Faure, *The Power of Denial Buddhism, Purity and Gender,* New Jersey, 2003.
43. *Therigatha,* pp. xxii, xxvi, xxxi, lxvi.
44. I.B. Horner, *Women in Primitive Buddhism,* Delhi, 1975, pp. 165-66.
45. Horner attributes the reason for this, as being that the order wanted to keep the friendship of the world, so it also made it a *pacittiya* offence for a women to be ordained unless she had her husband's permission. I.B. Horner, *Women in Primitive Buddhism,* Delhi, 1975, pp. 174-75.

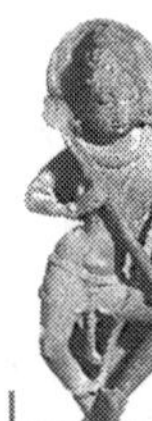

46. I.B. Horner, *Women in Primitive Buddhism*, Delhi, 1975, p. 173.
47. Kumkum Roy, "Of Theras and Theris: Vision of Liberation in Early Buddhist Tradition", in Vijaya Ramaswamy (ed.), *Researching Indian Women*, p. 93.
48. Allan Sponberg, "Attitude towards Women and Feminine in Early Buddhism", in J. Ignacio Cabezon (ed.), *Buddhism, Sexuality and Gender*, pp. 3-36, referred in Bernard Faure, *The Power of Denial, Buddhism, Purity and Gender*, New Jersey, 2003.
49. Rita M. Gross, *Buddhism After Patriarchy, A Feminist History Analysis and Reconstruction of Buddhism*, New York, 1993, p. 118.
50. Uma Chakravarti, *Gendering Caste through a Feminist Lens*, Calcutta, 2003, pp. 94-95.
51. Ian Astley, (A book review) of Rita. M. Gross, *Buddhism and Patriarchy: A Feminist History Analysis and Reconstruction of Buddhism*, Albany, State University of New York, 1992, in *Studies in Central and East Asian Religions*, Vol. 5/6, Copenhagen: *Journal of the Seminar for Buddhist Studies*, 1992-3, p. 208.
52. Uma Chakravarti, *Gendering Caste through a Feminist Lens*, Calcutta, 2003, p. 95.
53. See Diana Y. Paul, *Women in Buddhism*, p. 88.
54. Tessa Bartholomeusz, "The Female Mendicant in Buddhist Sri Lanka", in Cabezon (ed.), *Buddhism Sexuality and Gender*, 1992.
55. Chapla Verma, "The Wildering Gloom: Women's Place in Buddhist History", in Mandakranta Bose (ed.), *Faces of Feminine in Ancient, Medieval and Modern India*, Delhi 2000, p. 78.
56. It is suggested that the Buddha never proclaimed the eight strict rules – they are an addition of the editor of *Chullavagga*. See Tessa Batholomeusz, *Ibid.*
57. *Jataka*, IV. 48.
58. *Jataka*, VI. 468.
59. *Jataka*, II. 337.
60. *Jataka*, I. 28.
61. *Jataka*, V. 425.
62. *Jataka*, II. 367.
63. Chalmers, *Jataka*, p. 155.
64. *Ibid.*, p. 150.
65. Motichandra, *The World of Courtisans*, p. 18.
66. What Faure calls, 'politics of mensturation', as expressed through blood bowl in medieval Japan, acquired an important position in the male discourse on female sexuality. This goes to counter the basic Buddhist tenet of the role of intention in action. Women, after all, cannot be blamed for defiling nature of menstrual blood. Bernard Faure, *The Power of Denial – Buddhism Purity and Gender*, Princeton University Press, New Jersey, 2003.
67. Bernard Faure, *The Power of Denial – Buddhism Purity and Gender*, Princeton University Press, New Jersey, 2003.

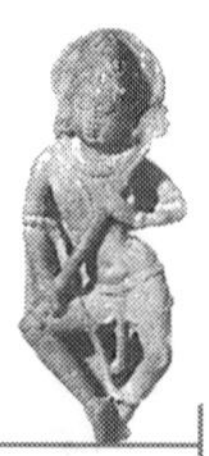

68. Gerda Lerner, *The Creation of Patriarchy,* New York, 1986.
69. *Anguttara Nikaya.* 3.37.
70. *AN* 3.295-98.
71. *Vin* 3.187-88; 191-92, 4.161-62, 1.290-91, 2.129-30; 169-70, 236, *DN* 3.80, *MN* 2.112, 3.1, 78, to 4, *SN* 1.77, 190, 5.216, 222, 269 *AN* 1.26, 193, 205, 21.83, 4.204, 255; Horner, pp. 325-61.
72. Vijay Nath, *Dana: Gift System in Ancient India (600* BC-AD *300): A Socio-Economic Perspective,* Delhi, 1987, p. 75.
73. *Vin* 1.231-33, *DN* 2.95-98.
74. Vijay Nath, *op. cit.*
75. *AN* 1.26, 2.62-63.
76. *MN,* 253-57. See finally, "Ananda's Case for Women, International Journal of Indian Studies 3.2 (July-Dec, 1993), pp. 1-31) Bernard Faure, *The Power of Denial- Buddhism Purity and Gender,* p. 6.
77. Bernard Faure, *The Power of Denial – Buddhism Purity and Gender,* Princeton University Press, 2003, p. 9.
78. *Ibid.,* p. 9.
79. *Ibid.,* p. 13.
80. Wallach Joan Scott, "Gender: A Useful Category of Historical Analysis", in J.W. Scott (ed.), *Feminism and History,* OUP, New York, 1996, p. 31.
81. K.T.S. Sarao, *Origin and Nature of Ancient Indian Buddhism,* printed for free distribution of The Corporate Body of The Buddha Educational Foundation, Taipei, Taiwan, p. 95.
82. Nancy Auer Falk, "The Case of Vanishing Nuns: The Fruits of Ambivalence in Ancient Indian Buddhism", in Nancy Auer Falk and Rita M. Gross (eds.), *Unspoken Worlds: Women's Religious Lives* 155-65, Wadsworth, 1989.
83. Junjiro Takakusu, *A Record of the Buddhist Religion as Practiced in India and the Malay Archepelago* (AD 671-695) by Itsing, Delhi, 1966 (1986), p. 81.
84. J.S. Walters, "A Voice from the Silence: The Buddha's Mother's Story" in *History of Religion,* p. 33, 4:358-79.
85. Liz Welson, *Charming Cadavers: Horrific Figurations of the Feminine in Indian Buddhist Hagiographic Literature,* Chicago, 1996, p. 146.
86. Geregory Schopen, "Deaths, Funerals, and the Division of Property in a Monastic Code" in Donald Lopez Jr. (ed.), *Buddhism in Practice,* Princeton, 1995, pp. 473-502.
87. Roth (ed.), *Bhiksuni Vinaya (of the Mahasanghikas): Manual of Discipline of Buddhist Nuns,* Patna K.P. Jaiswal Research Institute, 1970, pp. 106-07.
88. J.D. Wills, "Nuns and Benefactress: The Role of Women in the Development of Buddhism" in Yvonne Yazbeck, Haddad & Ellison Banks (eds.), *Women, Religion and Social Change,* 59-85, Albany New York Press, 1985, p. 77.
89. Diana Y. Paul, *Women in Buddhism: Images of the Feminine in the Mahayana Tradition,* California, London, 1985, p. 25.

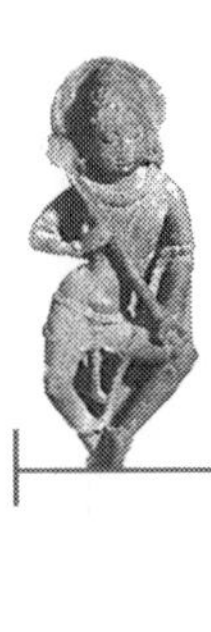

90. David R. Kinsely, *The Sword and The Flute: Kali and Krisha, Dark Vision of the Terrible and the Sublime Hindu Mythology*, Berkley and Los Angles University of California Press, 1975, pp. 81-159.
91. Diana Y. Paul, *Women in Buddhism: Images of the Feminine in the Mahayana Tradition*, London, p. 4, also Heinrich Zimmer, *Myths and Symbols in Indian Art and Civilization*, Princeton, 1946, Sepri 1962, pp. 90-92.
92. *Anguttara Nikaya.* E.M. Hare, *The Book or the Gradual Sayings*, London, 1952, I, pp. 1-2.
93. Diana Y. Paul, *Women in Buddhism: Images of the Feminine in the Mahayana Tradition*, London, 1985, p. 10.
94. *Mahaparinibbana – Sultana in Dialogue of the Buddha,* (tran.) T.W. Rhys Davids and C.A.F. Rhys Davids, London, 1966, II, p. 154.
95. *Vinaya Texts,* (tr.) T.W. Rhys Davids and Herman Olderberg, Delhi, 1968, pp. 7-8, 16-17.
96. Hoards of inscriptions also record women donors. For this see Chapter V on Gender in Inscriptions.
97. Rita M. Gross, *Buddhism After Patriarchy*, New York, 1993, p. 20.

Chapter III

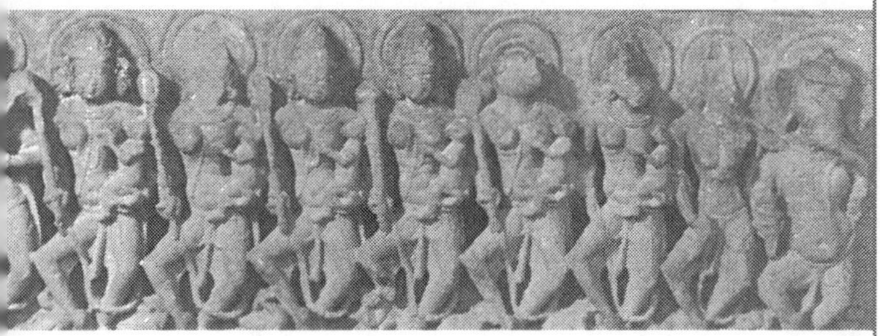

Images of Women in Sanskrit Texts

Given the diverse and culturally pluralistic environment of India, different interpretations can be applied to the images of women in Sanskrit literature. There are two paradigms of the goddess-women equation:

1. Myths and legends illustrating idealization of women in epic heroine Sita.
2. Ideal feminine and corresponding image of women in Shakta Tantras.

A. GENDER DIFFERENTIATION AND CONTENTIOUS FEMININE VOICE OF SITA IN THE RAMAYANA

Women and gender issues need to be recognized and addressed in early historical studies owing to their importance as well as their bearing on our understanding of contemporary society. Women have emerged as a force in history. Historians of women may differ from one another in the

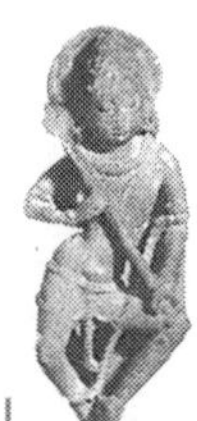

writings which have appeared, but writing women into history has had its impact on the broader discipline. Recently, there has been some effort towards developing methodologies and studying the texts, inscriptions and other archaeological artefacts. "Women's history has a dual goal: to restore women to history and to restore our history to women".[1] Human identity always determined in specific places and at specific times only can be the object of study within a historical perspective. Similarly, understanding of women's issues necessitates the procession dimensions of her social and cultural construction from a historical point of view.[2] Here we will discuss women in Valmiki's *Ramayana* with special reference to Sita.

H.D. Sankalia holds that the *Ramayana*, as a story in its present form, is a pure fancy or fiction, but its core contains gems of truth.[3] He further draws the inferences that the core of the *Ramayana's* story—viz. Rama, Sita, Lakshmana and the exile of Rama with Sita and her being kidnapped by Ravana—is true and was known in 1000 BC.[4] But Sankalia does not specify the grounds on which he thinks Rama, Lakshmana and Sita, etc. to be historical figures. Secondly, archaeologically the final dates are based on Sankalia's description of such cities as Ayodhya, Kiskindha and Lanka[5], which were built between the Kushana and the Gupta periods and are suggested to have existed around third-fourth century AD. Sankalia's excavations at the sites mentioned in the *Ramayana* do not show explicit coherence with the story of *Ramayana*.[6] The root of the *Ramayana* story may be traced to these *Rig Vedic* verses, and it is likely that the Vedic Indra was converted into epic Rama (the derivative meaning of the word Rama is also associated with cultivation and procreation) and Sita is simply the furrow, which bears crops for men, and she is connected with Indra.[7] In the *Ramayana,* Sita is said to have sprung from mother earth and in the end, she disappears again into her womb.[8] The beginning of the epic ornate poetry (*Adi Kavya*) can be traced back to the *Ramayana* and Valmiki has always been the model and the first ornate poet (*Adi Kavi*). Variant methodologies are utilized in analyzing the same text. It should be kept in mind that *Ramayana* as a text is the outcome of a century's long process of compilation, and as a result incorporates many diverse socio-economic, cultural and politico-religious milieus as also different groups and communities.

The *Ramayana* reflects the patriarchal notion of Indian society by reinforcing the ideal of strong man and weak woman. The epic tale echoes the notion of sex appropriate behaviour of women and has expectations of different behaviour from women than that of men. Men find the celebrated deeds of Rama elevating and his wise speeches exalting; women love and praise Sita as an ideal woman faithful to her husband, as the highest feminine virtue.[9] This view amounts to the sovereign authority of men as fathers and husbands over women.[10]

The second book, Ayodhya-Kanda describes the life and activity of a royal court and also the court intrigues. As Dasharatha felt old age approaching him, he decided to crown his favourite son Rama as his successor and asked his family priest, Vashistha to make all the necessary preparations for his coronation. Hunchbacked maid of queen Kaikeyi, Manthara notice this and incite her mistress to prevail upon the king to make her son Bharata successor to the throne. The king had once granted her two boons of her choice which he had not fulfilled till now. So, she asked the king to send Rama into exile for fourteen years and make her son Bharata his successor to the throne. The king was crushed to hear this. Kaikeyi brought her husband displeasure by asking him to honour his promises in this way. Kaikeyi proved to the audience the futility of women attempting to forcibly control their status and welfare. For all her entitlement to claim the fulfilment of Dasharatha's promises to herself and her father, she is condemned. But Rama himself, as soon as he heard about the matter, did not hesitate even for a moment to go into exile, in order that his father would not have to break his word. He did not heed the appeals of his mother Kausalya or brother Lakshmana to stay back and informed his wife Sita about his decision. He exhorted her to be kind to Bharata, to lead pious and temperate life at the court of Dasharatha and to serve his father and mother obediently. But Sita replied to him in a magnificent speech on the duties of a wife, that nothing would stop her from following him to the forest.

Rama described to her all the terrors and dangers of the forest, so as to dissuade her from her decision. But she remained firm and did not like to entertain the idea of a separation; like Savitri, once upon a time in the past followed Satyavrat, she would go with him. At last Rama consented that Sita would go with him to the forest. Here John Brokington states, "There are two main ways in which wife's subservience is emphasized, either by stereotyped statements that a husband is his wife's deity or by comparison with various mythical models such as Rohini and Savitri".[11]

So strong was the notion of patriarchy that when after the death of Dasharatha, Kaikeyi repented and exhorted him to come back and rule the country, Rama said he could not reproach his mother; but what the father had ordered was dear to him even now and he would never give up his resolve to spend fourteen years in the forest.[12]

Women's position, once married, was not only one of subservience to her husband but also one of insecurity, through the possibility or often the reality of competition from other wives, since polygamy seems to have been normal for rulers. This was indeed institutionalized in the *asvamedha*, which was performed by Dasharatha in the Bala Kanda.[13] It is vividly illustrated by Dasharatha's reaction of abandoning Kaikeyi as soon as he had kept his promise[14] and Rama's declaration that he could find another wife like Sita, but not another brother[15] presupposes the ease with which men could make successive or multiple marriages. Tensions and conflicts within such polygamous households were clearly regarded as a common occurrence, a fact that is made use of in the plot.[16] Manthara excited Kaikeyi's fears by suggesting how her situation would change if she was no longer the favourite of the reigning king but only a stepmother.[17] Sunder Kanda here rightly suggests that the author is using Manthara to give voice to the emotions that Kaikeyi should not express directly, since the royal family is expected to be free of negative attributes (which also facilitates her partial retribution later).[18]

Women are considered subordinate and mere possessions rather than partners. A virtuous woman in the story possesses exaggerated feminine qualities, while the immoral woman's actions more closely resemble the behaviour of a man. A woman is valued mainly for her beauty and the pleasure she can provide to her husband. Irrespective of whether the characters or happenings are purely legendry or not, fiction or history, they reflect the social reality of those ages. What is still more important is that these epic stories have been an actual moulding factor of thoughts and morals throughout the succeeding centuries. The attitude of later ages throughout these characters is in itself revealing. For instance, Hindu men, to this day, love Rama for the attitude he adopted in the end towards Sita. They say it was his duty, as a just and blameless king, to re-establish before his people beyond cavil or possible breath of slander the purity of their queen. But we may read into the incident another meaning. This overemphasis on the physical aspect of womanhood, this lack of confidence which is its natural result, attributed even to the noblest of Hindu kings, explains to some degree why it was possible for laws such as Manu's in time to gain complete ascendancy, and to wrest from women all other interest in life but those of sex and homemaking.[19]

At the time when Sita set out with her husband for the forest through the public thoroughfares of Ayodhya, a regret is expressed in the *Ramayana*, that a lady, who had so far not been seen even by the spirits of the sky, should now become the object of public gaze.[20] The *Ramayana* further observes that there is no objection if women come out in public on the occasions of marriages, *swayamvaras*, sacrifices and public calamities.[21]

Sita was held captive by Ravana, her ill treatment by him, her heroic endurance of all sufferings, her proud rejection of her enamoured King of Lanka shows her moral strength to stand alone in unfortunate times. She warns Ravana that great misfortune comes on all those who lust after the wives of others. Rama will come and destroy Lanka, slay them and set her free.[22] She further states to a *rakshasi* woman who was luring her, "Cut me up, tear me into pieces, make sherds of me, burn me into glowing fire—I will not come to Ravana".[23]

Altekar is of the opinion that "perhaps the best way to ascertain the attitude of society in this matter would be to find out its angle of vision towards women overtaken by the misfortune of falling in the hands of ruffians and enemies. Such a situation is a real touchstone to test the genuineness of society's sympathy towards the weaker sex; it enables us to find out how far man is prepared to rise above the prejudices of his sex and judge the woman by an equitable standard."[24] He talks about Rama who refused to accept back Sita after defeating Ravana. Rama told her that all his efforts to kill Ravana were only for the purpose of avenging the wrong done to him; he had no idea whatsoever of accepting back a wife, who had stayed so long in the house of the enemy.[25] There was suspicion concerning Sita's conduct with Ravana in Lanka. She had been touched by Ravana during kidnapping and afterwards. There is also an element of *rajyadharma* in Rama's thinking. He would soon be the king of Ayodhya and it would not be good for the kingdom if his wife's character was suspected. Therefore, he repudiates her against his own feelings, for the sake of what he conceived to be his highest dharma. Sita points out in reply that being in captivity, she was no longer the master of her own person; she could command only her mind and that was always faithful to her husband.[26] The crisis of character arises from the clash between the culturally normative attitude about and expectations of women, viz. Sita's abduction and action necessitated by her need to defend herself from Ravana's advances and preserve her chastity and Valmiki has created a situation from which the heroine cannot and does not escape without social censure. This explanation did not satisfy Rama, who accepted Sita only after *agni-pariksha* (a superhuman agency) vouchsafed her continuous chastity.

Altekar thinks that a critical student of the *Ramayana*, however, finds it difficult to believe that the sentiments expressed above really represented the views of Sri Rama. There are several passages in the epic citing his love for Sita when she was taken into captivity by Ravana.[27] Altekar ascribes this as later interpolation, introduced to facilitate the incorporation of superhuman proof of Sita's unbroken chastity.[28] Even John Brockington feels that Rama's cold rejection of Sita after the defeat of Ravana is totally out of character with the rest of narrative.[29] Whether the passage in question is original or interpolation, one thing is quite clear, i.e. unreasonable standards of purity were prescribed to women.

Sita of the *Ramayana,* as she is abducted and harassed or as she is rejected by Rama, always maintains in her accusations and lamentations a certain calmness and softness and in her words we find no trace of the wild passions, which we find so often in Draupadi of *Mahabharata.* Also, Kunti and Gandhari are mothers of the true heroes of a warrior race whereas in the *Ramayana,* Kausalya and Kaikeyi are more like the stereotyped queens of the classical dramas. In order to stress this sharply striking difference between the two epics, we must presume that the *Mahabharata* reflects the rude culture of western India whereas the *Ramayana* reflects the refined culture of eastern India and that the two epics represent, the poetries not of two different époques but of two different regions of India.[30]

The following is a *Ramayana* translator's summary of Yuddha Kanda, the sixth book of the *Valmiki Ramayana*, in which Rama rejects his wife Sita for having been kidnapped but eventually allows her to come back (although later Rama discards her again in the last book):

> The sixth book of the poem (Yuddha Kanda), as its name suggests, is chiefly concerned with the great battle that takes place before the walls of Lanka between the forces of Rama (Sugriva's monkey army) and the demon hordes of Ravana. Having received Hanuman's report on Sita and the military disposition of Lanka, Rama and Lakshmana proceed with their allies to the shore of the sea. There they are joined by Ravana's renegade brother, Vibhishana who repelled by his brother's outrages and unable to reason with him, has defected. The monkeys construct a bridge across the ocean, and the princes and their army cross over to Lanka. A protracted and bloody, though far from realistic, battle rages. The advantage sways from one side to the other until, at length, Rama kills Ravana in single combat. The prince then installs Vibhishana on the throne of Lanka and sends for Sita. But Rama expresses no joy on recovering his lost wife. Instead, he abuses her verbally and refuses to take her back on the grounds that she has lived in the house of another man. Only when the princess is proved innocent of any unfaithfulness through an ordeal by fire does the prince accept her. At last, travelling in the flying palace Pushpaka, which Vibhishana had given him, Rama returns to Ayodhya, as the period of his exile is now over and his long-delayed coronation is performed.[31]

Rama verbally abuses and discards Sita in Yuddha Kanda, the sixth book of the *Ramayana*, though he eventually forgives her for having been kidnapped against her will and they dwell in the palace of Ayodhya. The story doesn't end yet though; in Uttara Kanda, the seventh and last book of the *Ramayana*, he later dumps Sita again — and this time he trashes her while she is pregnant with twin sons. Rama, the *sat-purusa* (ideal man) and simultaneously the prime exemplar of an ideal husband every Hindu woman should hope to have, had to look out for his reputation; therefore, Rama, the great upholder of dharma, had to exile his wife Sita into the forest permanently even though he was sure she could easily perish. The following is a *Ramayana* translator's summary of the final part of the Uttara Kanda, the last book of *Valmiki Ramayana*: The seventh book, called Uttara Kanda, one-third of the book is concerned with Rama and Sita, and in particular the following is told:

> One day, Rama is told that the people are expressing their disapproval of the fact that he has accepted Sita even though she has sat (at the time of kidnapping) on Ravana's lap; they feared that this will have a bad influence on the morals of women in the country. Rama, the ideal king, is very much depressed at this; he cannot bear the reproach that he sets a bad example

> to his subjects and orders his brother Lakshmana to take her away and leave her outside the country. With a heavy heart, Lakshmana takes her in his chariot to the Ganges and brings her to the other bank of the river where he discloses to her that Rama has rejected her owing to the aspersions cast by the people. In profound grief but yet fully resigned to her fate, Sita sends Rama only her best regards. Soon after this children of the hermitage of Valmiki find Sita weeping in the forest and take her to the hermitage, where Valmiki entrusts her to the care of the womenfolk of the hermitage. There she gives birth to the twins Kusa and Lava after some time.[32] It was during Rama's horse sacrifice ceremony that Valmiki disclosed to Rama that Sita is blemishless and her twin sons Lava and Kusa are the actual sons of Rama. But Rama explains to Valmiki that although he himself is satisfied with the words of Valmiki, still he would like to purify Sita by means of an oath. Then all the gods descended from heaven but Sita spoke thrice folding her hands, "As truly as I have never even thought of another man than Rama—may goddess earth open her womb to me! As truly as I have worshipped only Rama in thought, word and deed—may goddess earth open her womb to me! As truly as I have spoken the truth here, and never known a man other than Rama – may goddess earth open her womb to me!" And then a heavenly throne rose out of the earth, borne by serpent demons on their heads and mother earth sitting on the throne embraced Sita and disappeared with her into the depths.[33]

Consumed by an inconsolable grief, Rama divides the kingdom between his sons, and then, followed by all the inhabitants of Ayodhya, enters the waters of the Sarayū River near the city and giving up his life, returns at last to heaven as Lord Vishnu. These events bring to a close both the book and the poem itself.[34]

The sex appropriate ideals are prominent throughout the *Ramayana*, which reflects the patriarchal values that structured the ancient Indian society. If we consider the *Ramayana* a post-Mauryan literature, whether mythical or real story, it is a reflection of the thoughts prevailing during the Kushana–Gupta period. The centre of attention in Valmiki's composition is, thus, quite fittingly Rama, the man. Celestial sages, other characters and women are so presented as to set off to advantage the greatness of this hero. Women appear in all possible relationships, as mothers, wives and daughters. Despite all odds, Sita is not meek and uncomplaining. She is willing to rebuke Rama for presuming to go to forest without her, for killing the *rakshasas* in the forest, for daring to question her moral purity, for sending her pregnant away from Ayodhya. Her final disappearance into the earth may be a final protest at the treatmented out to her. It is also an affirmation of her failing trust in Rama.[35] Sutherland observes that Sita's repudiation of Rama comes to represent to the vast majority of the audience, not merely a wife refusing a husband, but an expression of a socially acceptable and highly sublimated act of counter aggression against a figure of authority. Subordination of women is a common feature of almost all stages of history and is prevalent everywhere in the world, only the extent and form of that subordination has been conditioned by the social and cultural environment in which women have been placed. To understand the position of women in early India, we have to study women in their wider context.

B. *DEVI MAHATMYA* (*MARKANDEYA PURANA*) AND MYTHICAL AND THEOLOGICAL TRADITION OF GODDESS WORSHIP IN EARLY INDIA

The first major attempt to situate a universal theology of the goddess in the Indian religious tradition is to be seen in the *Devi Mahatmya*; this is an account of the glory of the goddess in a codified form, which forms a part of larger text, the *Markandeya Purana*.[36] Worship of divine feminine is one of the most religious expressions in India. What is special about goddess worship in the Hindu tradition? My survey here limits to the text *Devi Mahatmya* of the *Markandeya Purana* and the ethnographic material relating to this. For this, my approach has been to survey the few shrines of Durga/Kali Goddess in Chandigarh-Kalka-Shimla region, Jodhpur Sachia Mata temple, Vaishno Devi, Varanasi – Annapurna, Guwahati, Assam – Kamakhya.[37]

The recuperation of the Hindus Goddesses, or of a Hindu Goddess, a feminist is problematic at the present history junction, both for its assumption of an undifferentiated "woman power and for its promotion of a certain radicalized Hinduism". The connections suggested between goddesses and women in Indian society have been questioned. The distinction is made between feminization of certain attributes—righteousness, justice, wealth, earning—or more accurately their embodiment in the female form, and the elevation of strong and aberrant women with these attributes to divinity. The goddess is a product of the first process, not the second. The implication of this distinction lies in this: that the symbolic valuation of the form is not a reflection of the actual material and the historical condition in which they take shape.[38] A necessary corelation between powerful goddesses and empowered women would imply simplistic theories of role models and uni-gender projection.

In the recent years, conscious efforts have been made to make contact with the feminine dimension of religion. Scholarships on Hindu Goddesses have increased in recent years in the field of religion and anthropology on two accounts

1. Accord recognition to the previously ignored roles and contributions of women, and
2. Symbolization of the feminine.

History of Goddess Worship in India

Goddesses figure strongly in mythology, but not as major deities. Usually, goddesses are portrayed as wives of the gods, goddesses as supreme beings have not yet been legitimized and absorbed into the Sanskritic tradition. Vedic imagery is overwhelmingly masculine except for the notable exceptions such as Vagambhrini Sukta (*Rig Veda* 10.125), a hymn to the goddess of speech, *Vak*. Concept of Shakti occurs in Vedas and Upanishads[39]. Yet there is little evidence to suggest the Vedic origins of goddess cult. But the period of the epics, the *Mahabharata* and the *Ramayana* (400 BC to AD 400) is one of transition in the integration of goddesses into the Hindu Pantheon. It is during the period of the Puranas (AD 400) that goddesses as individual deities and the concept of goddess became prominent in Sanskrit literature. Between 400 BC–AD 800, cult of mother goddess was popularized in India (Figs. 3 & 4).[40]

Devi Mahatmya is also known as the *Durga Saptashati*, *Chandi* or *Chandi Patha*, where Patha "reading" refers to the act of (ritual reading), the text contains 700 (*saptashata* "seven hundred") verses, arranged into 13 chapters. By far, the most important text of Shaktism—sometimes referred to as the "*Shakta Bible*"—*Devi Mahatmya* is the first religious text to define the *Supreme Reality* (God) as a *female principle*. The text is a compilation and synthesis of far older myths and legends, skillfully integrated into a single narrative.[41] *Devi Mahatmya* is the base and root of Shakta religion. The oral tradition of the text plays an important role in

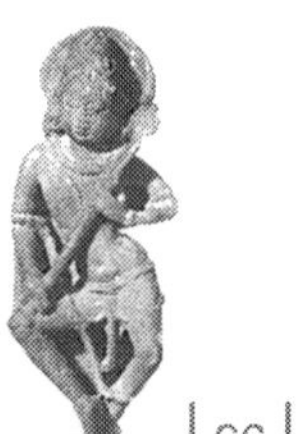

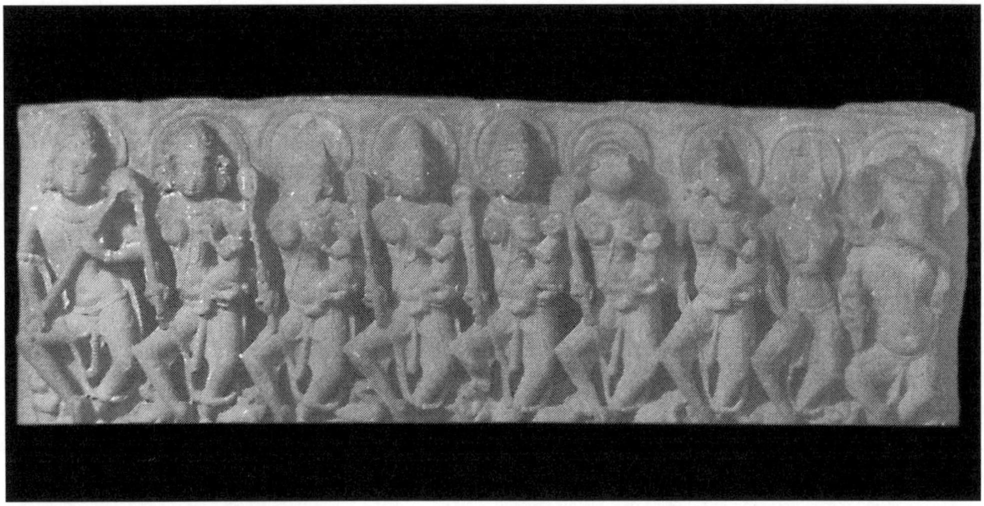

Fig. 3. Seven Matrikas, Mathura.

the ritualistic traditions of Shakta Hindus. The entire text is considered as one mantra. *Devi Mahatmya* was considered significant among the *Puranas* by Indologists. This is indicated by the early dates at which it was translated into European languages. It was translated into English in 1823, followed by an analysis with excerpts in French in 1824. It was translated into Latin in 1831 and Greek in 1853.[42] *Devi Mahatmya* has been translated into most of the Indian languages. There are also a number of commentaries and ritual manuals. The commentaries and ritual manuals followed vary from region to region depending on the tradition. *Devi Mahatmyam* has been called the Testament of Shakta philosphy,[43] and the base and root of Shakta doctrine.[44] It appears as the centre of the great Shakti cult.[45]

Devi Mahatmya is based on the Samkhya philosophy. It is a synthesis of the then prevailing local Mother Goddess cults of Aryan and non-Aryan origin. In it the goddess is Shakti, power itself, beyond the patriarchal relegation of consorting with any eclipsing male deity or patriarchal construct. The three episodes of the text may be considered allegories of outer and inner experience. Sanskrit *mahatmya*—"magnanimity, highmindedness, majesty" is a neuter abstract noun of *maha-atman* (great soul). The title *Devimahatmyam* is a *tatpurusha* compound, literally translating to "the magnanimity of the Goddess".

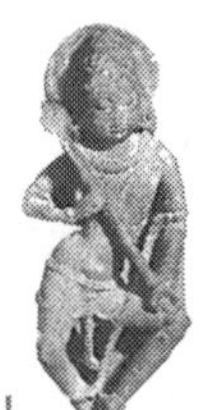

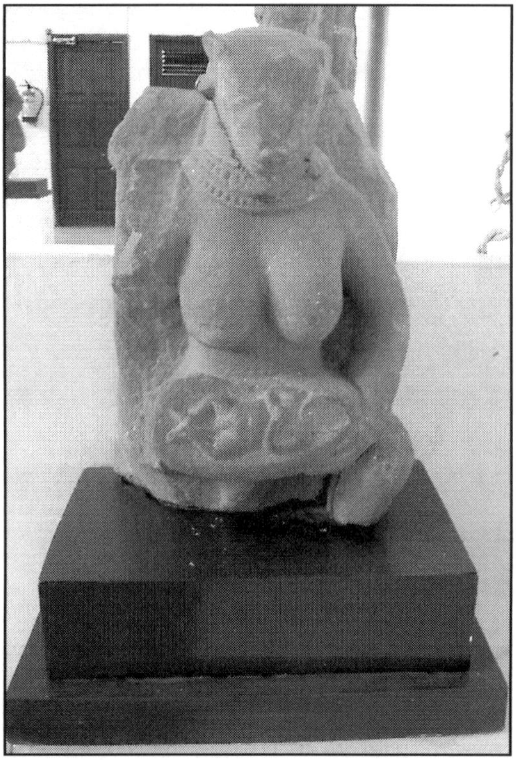

Fig. 4. Goat-headed Jaina Mother Goddess, Mathura.

The text is called *Saptashati* as it contains 700 shlokas. (*sapta*=7, *shata*=100) verses. This count includes even one-line sentences which are not strictly verses. There is another opinion that the name should be *Saptashati* as it deals with the story of seven satis or "pious persons". The *seven mothers* are Brahmi, Maheshwari, Kaumari, Vaishnavi, Varahi, Indrani, and Chamunda.[46]

Three Episodes

Devi Mahatmya (6th century AD) remains one of the most important Sanskrit sources central to Hindu goddess worship today. *Devi Mahatmya* contains thirteen chapters and these are organized into three episodes or *charitas* suggesting that Devi is the true cause of the triumph of good over evil.

V.S. Agrawala[47] analyses the *Devi Mahatmya* section of the *Markandeya Purana* and divides it into three parts: (i) Purva Charita, the divine conflict against Madhu and Kaitabha; (ii) Madhyama Charita, the battle against demon Mahisha; and (iii) Uttara Charita—having three constitutents: battle against ganda and Munda, battle against Raktabija and battle against Shumbha and Nishumbha.

The first half of the frame of story recounts how a king Suratha and merchant Samadhi, seek refuge from the turmoil of the world by retiring to the forest. There they encounter a Rishi Medhas, who informs them that their woes are due to the power of Mahamaya, a term that can mean either "she who possesses great deceptiveness" or "she who is the great deception". Pressed for further details, the sage then recounts the three myths.

In Purva Charita the 'great deluding' Mahamaya, immanent in all things as either wisdom or ignorance, is truly responsible for the victory against the demons Madhu and Kaitabha, whereas in other works Vishnu is credited to have defeated the two demons. In the first episode, Devi is characterized as maya, "the Madhu Kaitabha myth", earlier described in *Mahabharata* (3.194.8-30) has been retold in *Devi Mahatmya*, with several crucial modificiations. Vishnu is described as having entered into *yoganidra*, the twilight slumber of tranquility, a term not used in the epic. The demons Madhu and Kaitabha begin their assult upon Brahma, who again endeavours to awaken Vishnu. He does so here, however, not by shaking the lotus but by invoking Devi, who is addressed as *yoganidra*, that is, as personification of the state of sleep in which Vishnu has entered. The climax of invocation read:

"Whatever and whenever anything exists, whether it be real or unreal, O (you) who have everything as your soul, of all that you are the power (Shakti) how, then can you be (adequately) praised? By you the creator of the world, the protector of the world, who also consumes the world, is (here) brought under the influence of sleep (nidra); who here is capable of praising you? Since Vishnu, Shiva and I have been made to assume bodily form by you, who could have the capacity of (adequately) praising you? May you praised in this fashion, Devi with your superior powers confuse these two asuras (1.63-67)".

Devi then accedes to Brahma's request by withdrawing from Vishnu's various limbs thus awakening Vishnu and then *asuras* are killed. By the time of *Devi Mahatmya's* composition, the myth of Vishnu's killing Madhu and Kaitabha was well known; Madhusudan (killer of Madhu) is a common epithet of Vishnu in the *Mahabharata*. The *Devi Mahatmya* version is similar to *Mahabharata* version with a very important difference that Vishnu's capacity to act is shown to be derivative of the goddess, to be contingent upon the withdrawal of Yoganidra from his body. The epithet linking the Goddess to Madhu-Kaitabha myth is Mahamaya, the great illusion, for this deludes the two demons into thinking that they can overpower and outwit the divine. In the same way she deludes human beings for whose benefit the story is told and it is through her that they must seek a way out of this delusion. Thus, the story is both a cosmic creation myth and one that has relevance for the salvation of human beings.

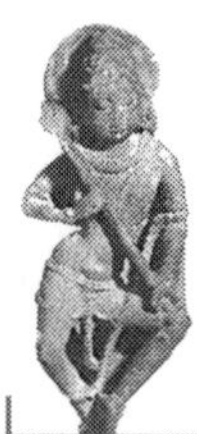

Madhyama Charita affirms Devi to be latent luminosity or power (*tejas*) in beings that when evoked from the gods themselves assumed female form to defeat the form changing buffalo demon, Mahisha. Earlier myth cycles credit the victory to another male God: either Shiva or his son Skanda. It would be argued that Devi killing Mahisasura is an adapted form of the Skanda myth. The motif of a goddess slaying a buffalo, however, is of considerable antiquity and iconographic evidence has been found that predates literary sources.

The episode thus begins: "Once upon a time, a battle between the gods (*devas*) and (*asuras*) was fought for full hundred years when (the buffalo demon) Mahisa was the leader of *asuras* and Indra (was leader) of the gods. The god's army was conquered and having conquered all the gods, the asura Mahisa became lord (literally Mahisa became Indra)" (2.1-2).

The second episode of *Devi Mahatmya* centres around the goddess's killing of the Mahisasura, the buffalo demon. Here the dynamic of the text moves from cosmic orientation of the first episode to the more mundane activity of preserving order in the created universe. The gods are unable to kill the demon Mahisa, who has usurped the power of gods. They approach Vishnu and Shiva for help. Through their anger emits a great brilliance (*tejas*) which fuses together "like a flaming mountain whose flame pervaded the entire sky" (2.11). The heap of brilliance becomes a beautiful woman, each part of the body formed from the brilliance of a particular god. Each god then gives her a weapon, ornament or other emblem: Shiva gives her a trident, Krishna a discus, the Himalaya a lion as her vehicle[48] and so on. Thus, she kills Mahisa. Gods praise her as the supreme protector and boongiver and they request her to return wherever they remember her. She agrees and then disappears.

The third story owes its origin to popular tradition associated with the ancient regional Goddess, Vindhyavasni. The defeat of twin demons Shumbha and Nishumbha in the Vindhyas is mentioned in many earlier Sanskirt sources, which describe her as Krishna-Gopala. The *Devi Mahatmaya* recasts the story.

In the *Markandeya Purana*, Devi is primarily conceived as the war goddess who not only bestows victory and success on her worshippers in the battlefield, but also actually participates in the war to deliver the world whenever it is oppressed by the demons. According to the *Devi*

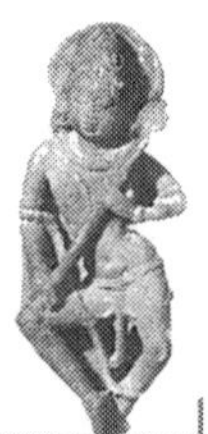

Mahamatya section of the said *Purana*, the gods oppressed by the demons Shumbha and Nishumbha went to the Himalayas and worshipped the Goddess, whereupon Shiva and Kausiki appeared from the *kosa* (muscle) of Parvati and said that it was she whom the gods were raising for killing the demons. This Kausiki is also identified with Katyayini, Vindhyavasini, Chandika and Nanda. The name Kausiki, as we have already pointed out, was connected with the Kusika tribe, and the legend of her coming out from the *kosa* of Parvati was evidently invented to rationalize the role of the tribal goddess into the framework of the Shakta conception of the Devi. The same also held good in the Katyayini, who probably belonged to the Katya tribe, but it is stated that a mass of energy produced from the flames of the god's *anga,* caused by the misdeeds of Mahisasura, who was thrown into the hermitage of the Sage Katyayana, who nourished it to create the goddess. The goddess thus produced came to be known as Katyayini, whom Shiva gave his trident, Vishnu his disc, Varuna his conch, Agni his dart, Yama his iron rod, Vayu his bow, Surya his quiver and arrows, Indra his thunderbolt, Kubera his mace, Brahma his rosary and pot, Kala his sword, Vishwakarma his sword, Himavan his lion, and other gods their various weapons. Vindhyavasini, as the name implies, was a regional deity, who came to be identified with Chandika, Kausiki, Katyayini and especially with Nanda, the offspring of Yasoda, in the house of Nandagopa, who was made responsible for the slaying of Shumbha and Nishumbha.[49] Before killing Shumbha and Nishumbha, the goddess kills Chanda and Munda, who were sent to fight with the Devi, thus gaining the appellation Chamunda. As the battle continues and the shaktis emerge from the bodies of the seven male gods, which are supposedly feminine essence of each god. These shaktis are famous seven mothers (*saptamatrikas*) of Brahmanical myth and iconography, designated in this text as Brahmani (from Brahma), Maheshvari (from Shiva), Kaumari (from Skanda), Vaishnavi (from Vishnu), Varahi (from Vishnu's boar incarnation), Narasimhi (from Vishnu's man-lion incarnation), and Aindri (from Indra)[50] (Figs. 5–11). In addition, goddess herself emits Shakti called Sivaduti because she enlists Shiva to challenge the demons to fight with her.

Of all the major achievements of the Devi, the story of her fight with Mahishasura became most popular as is proved by numerous *Mahishasurmardini* sculptures. The Mahishasura episode of the *Devi*

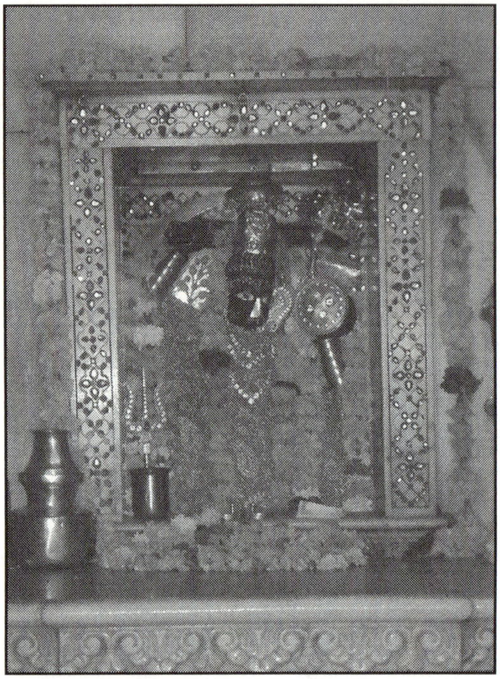

Fig. 5. Sachia Mata at Osian Temple, 8th-9th century AD (central shrine).

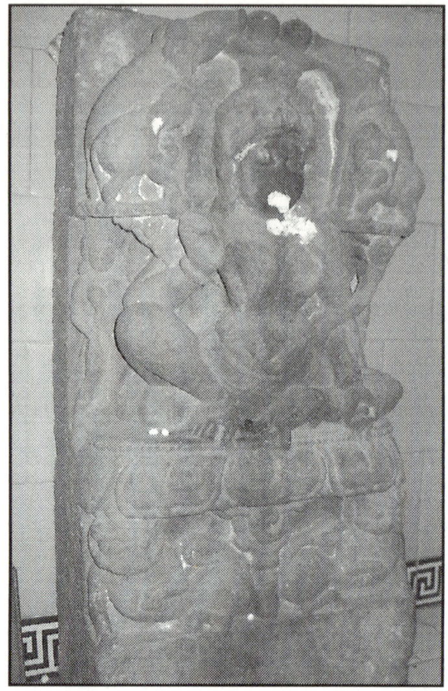

Fig. 6. One of the nine forms of Devi at Osian.

Mahamatya suggests in itself a nice outline of the Shakta conception of the Devi as the embodiment of an all-pervading power.

In these stories all the epithets of the Great Goddess occur and different names are identified or related to each other. In the Madhyama Carita, she assumes her Durga Mahishasurmardini and in Uttara Carita that of Kalika and Kausika. The Purva Charita conception of the Great Goddess does not get favour from the artists. It is only her *Mahisasurmardini* form and *Kalika* forms that attract popular worship.

The position of the great Mother Goddess is enhanced by the *Markandeya Purana (Devi Mahatmya* section), where it says that after the death of the demon king Mahisha all the gods headed by Indra began to praise her, bending their necks in humility.[51] They lauded her thus: we bow down with devotion before that Goddess Ambika, who stretched out of this world by her own power, in whom are impersonated the various energies (Shakti) of all gods, who is to be adored by all the deities and Rishis, may she confer upon us blessings. May Chandika whose unequated

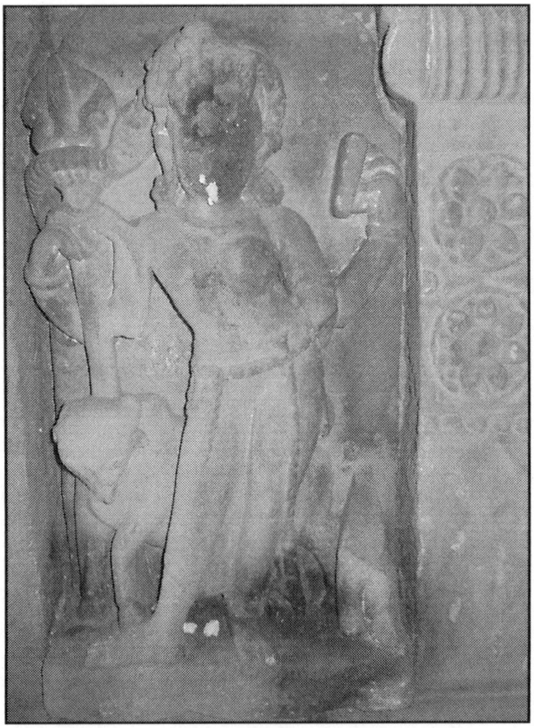

Fig. 7. One of the nine forms of Devi at Osian.

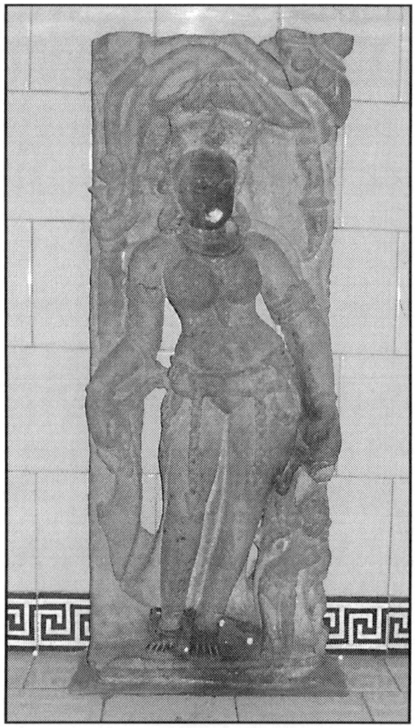

Fig. 8. One of the nine forms of Devi at Osian.

majesty and might neither the divine Ananta (Vishnu) nor Brahma, nor Hara (Shiva) is competent to express, determine upon the preservation of the world, and the destruction of the fear of evil.[52] Muir, therefore, observes that "these specimen may suffice to show the dignity to which this Goddess has eventually been elevated in the estimation of her worshippers and she has attained now a higher rank in Indian pantheon than was originally enjoyed by the daughter of Daksha and Himavat.[53] The name of the great Goddess Durga has been conceived as powerful, in the Harivamsa, as Brahma, Vishnu Rudra, sun moon and wind... all were uttering her name.[54]

The earliest representation of the Goddess Mahisasurmardini is in terracotta plaques discovered at Nagar near Uniyana in Tonk distt., Rajasthan. One of these has been dated from the first century BC to first century CE.[55] Another plaque found in period IV levels of Sonkh (Mathura)

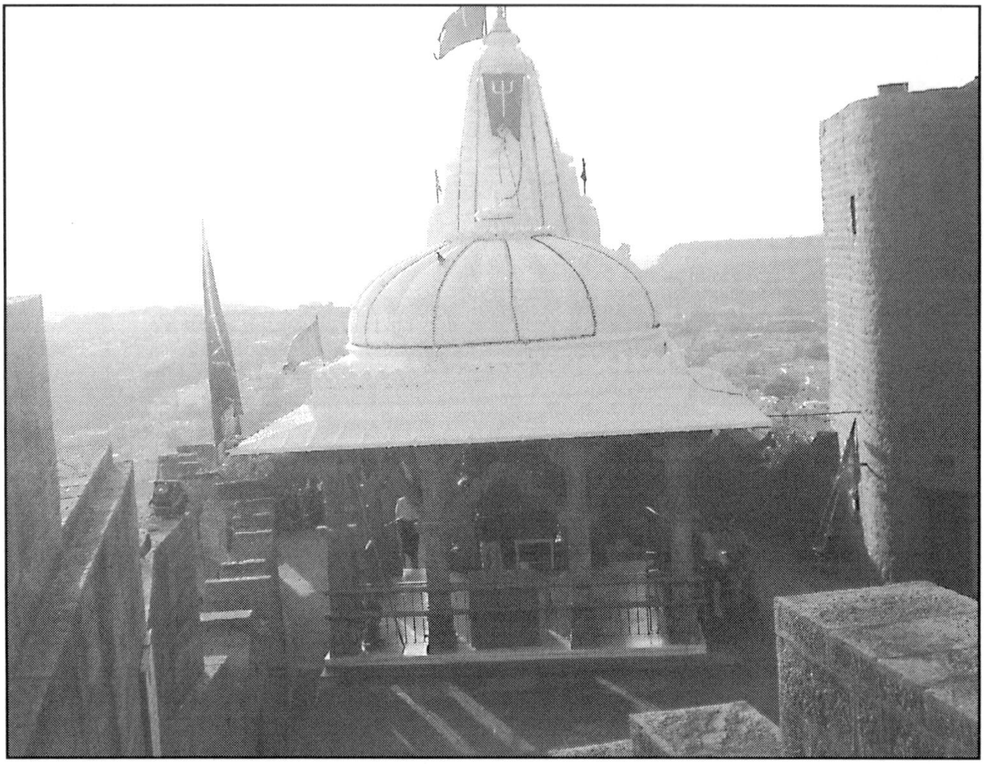

Fig. 9. Medieval Durga Mandir at Jodhpur.

represents Durga Mahisasurmardini[56]. The widespread distribution of the Mahisasurmardini sculptures, the popularity of the concept of Goddess slaying the demons, must have social significance. While dealing with the political, economic and social changes in India before and during the time of Guptas, we have seen that from about the beginning of Christian era, a plural society based on functional interdependence came into existence with the increase of the state power, welfare for wealth, commercial enterprises, agricultural development, specialization in the field of occupations, detribalization and other socio-economic factors. While these factors led to a general economic progress and social mobility conducive to multifarious activities in different walks of life, they could not remove oppression and injustice, social and economic inequations, the tensions and frustrations of the common men, the toiling masses who were really responsible for the production of social wealth, the benefit of which was enjoyed only by the ruling classes and the upper echelon

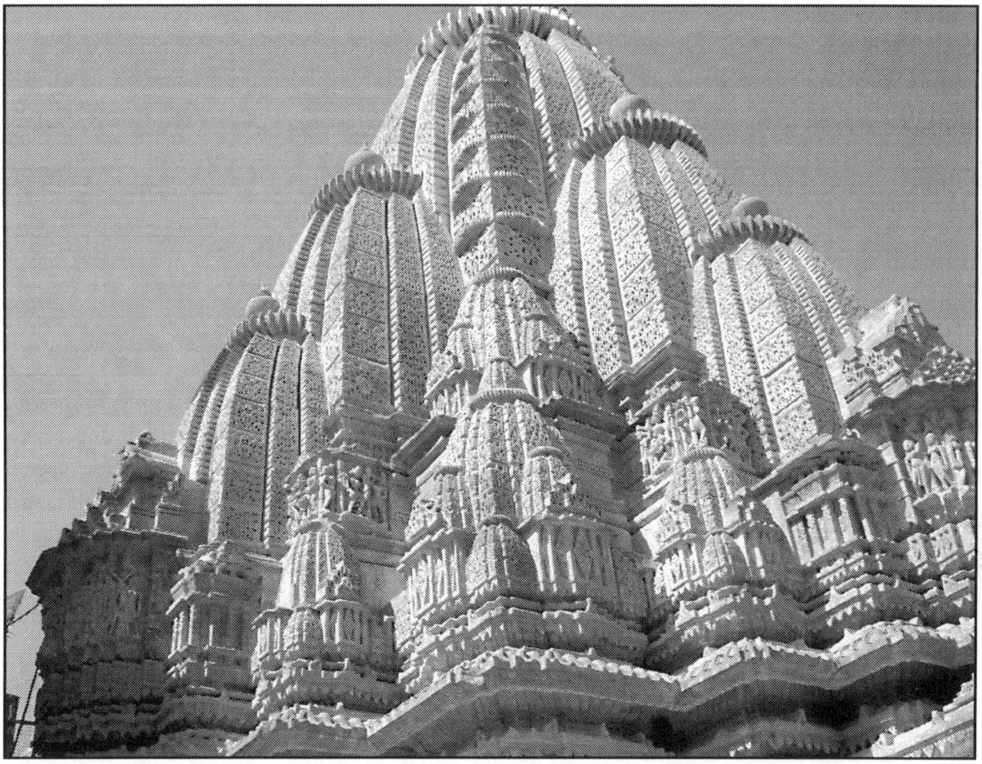

Fig. 10. Osian Temple also known as Sachia Mata Temple, Osian village, Jodhpur.

of society. The Devi's fight with the demons, symbolizing the ultimate triumph of good over evil, must have provided the toiling masses with the illusion of a cherished reality, when the existing reality went against their hopes and aspirations. Though gods like Vishnu or Shiva are also said to have killed many demons to save the world from oppression and injustice, their legends failed to attract popular imagination. But in the case of exploits of Devi, the situation was different, because of the closest association of other goddess with the common people, with the facts of their daily life, in her capacity of being the goddess of vegetation and fertility, the producer of life and protectors of children, the healer of diseases, the mistress of cattle, the guardian of forest and wild life, the best power of success and fortune and the troubleshooter of all types. The association of the goddess with the hopes and aspirations of the common people since the time immemorial must have given a new dimension to the Puranic Devi legends.[57] Essentially, the developments

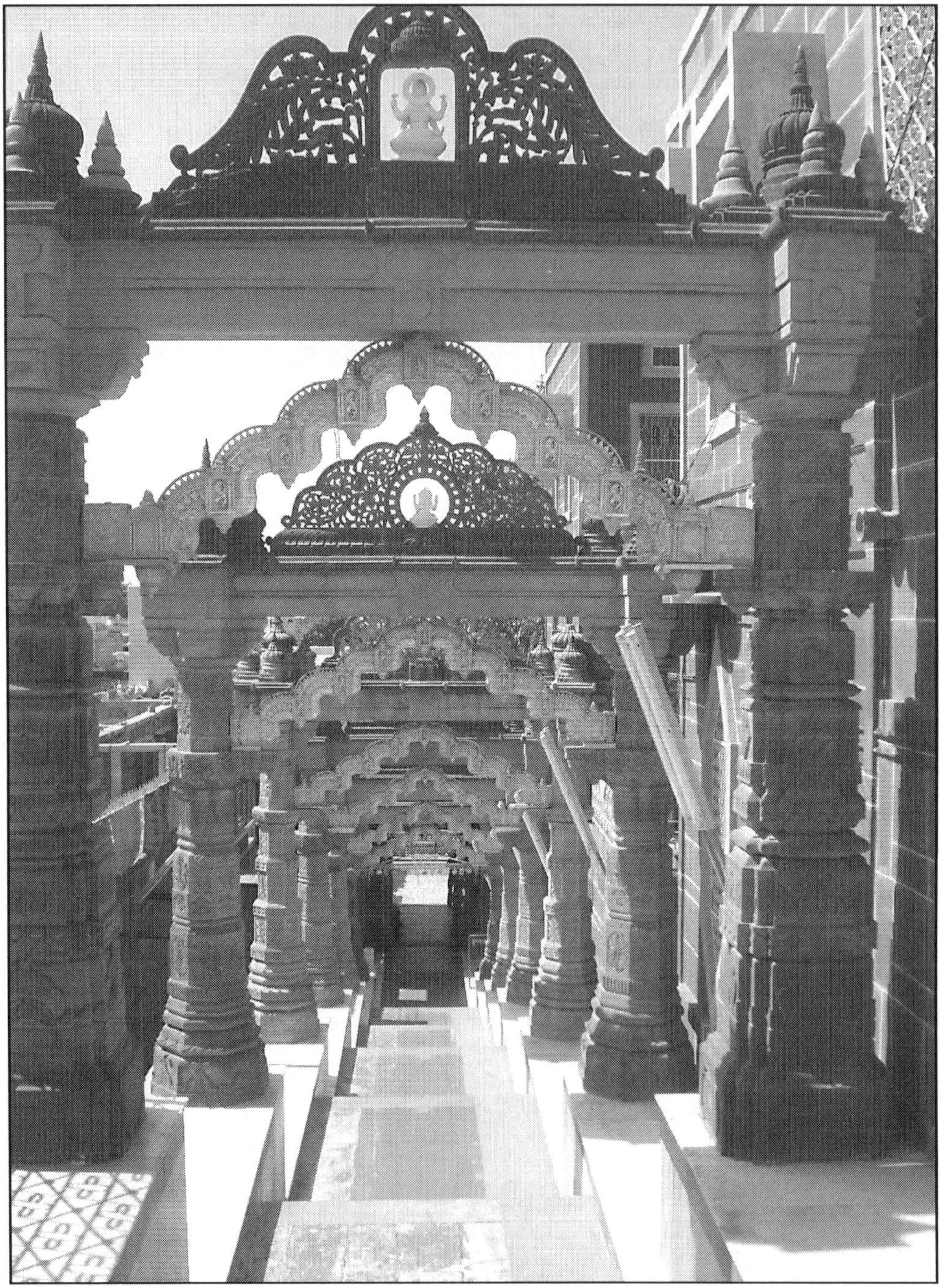

Fig. 11. Entrance of Osian Temple, Osian village, Jodhpur.

in the religious sphere were the outcome of the social processes and mutations.

Durga Mahisasurmardini form is depicted on the gold coins of Gupta King Chandragupta-Kumaradevi type[58], showing on the obverse the lion-slaying goddess. On the reverse, the goddess is shown seated on the lion holding a lotus in her hand. Indira S. Aiyer suggests that though the devise could have been influenced by the Nana-Adrokosho coins, the theme of Narayani Stuti could have contributed towards its evolution.[59]

Devi Mahatmya appears to be the first Sanskrit text to provide a comprehensive vision of that the ultimate realty in the universe is understood to be feminine Devi, the goddess, though from the time of *Rig Veda* various goddesses have figured in Sanskrit tradition. The goddess' varied and often highly nuanced relationship to male deities is particularly revealing of her nature, which is vividly presented in the three episodes mentioned below.

L.A. Babb[60] contends that the Hindu pantheon is differentiated on the basis of gender, with male deities being generally benevolent and female deities being generally malevolent unless controlled through marriage. This distinction between the consort or domesticated goddesses as benevolent and single or independent goddesses as malevolent is one that has been accepted by A.R. Ramanujam, who has also distinguished between two types of Indian goddesses; breast mother or consort Goddesses and tooth mothers or virgin Goddesses.[61] He considers Goddess Durga of *Devi Mahatmya* to be malevolent. As she is represented in the *Durga Saptashati*, the only discernable emotion of the goddess is anger; black, implacable and bloodthirsty. She is something emerging from the highest gods; she is the very essence of their anger. But the description of goddess as black and bloodthirsty is only valid for Kali, a Shakti whom goddess produces from her brow during the third episode to drink the blood of the demon Raktabija. Throughout her battle, the goddess remains beautiful and smiling, exerting a self-controlled energy. She releases the energy and absorbs it at will. The anger of the gods has been transformed into the protection power of the goddess. She kills demons to protect the gods and restore order to the universe. The two names besides the generic Devi, i.e. Chandika and Ambika, demonstrate both her fierce, distinctive and motherly protective qualities.[62]

David Kinsley suggests that not all goddesses in all contexts and situations throughout the history of Hinduism can be reduced to a single

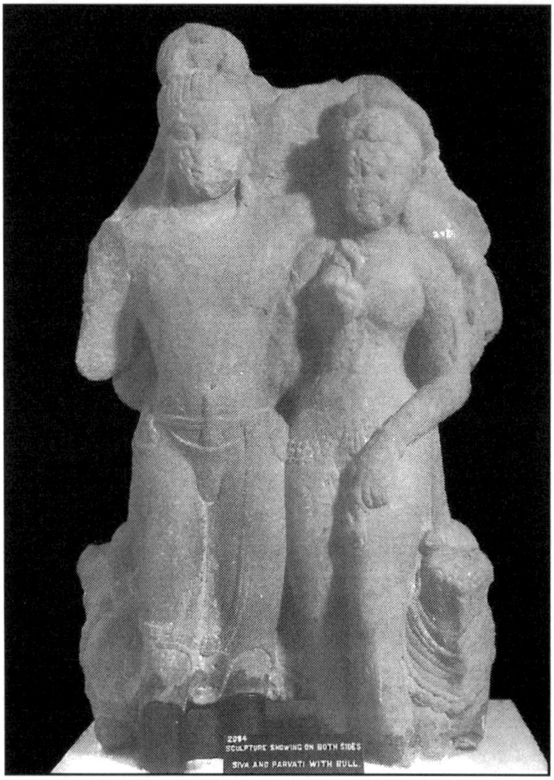

Fig. 12. Shiva and Parvati with bull.

'feminine principle' just as not all gods can be reduced to single masculine principle:

"The Goddess... often illustrates the important idea of the Hindu tradition, ideas that underline the great Hindu philosophic visions. Several Goddesses, for example, are unambiguously identified with or called Prakriti, a central notion on most philosophical systems....Other Goddesses such as (Radha and Sita) explore the nature of devotion and the divine human relationship..... Laksmi expresses Hindu thinking about kingship and the relationship to the ruler about the fertility of the world.... Many Goddesses associated with the geographical features of the Indian subcontinent suggest Hindu thinking about the relationship between sacred space and spiritual liberation.... Several Goddesses are cast in untraditional, 'masculine' roles that express unconventional, perhaps even experimental, thinking about sexual roles. Other Goddesses in their myths and personalities, express central tensions that characterize the Hindu tradition".[63]

There is evidence of systematic attempts to connect the principal male Puranic deities with the goddesses. This has been described as a process of spousification (Fig. 12),[64] whereby autonomous female deities were brought into association with a god, either Vishnu or Shiva which may be viewed as either representing a process of incorporation and/or subordination of the female principle.

Couburn remarks that the *Devi Mahatmya* is "not the earliest literary fragment attesting to the existence of devotion of a Goddess figure, but it is surely the earliest in which the object of worship in conceptualized as Goddess with capital G."[65]

"But it is important nonetheless, to look at the *Devi Mahatmya* in the general context of the Brahmanical tradition, and specially the *Puranas*, for the *Devi Mahatmya* does not exist in a vacuum. The formulation of the great Goddess, in this text, is already somewhat influenced by Vedic Brahmanical themes and narrative structure of the type that we have seen and the identification of Goddess as *Shakti, Maya,* and *Prakriti* in this text must be understood in relation to these larger patterns. In terms of the way in which it depicts the essential identity of the Goddess, *Devi Mahatmya* is not anomalous. It is the earliest and among the most forceful expressions of a theology of a Great Goddess, but this theology is adopted and adapted to at least some degree by later texts, both Shakta and non Shakta".[66]

Does the strong goddess tradition in Brahmanical texts and scriptures has anything to do with real gender relationships? Coburn notes, "One of the clear early lessons emerging from feminist study is that one cannot assume that the existence of Goddess, or Goddess texts, in a given culture corelates with favourable social status for women—*Devi Mahatmya* is a part of a broader Indian context whose thinking about gender is shaped by many factors other than the fact that *Devi Mahatmya* happens to be the text praising the Goddess.

In his scholarly analysis of the text *Devi Mahatmya,* Coburn[67] arrives at the conclusion that this anonymous Sanskrit text articulates the view that ultimate reality is feminine. He supports this with detailed studies of Puranic texts and of the *Durga Stava* and the *Durga Strota* from the *Mahabharata.* His arguments are cogent and based on keen insights into the literary texts that he examines. But the purpose of this study is not to deal with religious texts per se, but to consider literary characters presented to us as human, taking part in ordinary human pursuits, albeit at times in a somewhat extraordinary manner, and to discover in them greater or lesser degree of divine identity or at least evidence of their being special foci of their divine predilection. We find in the lives of these epic women characters, a frequent, sometimes constant intervention of the divine, often at the cost of pain and shame, at other times bringing comfort, reassurance and ultimate glory.[68]

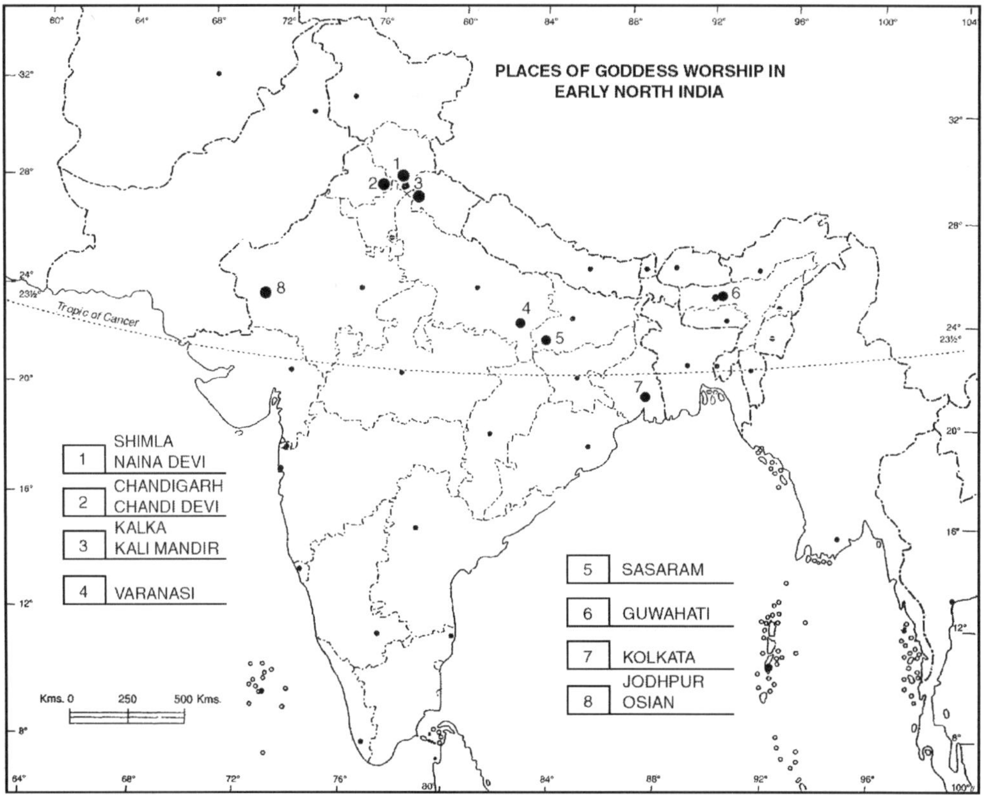

Map 2. Places of Goddess worship in early north India.

The story of Devi is quite unselfconsciously woven into the very fabric of the social order and of the daily behaviour. Other than mythological, theological analysis, there are two more aspects of Devi worship, i.e. an anthropological and psychological analysis. Recent anthropological study has demonstrated text based ideas about Devi as interwoven into popular practice in complex, non-linear ways. Akos Ostor[69] discovers a striking and close correspondence between the categories Bengali villagers use to understand their everyday experience, particularly during the great annual Durga Puja featival, and the categories employed in the popular understanding of *Devi Mahatmya*. William Sax in his recent study of goddess pilgrimage in the Himalayas, has explored how different regional traditions rework the basic aspects of Devi's mythology in the light of local approaches to politics, social order, gender relations and ritual practice.[70]

The images of female goddesses have been analysed as evidence of the male fear of female potency, as the embodiment of the ambiguous attitude towards women and female power in the society that was increasingly becoming sex-segregated, and as symbols of female empowerment. For the historian they reflect the re-emergence of female goddesses from pre-Aryan cultures and the continuing interaction among the multiple cultures eventually labelled "Hinduism" by outside observers (Kinsley, 1996; Pinchman, 1994)[71].

I agree with the opinion of Cynthia Ann Humes,[72] who writes, "To ask, if *Devi Mahatmya* is a feminist scripture is to ask a question which pre-occupies persons within a specific time, place and mindset. The authors never intended to answer all questions on men's or women's nature. They were interested in religious goals, not worldly goals, by which I mean they were preoccupied with what they believed to be the ultimate human concern, enlightenment and salvation from suffering".

We do not make any claim that the Shakta women are not or were not under patriarchal structures of brahmin orthodoxy. Scholarships on interpretation of role of Hindu goddesses point to an emphasis on the goddesses as part of a general movement of academia to accord recognition to previously ignored or denigrated aspects of culture, particularly the roles and contributions of women and the symbolization of the feminine.

Places of Goddess (Shakti) worship in north India

Vindhyachal	The goddess who reigns there is known as Vindhyavasini - "One who dwells in the Vindhyas". It contributed to the general formulation of 'goddessness' that is found in the *DM*. Vindhya Mahatmya is localization of the text *DM*
Jodhpur	Sachia Mata temple
Jaipur	Devi Mandir
Assam	Kamakhya
Benares	Annapurna
Jammu	Vaishno Devi
Kolkota	Kali temples
Sasaram	Tarachandi

13 Epithets of Goddess in *Devi Mahatmya*

1.	Durga	feminine Goddess as a protector of her devotees from worldly calamities.
2.	Chandika	this is a most popular epithet in *DM.*
3.	Ambika	emanates from the kosa of Parvati and all fighting hosts merge in her.
4.	Mahamaya	who possesses delusive power.
5.	Nitya	in *DM* Nitya is applied to the eternality of the Goddess.
6.	Shivaduti	it is a Goddess who put forth Shakti.
7.	Gauri	is said to have emanated from Parvati.
8.	Kritya	this epithet in Narayani Stuti emphasizes the malevolent origin of the Goddess, and her association with Shiva and Agni
9.	Prakriti	in *DM* means material earth and the Goddess identifying herself with it raises it to divine heights
10.	Yoganidra	is the creator and destroyer of the world
11.	Vishnumaya	she is the power of Vishnu and is also praised as Parvati, wife of Shiva.
12.	Parameshwari	ultimate principle and creator of the world
13.	Katyayini	has Shiva connotation

NOTES AND REFERENCES

1. Joan Kelley, *Women, History and Theory: The Essays of Joan Kelley,* London, 1984, p. 1.
2. Merry E. Wiesers, *Women and Gender in Early Modern Europe*, 2nd edn., 2000, London.
3. H.D. Sankalia, *Ramayana- Myth or Reality,* New Delhi, 1973, pp. v-vi.
4. *Ibid.*, pp. 62-63.
5. *Ibid.*, p. 46; The internal evidence alone of the Ramayana on the city of Ayodhya, as available in the *Balakanda,* gives a crucial clue for dating which may correspond to its description: *Samantara asarighaischa Balikarmabhiravritam/ Nanadesanivasaischa vanighbhirupanobhitam, Ramayana,* 1.5,9, Baroda Oriental Institute Edition, I, 1960. Here more than the description of the city, it is the expression *Samantarajasamgha,* which is important. The expression *Samanta,* in these verses used here, cannot be earlier than the Gupta period.

See B.D. Chattopadhyaya, "Indian Archaeology and Epic Traditions", *Purattatva*, no. 8, p. 68 fn. A.L. Basham, *The Wonder That Was India*, (Delhi, 1967, 1992, p. 415) states, 'the fact that the Theravada Buddhists preserved in the *Jataka*, a version of the tale in which there is no mention of the abduction of Sita and the war with the demons, the most exciting part of Valmiki's story, suggests that the author conflated two separate traditions, the first that of righteous prince who was wrongly banished and the second of the conquest of Ceylon. The story of Rama's adventures in exile has, thus, no historical basis whatever, if we rationalize his monkey allies into aboriginal tribesmen with a monkey totem. p. 415.

6. H.D. Sankalia, *The Ramayana in Historical Perspective*, Delhi, 1979.
7. *Rig Veda*, IV.57
8. *Valmiki Ramayana*, I.66.13-14; VII.110.14-16. The similarity of Demeter-Percephone myth with the main story of *Ramayana* is too striking to be ignored. The heroine of the epic is born of a field furrow, abducted by a Pluto of the underworld, and after all her adventures she returns to the earth. The story of the quest of Sita by Rama and his troops resembles that of Demeter's quest of Isis for the body of Orisis; See N.N. Bhattacharya, *History of Sakta Religion*, 1996 (2nd edn.), Delhi, p. 48.
9. Maurice Winternitz, *The History of Indian Literature*, Vol. I, Delhi, 1996, p. 455.
10. Alongside the role model legends is a vast body of literature dealing with *stridharma*, or the normative dharma, outlining the conduct and postures of good and evil to be followed by Hindu women, reinforced in the *Dharmashastras* and *Smriti* literature. The laws of Manu compiled in second century CE laid the foundation of brahmanic social, legal and moral code and introduced several innovations that concerned women. See *Manusmriti*.
11. John Brokington, *The Sanskrit Epics*, Brill, 1998, p. 431.
12. Maurice Winternitz, *The History of Indian Literature*, Vol. I, Delhi, 1996, pp. 462-64.
13. *Valmiki Ramayana*, 1.13.27-28.
14. *Ibid.*, 2.12.11 and 37.6-9.
15. *Ibid.*, 6.39.5-6.
16. John Brokington, *The Sanskrit Epics*, Brill, 1998, p. 431.
17. *Valmiki Ramayana* 2.6.17.26.
18. Sally J. Suderland, 'Seduction, Counter Seduction and Sexual Role Models in the Sanskrit Epics", *Journal of Indian Philosophy*, 20. pp. 243-51.
19. F. Haiswirth, *Purdah: The Status of Indian Women*, London, 1932, pp. 48-49.
20. *Valmiki Ramayana*, II, 33, 8.

21. *Ibid.*, IV, 116, 28.
22. Quoted in Johann Jacob Meyer, *Sexual Life in Ancient India: A Study in Comparative History of Indian Culture*, Delhi, 1971, p. 425.
23. *Ibid.*
24. A.S. Altekar, *The Position of Women in Hindu Civilization*, Delhi, 1959, p. 305.
25. *Valmiki Ramayana*, VI, 118, 15ff.
26. *Ibid.*, VI, 119, 6-8; A.S. Altekar, *The Position of Women in Hindu Civilization*, p. 306.
27. *Valmiki Ramayana*, IV, I, 103.
28. A.S. Altekar, *The Position of Women in Hindu Civilization*, Delhi, 1959, rep. 2005, p. 307.
29. John Brokington, *The Sanskrit Epics*, Brill, 1998, p. 431.
30. Maurice Winternitz, *The History of Indian Literature*, Vol. I, Delhi, 1996, p. 486.
31. Robert P. Goldman, *The Ramayana of Valmiki: An Epic of Ancient India*, Balakanda (Vol. 1), Introduction, Princeton, 1999, pp. 11-12.
32. Maurice Winternitz, *The History of Indian Literature*, Vol. I, Delhi, 1996, pp. 473-75.
33. Maurice Winternitz, *The History of Indian Literature*, Vol. II, Delhi, 2002, p. 475; her name means ploughshare, she is born out of earth and mother earth admits her into her womb again.
34. Robert P. Goldman, *The Ramayana of Valmiki: An Epic of Ancient India*, Balakanda (Vol. 1), Introduction, pp. 12-13.
35. *Valmiki Ramayana*, VIII. 97.
36. Thomas B. Coburn, *Devi Mahatmya: The Crystallization of the Goddess Tradition*, Delhi, 1984.
37. Map no. 2, Places of Goddess Worship in North India.
38. Rajeshwari Sunder Rajan, "Real and Imagined Goddesses", in A. Hiltebeitel and K.M. Erndl (eds.), *Is the Goddess A Feminist*, p. 272.
39. L.A. Babb, *Hierarchy: Popular Hinduism in Central India*, New York, 1975, p. 221.
40. See one such iconic representation of Mother Goddess in Kushana Mathura no. 3.
41. Kali, Davadatta, *In Praise of the Goddess: The Devi-mahatmya and Its Meaning*, Nicolas-Hays Inc., Berwick, Maine, 2003.
42. *Ibid.*, p. 52.
43. Sibendu Manna, *Mother Goddess*, Punthi Pustak, Calcutta, India, 1993.
44. Swami Sivananda, *Devi Mahatmya* (with a lucid running translation), The Divine Life Society, Shivanandanagar, India, 1994.

45. Thomas B. Coburn, *Devi Mahatmya: The Crystallization of the Goddess Tradition,* South Asia Books, 2002, p. 95.
46. S. Sankaranarayanan, *Glory of the Divine Mother (Devi Mahatmyam),* India, 2001, p. 7. See Mother Goddesses in the Fig. 3.
47. V.S. Agrawala, *Devi-Mahatmyam: The Glorification of the Great Goddess,* Varanasi, 1963, p. 69.
48. Later associated with the local cult of Sherawalin or Vaisno Devi shrine in Jammu.
49. N.N. Bhattacharya, *History of Shakta Religion,* New Delhi, 1996, p. 100.
50. Some of them are shown in the photographs of statues of Mathura, Osian etc. Figs. 5–8. Photo of Durga Mandir at Mehrangarh Jodhpur, no. 5 and photo of Sachia Mata Temple at Osian, Jodhpur, Figs. 9–11.
51. *Markandeya Purana,* 84.1.
52. J. Muir, *Original Samskrit Texts* (5 vols.) IV, p. 436, London, 1860-71.
53. J. Muir, *Original Samskrit Texts* 1860-71.
54. *Harivamsa* V, 10256 ff.
55. D.C. Sircar, "Shakti Cult in Western India" in D.C, Sircar (ed.), *The Shakti Cult in Tara,* Calcutta, 1967, pp. 87-91.
56. H. Hartel, *Excavations at Sonkh,* 1993, p. 88ff.
57. N.N. Bhattacharya, *History of Shakta Religions,* Delhi, 1996, p. 105.
58. See the coin, no. 1 & 2.
59. Indira S. Aiyar, *Durga as Mahisasurmardini: A Dynamic Myth of Goddess,* Delhi, 2005, p. 311.
60. L.A. Babb, *Divine Hierarchy: Popular Hinduism in Central India,* NY, 1975, p. 221.
61. A.R. Ramanujam, *Two Realms of Kannada Folklore,* pp. 56-58.
62. Katherine M. Erndl, *Victory to The Mother,* Oxford, 1993.
63. David Kinsley, *Hindu Goddesses,* California, 1988, p. 35.
64. Lyn E. Gatewood, *Devi and the Spouse Goddess: Women Sexuality and Marriage within India,* Delhi, 1985. We have iconic representation of God with his spouse (Shiva and Parvati), Mathura. See Fig. 12.
65. Thomas Coburn, *Devi Mahatmya: The Crystallization of the Goddess Tradition,* South Asia Books, 2002.
66. *The Feminine Principle in Puranic Cosmogony,* p. 121.
67. Thomas Coburn, *Devi Mahatmya*: A translation of the *Devi Mahatmya* and a study of its interpretation. New York, 1991, p. 172.
68. Sister Maeve Hughes, *Epic Women: East and West,* Calcutta, 1984, p. 38.
69. *The Play of Gods,* Chicago, 1980, referred in *Encountering the Goddess,* pp. 154-56.
70. William S. Sax, *Mountain Goddess: Gender and Politics in a Himalayan Pilgrimage,* New York, 1991, referred in Thomas Coburn: Devi The Great

Goddess, in John S. Hawley and Donna M. Wulff (eds.), *Devi: The Goddess of India*, London, 1996, p. 43.

71. Barbara N. Ramusack and Sharon Sievers, *Women in South Asia: Restoring Women to History*, Bloomington, 1999, p. 33.
72. Is Devi Mahatmya a Feminist Scriptures, in A. Hiltebeitel and K.M. Erndl (eds.), *Is the Goddess a Feminist?* p. 125.

Chapter IV

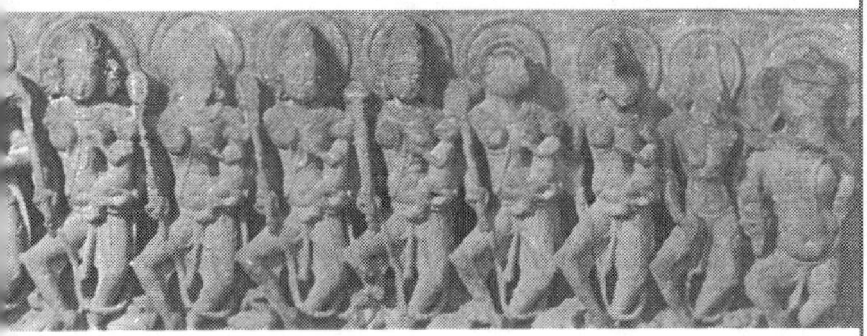

Gendered Identity
The Case of Queen Didda of Historical Kashmir

"Who else but poets resembling prajapatis (in creative power)
And able to bring forth beautiful compositions,
Can place the past times before the eyes of men".

(*Rajatarangini*, I, p. 2)

A. INTRODUCTION

The study of women in India explores some of the less frequented areas in early Indian history. In recent years, studying women's issues or revaluating literature by and about women has been a major activity. The

Original Sources: The source used for this article is mainly English translation of Kalhana's *Rajatarangini* edited by R.S. Pandit. M.A. Stein's English translation and critical Sanskrit edition have also been used.

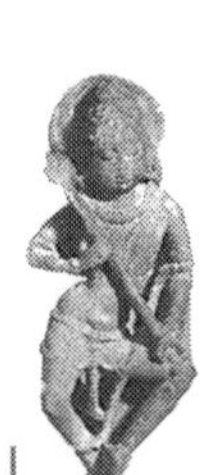

notion that women are unfit for political leadership has denied them public presence. This is an attitude found far beyond ancient South Asia. Throughout the complex societies of Euro Asia, we observe a similar official prohibition of female participation in political affairs. While attempting to explain the widespread restrictions placed on the political activity of women, historians and anthropologists have relied heavily over the past two decades on the concept of gendered public and private domains where power resided in the public arena was reserved for men, whereas women were at home only in the limited domestic realm. It was the exclusion of women from the possession of public political power that led to almost universal devaluation of women.

Recovering the lives of women from the neglect of historians was the goal of women's history from its inception. Its methodology and interests have evolved over time as it has become established as an academic discipline. From its early origins in cataloguing great women in history, in the 1970s it turned to recording ordinary women's expectations, aspirations and status. Then, with the rise of the feminist movement, the emphasis shifted in the 1980s towards exposing the oppression of women and examining how they responded to discrimination and subordination. In more recent times, women's history has moved to charting female agency, recognizing women's strategies, accommodations and negotiations within a male-dominated world. Although it developed out of the feminist agenda, gender history has somewhat different objectives. Recognizing that feminity and masculinity are to some extent social constructs, it investigates how institutions are gendered and how institutions gender individuals. In a short space of time, gender has become an indispensable category for historical analysis alongside class and race. While this is to be applauded, gender history is not without its problems. One of its most prolific areas of research is the history of men as a sex and the changing nature of masculinity. Though gender is a relational concept, women and femininity have been marginalized in some of these studies. The study of gender explodes order and restores ambiguity, contradiction, diversity and possibilities to the centre of social process.[1] The time is ripe for the assessment of ways in which gender in the past was being studied, to consider which avenues of research are most fruitful and productive and reciprocally in what ways the study of the past gender construction is important for other kinds of feminist research.[2]

Indeed one historian of masculinity, Toby Ditz, has recently warned that this risks 'restoring men—however particularized, differentiated and socially constructed—to the centre of our historical narrative'.[3] But scholars are asking conceptual and methodological questions about both genders and women's history reveals the vitality of both fields and points to their continuing evolution. Such questioning should avoid the fate of obscuring women in history and instead lead to new opportunities for more research about women. For instance, scholars entering the field will inevitably need to engage with recent claims that masculinity is only comprehensible when fully integrated with the history of women and, in the view of some, with feminist concepts of male-female power differentials.[4]

Since gender like caste and class is a relational category of analysis, it is time to ask whether gender history is 'hiding' women from history again. But answer to this query lies in much of the available literature authored and published in the name of gender approach of history which is concerned chiefly or exclusively with women. J.W. Scott points out "in its simplest recent usage, 'gender' is a synonym for women. Any number of books and articles dealing with women's history has substituted 'gender' for women to acquire political acceptability in the field of enquiry".[5]

Women and gender issues need to be recognized and addressed in early historical studies owing to their importance as well as their bearing on our understanding of contemporary society. Women have emerged as a force in history. Historians of women may differ from one another in the writings which have appeared, but writing about women in history has had its impact on the broader discipline. Recently, there has been some effort towards developing methodologies and studying the texts, inscriptions and other archaeological artefacts. Understanding of women at a certain level of depth necessitates the use of biographical and case study methods. The biographical accounts of women should be analysed to understand the institutional, structural and cultural sources of her life. I propose to extend this work, especially in the context of early India. Following Scott's principles in the study of gender, my first aim is to show that some women did acquire political power and authority in medieval India and the second is to explain how this was possible given the dominant patrilineal norms and ideology of kingship.

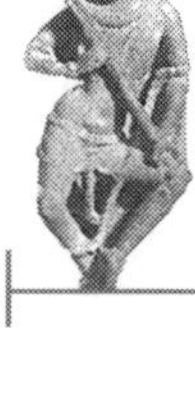

Kalhana wrote the history of Kashmir well known as *Rajatarangini* or 'River of Kings'. It is a poem in Sanskrit in eight cantos composed in the 12th century AD. In *Rajatarangini* we find that the women who had already emerged from the domestic stage and went onto the political stage, were free, owned immovable property, managed their own estates and even fought as the head of their troops.

First of all, we need to locate social sanctions from the authority of texts which may have allowed people of Kashmir to accept the dominance of women rulers in the valley. This can be traced from the verse in the *Mahabharata* which authorizes the coronation of a vanquished ruler's daughter in the absence of suitable male candidates, though it was rarely executed in practice.[6] In the past, Kashmir had a woman ruler Yasovati, whose crowning was justified as Goddess Parvati's incarnation by underlining Kashmir's spiritual importance, as Goddess Parvati's incarnation and declaring its king to be a portion of Lord Shiva,[7] to be respected by all who desired prosperity.[8] Women of Strirajya[9], which Chakladar, following the identification of that country by Varahamihira's *Brihat Samhita* and Kalhana's *Rajatarangini*, locates in the region of north-west beyond Himalayas, practised polyandry. Hieun Tsang informs us that in this country, women administered executive powers, and it was ruled by succession of women. The queen's husband was the king, but he did not hold the reigns of the government.[10]

We do not have many epigraphic records throwing light on the women rulers and administrators, during the period of our study. But we have stray literary references which indirectly suggest, that in certain countries, women were authorized to discharge executive/political functions.

We notice in the *Rajatarangini*,[11] departure from the traditional role which women played in the early history of India. In this text, a notable feature of the political history of Kashmir is the administrative ability displayed by the queens in the affairs of state. Though, unfortunately, in most cases this was accompanied by dissolute character[12], still the careers of Sugandha, Didda, Suryamati and Kota and a host of minor ones, throw interesting light on the opportunities afforded to women to take effective part in public life. Here the prevailing feminist notion of public/private domain for men and women respectively does not apply in the case of ruling class women in Kashmir, especially in the context of the above-mentioned queens, as general patriarchal dominance is missing in these contexts. Bilhana also extols the women of Kashmir for their learning which allowed them to speak fluently both in Sanskrit and Prakrit.[13] Perhaps the ladies of the royal families were given administrative training. There are examples of justice and good administration. The queens of Kashmir, pursuant to the ancient law and convention, were sprinkled with the sacred waters of the coronation side-by-side with the kings, who shared the throne with their consorts. The queens were not always of royal origin. Sometimes, they were daughters of feudatories, traders, merchants, spirit distillers and also untouchables. Prevalence of *anuloma* and *pratiloma* marriage was there in Kashmir as it was practised among the ruling classes of ancient and medieval India. King Chakravarman married an untouchable Domba woman and made her 'the premier queen who enjoyed the privilege among royal ladies and visited the temple of Vishnu. But whether marrying an untouchable woman (Domba) was revolutionary or not for King Chakravarman is not shown anywhere. In other instances, there were spaces where queens could choose Chandala lovers,[14] sisters of queens could be married to the Kayasthas.[15] But we do not find any reference to opposition from any quarters for breaking the caste barriers. Though it is evident that while Kalhana himself idealized and valorized the Varna-Jati order, it was by no means firmly entrenched as is seen in this and many such cases suggesting that brahmanical claims and pretentions were by no means universally accepted. What is more, the categories which were viewed as despicable from the brahmanical perspective, including Dombas and Chandalas, evidently exercise influence in the royal court. In such cases, it may be possible to argue that women may have found it esier to claim and exercise power in situations where Varna-Jati order was relatively weak.[16]

In sociological traditions 'the distinction between power and culturally legitimate authority, between the ability to gain compliance and recognition that it is right, is crucial to our study of women. Social scientists by and large have taken male authority for granted; they have also tended to accept a male view that sees the exercise of power by women as manipulative, disruptive, illegitimate, or unimportant. But it is necessary to remember that while authority legitimates the use of power, it does not exhaust it, and actual methods of giving rewards, controlling information, exerting pressure, and shaping events may be available to

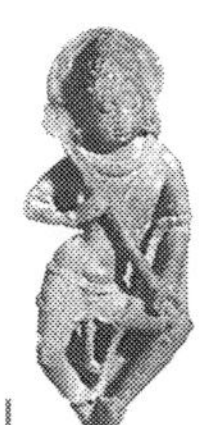

women as well as to men'.[17] But despite acknowledging the universal fact of male authority, we cannot deny the importance of role of women rulers in historical Kashmir. *Rajatarangini* mentions several administrative and public works performed by the queens independently or with their husbands such as building of temples, monasteries, grant of village to brahmanas, founding of towns, etc. In this background of the dominance of queens of Kashmir, we shall be discussing Didda's role in Kashmir's history.

B. DIDDA AS QUEEN CONSORT, REGENT QUEEN AND THE RULING QUEEN

According to Kalhana's *Rajatarangini*, the most prominent queen of Kashmir, Didda[18], daughter of Simharaja chief of Lohara, had such great influence on her husband Kshemagupta that the latter "became known by the humiliating appellation of Kshema".[19] Kalhana's appellation is supported by the copper coins of Kshemagupta, which bear the legend, 'Di-Kshema', apparently a contraction of the above name (Fig. 13).[20] The numismatic specimen clearly reveals the great influence exerted by the granddaughter of Sahis upon her husband. D.C. Sircar mentions that the coins bearing the name Kshemagupta alone are rare, whereas the other type with *di-kshemagupta de (va)* is common.[21] During the lifetime of her weak and effeminate husband, Kshemagupta, she was the virtual head of the state and wielded sovereign powers. Whatever the reason might

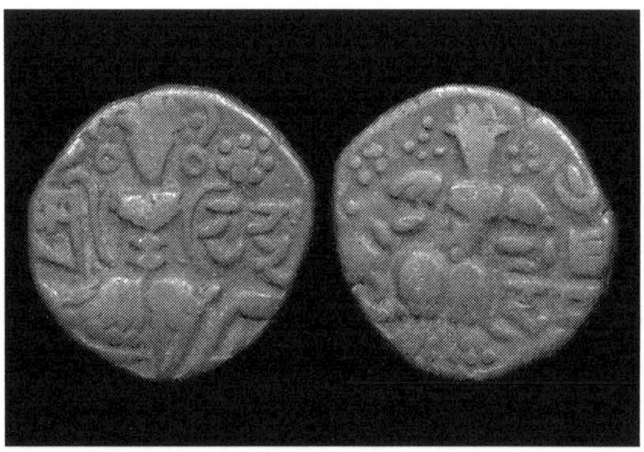

Coin 1

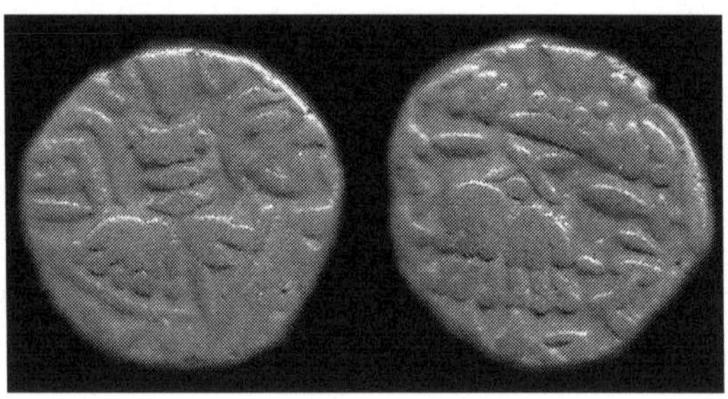

Coin 2

Fig. 13. Coins of Didda Rani, Ruler of Kashmir.

have been which led Kshemagupta to inscribe the queen's name on his monetary issues, the unusual procedure adopted is in itself sufficient to account for the use of the nickname casting reflections on his political impotency as against his powerful queen, who acted for him and ruled like the real king. We may take into account the fact that even in the past queens have been represented on Gupta gold coins: 1. Chandragupta-Kumaradevi type; 2. Asvamedha type of coins of Samudragupta and Kumaragupta and 3. King and Queen type of Kumaragupta[22]. But we do not have matching epithet on the coins of Gupta rulers.

When Kshemagupta died, all his co-wives followed him to the funeral pyre. Didda, through ostentation, began to prepare to die after him and Prime Minister, Phalguna, gave his consent readily. When she repented in pursuance of her desire near the funeral pyre, however, she was prevented from dying by the tender-hearted minister Naravahana[23]. G.M. Rabani puts it as "Naravahana, the prudent minister of the state who realized the value of Didda's services to the people and what she was capable of doing for their welfare, dissuaded her from ending her life."[24] We see the same theme in one of the traditions about Rudrama Devi where she is identified as widow queen. In the *Sidhesvara Charitramu* (essentially a later version of the *Prataprudra Charitramu*), Rudrama Devi was dissuaded from killing herself following the death of Ganapati (her husband in this account) by her religious preceptor, a Shaiva guru who advanced a number of religious and pragmatic arguments in favour of her remaining alive. One of these rationales concerned the security of the kingdom which would fall into the state of anarchy without a ruler.[25] In a different context, Kathryn Hansen reports that several stories in popular Indian culture about regent queens directly address their failure to commit sati after the king's death. Typically, the queen is depicted as foregoing the attractive option of sati because of her sense of responsibility towards her family and kingdom, often threatened by imminent attack.[26] Later, after the death of her husband, she chose to become regent queen of her young son and exercised all royal powers herself. Didda's legitimacy as a ruler was derived from her husband. Despite the dichotomy of a widow queen's situation—cast in the dual role of a good wife and a capable ruler—the number of widow queens who actually ruled is far greater than the number of daughters succeeding to the throne. The regent queen may have been a more acceptable type of woman ruler, as they were far less threatening to the patriarchal order than the female kings like Rudrama Devi or Razia.[27] But Didda's deviance from societal norms for good wife still had to be vindicated. We see departure from the Kashmiri tradition of queen being sati after the death of the king. Kalhana has appreciation for those queens who 'preserved the honour of their country from being lost' by being sati. This practice was so deep rooted that even the humble attendants who performed this supreme act of devotion for their masters are mentioned in high praise. Very characteristic of this attitude is the contrast between the two dancing girls, one of whom, belonging to King Kalasa's train, 'disgraced the whole women kind' by yielding herself after the king's death to a village official,[28] while the other belonging to Utkarsha's household followed him on the funeral pyre, thus displaying a noble conduct which makes women who are beloved by their husbands carry their heads high even in this day.[29] Equally characteristic is Kalhan's enthusiastic admiration of the noble wife of the Damara Kosthesvara. Finding her husband lying wounded by the king's orders, she paid no heed to those who told her that she might yet get back her husband alive and committed sati by entering the fire. The fire itself, so runs the chronicler's tribute, was purified from its sin by the feet of one who was proceeding towards the world of the virtuous women.[30] Kalhana does not admire those queens who did not immolate themselves with their husbands. Referring to the ascendancy of Naravahana, Didda's minister, he contemptuously uses the word *randa* for queen Didda.[31] Here Didda may have been seen as *anamoly*, because the societies that define women as lacking legitimate authority have no way of acknowledging the reality of female power. The difference between rule and reality is reflected in our own society, when we speak of powerful women as 'bitches'.

Didda had gradually assumed the control of administration even during her husband's time and in course of time her potentialities to handle the statecraft were fully unfolded. She ran the government and attended to every detail of administration. She was in direct charge of civil departments as well as armed forces; nothing could be done without her consent and permission. Kshemagupta was succeeded by his infant son Abhimanyu in AD 958 who ruled up to AD 972. During her time, Didda overcame many revolts successfully. Her prime minister Phalguna, who had revolted later either through the dexterous negotiations of Didda or through his own sense of loyalty to the crown, abandoned his plan to attack Srinagar and laid down his arms in the temple of Varaha (now Kothi Tirtha Baramulla on the right bank of Jhelum). The other revolt was by Mahiman and Patala, who had formed a powerful league with feudal barons and encouraged people to rise to rebellion against Didda. When civil war broke out the ministers began to waver their loyalty to the crown. Only Naravahana remained steadfast. Didda herself took up the responsibility of operations against the advancing rebels. Unmindful of her own personal safety and life she appeared on the battlefield determined either to vanquish the enemies or get killed herself. But she was conscious of the numerical superiority of the rebel forces. Therefore, she employed the weapon of diplomacy to frustrate the designs of the rebels. She created a rift among them by offering the brahmana rebels heaps of gold. With the defection of the brahmanas, the rebellion fizzled out and most of the enemy troops dispersed. Kalhana expressed in *Rajatarangini*, "She whom none believed had strength to step over a cattle track, the lame lady traversed in the manner of the son of the wind (Hanuman) the confederate forces." She appointed Yasodhara as supreme commander of the army and got Mahiman killed and thus became the undisputed leader of the state. "This was the first critical period in the long life of Didda which tested her merits, forbearance, fortitude and statesmanship. As the events proved, she rose equal to the occasion and scaled heights of diplomacy while dealing with the enemies and facing the odds".[32] When Yasodhara rebelled, Didda tackled the rebellion by commanding her army in person and defeating and killing him. She was liberal in conferring titles to her loyalists and at the same time she was suspicious of them too. She conferred the highest title of *Rajanaka*[33] on Naravahana for his loyalty to the queen, but when she was told by officials that he had absorbed all powers in himself, it made her apprehensive and she refused to forgive Naravahana who ultimately committed suicide. Her character is defined by Hussnain as kind and generous but at the same time cruel and suspicious'.[34] She showed her decision-making ability when her commander Rakka died. She quickly invited her old Prime Minister Phalguna, who joined her and suppressed the Damara revolt. She had a wonderful capacity for organization, which turned many a near defeats and failures into victories and successes. Hussnain[35] describes her as diplomatic, cunning, ruthless and energetic by nature, possessed of inborn qualities of rulership, which smoothened her path to the throne of Kashmir.

In the meanwhile, King Abhimanyu died in AD 972 due to consumption, as Kalhana says. But Mohammad Azam asserts that he was poisoned by his mother. Kalhana's account is trustworthy, which shows her as engaged is construction of religious and charitable deeds. A period of creative activity followed when Didda was occupied in founding towns, constructing edifices and building shrines.

After the death of her son, Abhimanyu, sorrow overshadowed her cruelty and through composure, she cooled down like the crystal when darkness had screened its radiating heat[36]. The grief of her lost son softened the heart of Didda for some time and she, in expiation of her immoral acts, founded several temples and villages in different parts of the kingdom, amongst which are the Diddamatha, now known by the name Diddamar, a mohalla in Srinagar on the right bank of the river near the seventh bridge[37]. From that time onwards by her wondrous acts of piety, her wealth, though acquired by evil deeds, gained sanctity.[38] The commissioner of Srinagara Bhuyya, brother of Sindhu, a man of good conscience fostered in her a philanthropic spirit.[39] He created in her mind the inestimable love for the people and from that time onwards the queen, who had given up evil ways, came to be respected by all the people.[40] The queen founded, in order to add to her deceased son's pious acts, the shrine of Abhimanyusvamin and the town of Abhimanyupura.[41] She founded her capital town, Diddapura. Further near Diddapura, Diddasvamin was founded by her and the convent as a resort for the people of Madhyadesa, Lata and Saurashtra.[42] To augment the merit of piety of her husband, "the rainer of armlets", this beautiful woman who showered gold, founded the town of Kankanapura.[43] She built of white stone another temple of Diddasvamin, which gleamed as if bathed with the waters of Ganga emerging from its feet.[44] As a lodge for Kashmiris and people of the plains, a vihara with a very high quadrangle was constructed by this charming and fortunate lady.[45] She built a shrine called Simhasvamin after her father Simharaja, as well as a convent for the residence of the Brahmans of the plains.[46] By her pious acts such as the consecration of the chapel of Vishnu and convents, the confluence of the Vitasta and the Sindhu was made very sacred by her.[47] Despite the state's pre-occupation with internal feuds and in repulsion of attacks from Rajouri or other lands, numerous religious shrines were built keeping in view the interest of her subjects. As an attribute to the loving memory of her grandfather, she built a Vishnu temple known as Bhima Kesava[48] on the left bank of river Lidder in a village out three kilometres to the north of sacred springs of Matan on Srinagar Pahalgaon road.[49] It is needless to enumerate her manifold good works in the various localities, she consecrated sixty-four foundations, and such is the report.[50] Nearly all the temples of the gods, the encircling walls of which had been damaged by fire, were saved from dilapidation by the queen and provided with stone enclosures.[51] She also built a grand matha after Volga, the woman who carried the lame queen on her back at the games and called it Volgamatha. She also repaired Jayavindara Vihara which had been badly damaged by her husband Kshemagupta, who had also plundered this vihara. Buildings of viharas and finds of Bodhisattvas, Padmapani with six arms having Dhyani Buddha, Amitabha with his spiritual ego on his head and two goddesses Tara and Bhrikuti on his either side, have been discovered, which are slated to have been made in Didda's time, which shows that Buddhism had survived at least until eleventh century and also continued to receive royal patronage[52]. Female patronage figures prominently in other religious traditions as well.[53]

But this conduct of her lasted only for a year. She then forgot her grief, and her lust for pleasure and power returned. She destroyed her grandson Nandigupta (AD 973-75) by witchcraft as also her another grandson Tribhuvana, who had ascended the throne after his brother's death. Her treacherous and faithless character has been described in *Rajatarangini* as follows,

> Although residing in a sacred pool and observing the vow of silence, the Timi fish is addicted to eating up its kind; the peacock while living solely on drops from the cloud daily swallows the snakes, the stork ostensibly given to meditation makes the meal of the unsuspecting fishes which approach the edge; even while acting piously there can be no certitude about a relapse into evil in the case of sinners[54].

After putting her last grandson to death, Didda then ascended the throne herself (AD 981–1003). Didda is referred to as a queen who killed her three grandsons for power. M.K. Dhar talks about frequent and gruesome involvement of queens in counterplot tracing this to their being neglected in large harems and their consequent desire for attention. Dhar links this reason with Didda's frustration.[55] But this is not true. As noted earlier, Didda was Kshemagupta's chief and most desired queen and in fact was a widow by the time she murdered her grandsons. In her passion for Tunga, she also put Bhuyya to death.[56] In the annals of the T'ang ruler of China, there was Wu Tse-T'ien, the prototype of queen Didda in China. She murdered her own child, deposed another son and proclaimed herself emperor in AD 690. She crushed revolts and cut off the heads of those who rebelled against her, and satisfied her every whim. She appointed a young priest as the abbot of the monasteries of Lo-Yang "giving him official license to enter and leave the palace at any hour of the day and night". Piety went hand-in-hand with her sudden burst of cruelty and lust. It was she who, from AD 672 to 675, caused to be sculptured in the grottos of Lungmen, the celebrated Great Buddha of the Rocks with his company of boddhisattvas, monks and lokapalas.[57] During Didda's reign of 25 years, there were political intrigues, murders, banishments and denunciations. Her character in *Rajatarangini* has been described as follows, "Even in the case of those who are born in high families, alas! The natural bent of women, like that of rivers is to follow the downward course".[58] Kumkum Roy[59] highlights the fluidity of sexual relations represented in the *Rajatarangini*. The ministers present their wives to kings, and queens such as Sugandha and Didda consolidate their power by entering into relations with ministers.

Later, she ascended the throne herself and reigned for 22 years. After Didda became full fledged sovereign in AD 980, it was a critical period as she had to face the rebellions of greedy brahmanas, unruly landlords, nobles comprising with outside forces for dethroning her, but with her diplomatic talent, she was bold enough to crush them all. And thus she was able to maintain her autocratic hold over the land. Didda elevated her paramour Tunga[60] to the post of chief minister and his five brothers to other important offices of state. Her relation with Tunga can be explained in the light of Shalini Shah's discussion on the sexual access of women in the northern quarter (Uttaradisa), which as per brahmanical description, is the land of free behaviour populated by licentious, self-willed women.[61] The discontented ministers and officials who were ousted entered into league to raise a rebellion. They brought Vigraharaja, Didda's brother's son, into the conspiracy and spread disaffection among the brahmanas of the principal *agraharas*, inducing them to hold solemn fasts (*prayopavesa*) against the queen and Tunga.[62] But Tunga's valour and Didda's cunning diplomacy and bribes defeated these attempts.[63] Shrewdness of Didda is shown in her 'Bribe and Placation Policy'.[64] During her reign of 25 years, there were political intrigues, murders, banishments and denunciations, ad infinitum.

Didda being a good statesman responded quickly to the services of her faithful men. When chief of Rajouri, Prithvipala revolted against Didda, Tunga managed the show. Tunga, together with his brothers, entered Rajapuri by another route and set fire to the town.[65] By this successful attack, Prithvipala was forced to surrender and pay tribute to Tunga, who victorious and triumphant, returned to Srinagar and in recognition of the victory was also made commander-in-chief of Didda's army.[66]

Didda had an inordinate lust for power with a statesman-like sagacity, political wisdom and administrative ability. H.C. Ray unhesitatingly refers to Didda as a fickle-minded queen on one hand, and on the other he also states that despite the gross immorality and other defects in her character, her claim of being one of the ablest sovereigns of the valley can hardly be denied. He adds that "while the lust for power motivated her to perform acts of great cruelty, this does not indicate that she was lacking in humanity".[67] H.C. Banerjee[68] calls Didda "a ruthless and immoral lady but nevertheless an able queen". M.L. Kapur[69] labels her as "masterful personality". Among the ruling class in Kashmir, unlike other social groups, many queens had access to public power. The equality and high status enjoyed by queens like Didda point to their control over the kingdom. Didda died in AD 1003, after half a century of ruthless government, first as queen consort, then as regent and ultimately as sovereign. She remained to the last in possession of the Kashmir throne, and was able to bequeath it to her family in undisputed succession. She appointed Sangramaraja, son of her brother, Udayaraja, the ruler of Lohara, as heir apparent and the crown passed quietly and without a contest and convulsion to the new dynasty, the house of Lohara.[70] She chose him amongst a large number of other nephews. She placed a heap of apples before them and spoke "how many fruits can each one secure in here".[71] There was a scramble among the youngsters, but she noticed that Sangramaraja had picked up not only the largest number, but was quite unhurt. 'He was asked by her in her surprise how he, while securing numerous fruits, had escaped injury, whereupon he replied to her as follows "By making them

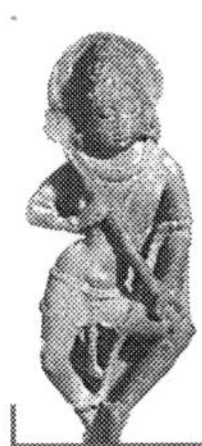

engrossed in the struggle with one another while remaining apart I secured fruits and at the same time was not hurt".[72] On hearing this, adept in statecraft, Didda considered him the wisest and fittest of them all for the throne of Kashmir. This territory, which has left its name to the present valley of Loharin, comprised the mountain districts immediately adjoining Kashmir valley on the south-west and now included in the Poonch district. Kapur talks of Didda's ability as a statesman in transferring power to Sangramaraja and concedes that while subsequent rulers were immoral/ guilty, there were none as competent as Didda. He further concedes that Didda's reign was significant, as it was rare for women to rule.[73] Didda's bestowal of throne to Loharas rather than that of Yashakaras, with whom the sovereignty was associated is unorthodox.[74] She demonstrates remarkable political sagacity by emphatically determining the future of Kashmir through maternal home.[75]

C. CONCLUSION

If we go by the description of Didda in *Rajatarangini*, Kalhana has painted Didda in black colour and others who followed him have done the same without caring to investigate the facts. Contrary to how Kalhana portrayed Didda, P.N. Bajaj remarked, "She ranks among the remarkable personalities in the medieval period, not only of Kashmir state but also of the Indian subcontinent." That she was a capable organizer, a clever diplomat, and a determined administrator and a bold fighter, no fair-minded critic can deny. Didda's crime in the eyes of Kalhana and others who were custodians of sacred traditions is that she declined to cremate herself as sati. This was looked upon as the height of unfaithfulness to the departed husband in ancient and medieval ages. But in modern times, she cannot be denounced on this account. The other charge labelled against Didda is her intimacy and affection for Tunga. It is said that she had fallen in love with him and accepted him as a 'paramour'. The charge does not bear any validity as there is ample proof to support the view that Tunga's efficiency may have allowed him to reach to that position, as even after Didda's death, Tunga maintained high position for many years under the succeeding regimes. Kalhana has been criticized by Vina Mathur for his attitude towards women in her following remarks, "Kalhana did not like the dissolute conduct of certain queens, but there were kings who were equally immoral. Kalhana has taken them to task individually but women, as a class, has been subjected to his criticism. He is harsh towards them.... He was an orthodox, conservative brahmana, allergic to women outstepping their limits".[76]

In spite of charges of gross immorality and other defects of character, queen Didda's claim of being one of the ablest sovereigns of the Valley can hardly be denied. As Rabani rightly puts it, "Didda's rule is significant from yet another point of view. The share of women, we may admit, was limited in the administration of the country. The succession of throne was confined to males, and as a consequence of the history of Aryans, India does not furnish us with many names of female sovereigns. Sugandha and Didda are the two females who occupied any place of significance in Indian history"[77]. M.L. Kapur's[78] assertion that there is nothing surprising if her rule was characterized by "petty politics, intrigue, treachery, cruelty, debauchery and murder", but it shall have to be conceded at the same time that while in the subsequent history of Kashmir, we come across many rulers who were no less guilty of moral and other lapses, there was none as able and competent as Didda' seems to be correct.

Didda was one of the most significant queens of Kashmir, who emerged from the 'veil of traditional history' and exercised her agency and political power[79]. She was so strong a ruler that her rule is shown to be parallel and even better than many of the male rulers of later period. Kalhana himself while comparing her with the male ruler Silhana (AD 1111-AD 1112) mentions, "on that (throne) on which even a lame queen (Didda) had maintained herself for a long time in a spirited manner, he though a man had his mind distracted by fears".[80] But she is not an isolated instance. Although the Hindu gender ideology mandated that rulers be males, it was flexible enough to accommodate female rulers. Women in men's role, however, tend to constitute an elite segment of humanity; few women in history have achieved a dominant position, and even fewer have competed with males to become queens or leaders. We have references to Rudrama Devi of Kakatiya dynasty.[81] In a study on Rudrama Devi of Kakatiya dynasty (in Andhra), Cynthia Talbot points out the need to recognize the flexibility of Hindu construction of identity. One did not actually have to be a male to fulfil the masculine functions of a ruler. The *Mahabharata* condemns women stating that the country where a woman, a child, or a gambler rules sinks helplessly as a stone raft in a river.[82] Kalhana too has seen Didda's dominance over her husband Kshemagupta as humiliating because in our gendered society, women are always termed as submissive figures. Whenever in the past we have such references to dominant women, authors of literature and history have never appreciated it. B.N.S. Yadava, who too blames Kashmir's ambitious queens rather than ambitious kings for vitiating the political atmosphere, omits the names of the important women and then talks of apprehension of the social decline in that period where he could be applying gender transgression as well.[83] But Kalhana applies the same morality to male and female rulers objectively as he criticizes Didda and Sugandha for their unconventional liaisons in much the same way as he criticizes Chakravarman's involvement with a Domba woman or later Lalitapida's affair with Jayadevi.[84] Hoards of authors, in secondary texts also, do not give dominant place to Didda in the history of Kashmir. Saroj Gulati refers to Dharmanika of Srinagar inscription as Didda's son, who apparently was dominant not Didda. She, thereby, tries to show that Didda was one of the common women in the ruling class of Kashmir where princes respected their mothers and engraved inscriptions in their honour.[85] But careful reading and interpretation of the inscription would suggest otherwise. The inscription engraved on stone slab, dated to the year 68, i.e. AD 992 in the reign of queen Didda mentions, "a certain lady whose name is not traceable in the text, gave birth to a son named Harmonica lovely as Marana and a great benefactor of cows". The second verse of the inscription describes "Dharmanika as devoted son who gladdened his mother as Kartikeya, Ganapati, Aditya and Krishna gladdened theirs, by charitable diggings which made the lord of Gods and people rejoice". The third verse is important as it records the date. It informs that "in the bright fortnight of the month of suchi, in the year 68 of the Laukika era, corresponding to AD 992 in the reign of queen Didda, he (Dharmanika) honoured his mother with utmost devotion (by dedicating some charitable works to perpetuate her memory)".[86] Dharmanika, the donor of the record, does not seem to be a prominent personality. However, the chronicle mentions Dharmanika, who was an official under Tunga and well-known prime minister of the queen and her successor, Sangramaraja. The other inscriptions mention Didda by masculine appellation of Deva rather than Devi (Diddadeva rajye)[87] for which Deambi provides an interesting explanation—"Didda's energy, political acumen, and essentially masculine traits of character caused people to view her more as a powerful king than as a mere queen"[88]. Earlier views that women were largely powerless have thus been revised in the light of new interpretations and evidences. Devika Rangachari correctly suggests, "Didda represents the female power at its vibrant peak in the *Rajatarangini.* Her rule spanning nearly 50 years, including her husband's Kshemagupta's lifetime, the period of her regency, and her actual accession to the throne as formal ruler of Kashmir (AD 980/1). The tenacity of Didda's rule witnessing a consistent overcoming of obstacles is a striking feature of Kalhana's account".[89]

The ideological barrier against the ruling queen was breached on several occasions such as in the case of Didda, Rudrama Devi of Kakatiya Dynasty in the 13th century, Raziah Sultan of Delhi, etc. Cynthia Talbot observes[90],

> The historical records from medieval Andhra, Orissa and Kashmir indicate that women were allowed to exercise supreme political authority on a number of occasions, as the only option that would ensure the retention of a throne or chieftaincy within the immediate kin group. I would argue, therefore, that the centrality of family in certain political cultures of Indian middle ages is the main explanation for the phenomenon of the ruling queens. By family, I mean a small unit including male and female kin, both by birth (consanguine) and by marriage (affine).This thesis that the immediate kindred, including women, took precedence over the patrilineage, contradicts the patrilineal kinship models of the brahmanical law books, which scholars of pre-modern India have tended to regard as hegemonic in their influence, at least among elites.

Even in early European History, we have examples of such queens who were as powerful as Didda of Kashmir. Ross Balzaretti's study of Italian queen Theodelinda, queen of Lombard for 38 years (AD 590–628) [91] points towards this fact. She is the most famous woman in Italian history and has been remembered for a variety of roles.[92] She had outlived three kings, her two husbands Authari (her marriage to him was 'political' and one arranged by abduction) and Agilulf and her son Adaloald (with whom she ruled presumably as regent queen/queen mother). She appears to be the first Lombard queen to construct and patronize churches and palaces (the most important project was the Church of Monza).[93] She achieved a position of real authority in a world almost entirely controlled by men. Theodelinda has a lot to contribute to current debates about the nature of queenship and gender ideology in early medieval times.[94] Here we can conclude that female ruler in Early Medieval times in general and Historical

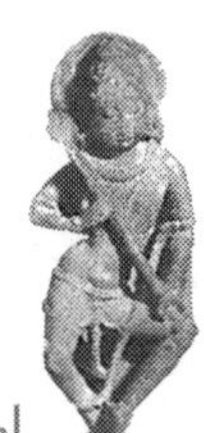

Kashmir in particular could be reconciled with an ideology that excluded women from political authority and analyse the specific social conditions that enabled certain queens to obtain power. In case of Kashmir, to what extent did these women pursue policies that were distinctive? There are no easy and immediate answers to this question, but it is clear that their legitimacy as a ruler was never readily accepted. As such they would have faced unique problems, and perhaps confirming to the ideals associated with male rulers, may have been an option for survival and success.[95] Kalhana's text *Rajatarangini* highlights the power and agency of women in royal court culture in two essential ways; as sovereign rulers in their own right and as powers behind the throne. Power is wrested and executed by them in what is essentially a patriarchal edifice, thus causing a certain amount of tension and ambiguity, not only in specific phases of Kashmir's history but also in Kalhana's portrayal of them. On the other hand, the text makes it very clear that the queen had a very definite political role to play—whether as a part of policy dictated matrimonial alliances or as a popular choice of wielding power. In this sense, the notion that "the kingship or the state was associated with the control of women and was an instrument of their subjugation"[96] does not hold true for women in *Rajatarangini.* The questions which arise here are that is the force of patrilineal ideology and norms has been over rated? Have we imputed greater hegemony to patrilineal orthodoxy than is warranted? Continuous research and close scrutiny of source material is needed to bring real people in the past alive and to arrive at a fresh understanding of the history of women in early Kashmir.

NOTES AND REFERENCES

1. Irevs Silverblatt, "Women in States", *Annual Review of Anthropology,* USA, 1998, pp. 454-55.
2. Wallmans, "The Epistemologies of Sex", in Lionel Tiger and Heather T. Flower (eds.), *Female Hierarchies,* Chicago, 1978, p. 22.
3. T. Ditz, "The New Men's History and the Peculiar Absence of Gendered Power: Some Remedies from Early American Gender History", *Gender and History,* 16.1 (2004), 1-35, p. 7.
4. Joanne Bailey, "Is the Rise of Gender History 'Hiding' Women from History Once Again?" *History in Focus,* 8, (2005): Articles in Gender History, New Hall, Cambridge, source: http://www.history.ac.uk/ihr/focus/gender/articles.html accessed on 10th March 2007.

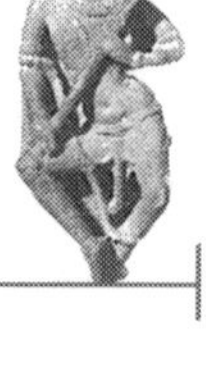

5. J.W. Scott, "Gender: A Useful Category of Historical Analysis", in J.W. Scott (ed.), *Feminism and History*, OUP, New York, 1996, p. 155.
6. Rajyadharma Santiparva, 33.43-46; also see Beni Prasad and R.C. Mazumdar, "Political Theory and Administrative System", in R.C. Mazumdar (ed.), *The Age of Imperial Unity,* 4th edn., Bombay, 1968.
7. Here the ruling queen, like the king, is considered to be a portion of Siva.
8. Ved Kumari, *Nilmata Purana,* Vol. I, Srinagar-Jammu, 1968, pp. 12-13.
9. *Kama Sutra of Vatsyayan,* Devidutt Shastri (ed.),Varanasi, 1964, pp. 126, 294, 295. Ancient Indian literary tradition refers to *strirajya* or 'women's kingdoms'. Jaiminibharata account for the kingdom of Pramila, Queen of the land of the Amazon may be mythical, but the existence of *strirajyas* in Ancient India was not merely a flight of fancy, as it seems to be supported by works such as the Si-yu-ki of the seventh century Chinese pilgrim, Hiuen Tsang, in which it is stated that to the north of Brahmaputra in the present Kumaon-Garhwal region, lay the Suvarnagotra country (Su-fa-la-na-kin-ta-lo), which was the 'eastern women's country' where according to the Chinese pilgrim, "for ages woman has been ruler, and so it is called kingdom of women (Watters, YCTI, I.330). Hiuen Tsang also mentions another *strirajya* called by him as 'western women's country' near Langalain, the present Baluchistan region Watters, II.257. Long before Hiuen Tsang, Megasthenese heard of queen rulers in the Pandya country. Arrian says that Pandaia was the daughter of Heracles, who entrusted her with the sovereignty of the land in which she was born. According to Polyaenus, her empire comprised 365 villages. According to Solinus the Pandeon nation was always governed by queens. Majumdar CAI,222-23,456-58. The *Markandeya, Garuda* and *Skanda Puranas* mentions *strirajyas* or women's kingdom. See N.N. Bhattacharya, *History of Sakta Religion,* Delhi, 1974, pp. 4-5.
10. T. Watters, *On Yuan Chang's Travel in India,* p. 330.
11. The literal meaning of *Rajatarangini* is the "river of kings" which expresses the aura of male dominance. But contrary to this it also talks about women queens who actually ruled Kashmir in early medieval times.
12. See Kumkum Roy, *Turbulant Waves: Construction of Gender Relations in the Rajtarangini of Kalhana.*
13. *Vikramanakdevacarita,* XVIII, 6.
14. *Raj,* 6.78.
15. *Raj,* 7.150-152.
16. Kumkum Roy, "Gender Relations during the first Millennium: An Overview", in B.D. Chattopadhyaya (ed.), *A Social History of India, History of Science, Philosiphy and Culture in Indian Civilization,* Gen. Ed. D.P. Chattopadhyaya, Delhi, 2009, p. 226.
17. Michelle Zimbalist Rosaldo, "Women, Culture and Society: A Theoretical Overview", in Michelle Zimbalist Rosaldo and Louise Lamphere (eds.), *Women, Culture and Society,* California, 1974, p. 21.

18. Didda is a term of respect for elder sister (*Raj.* VII.225), which still survives among Kashmiri Brahmins. This romantic grand daughter of the Sahis was a remarkable woman and stories of her armours survive in Kashmir to the present day. When she repented at one time for her sins, she founded shrines and monasteries and her piety recalls that of the Brunhilds, the freedegunds and Irenes in the west.
19. *Rajtarangini* (henceforth RT), R.S. Pandit (ed.), VI, 177.
20. This class of copper coins has been issued in the joint names of queen Didda and king Kshemagupta on which the figure of seated goddess appears on the obverse of this variety of coin; the letter Di which is in the first syllables of the queen's name and the letters 'ksema' which constitute the first part of the king's name occupy the left and the right field respectively. The reverse contains the figure of the standing king in regal attire; the word 'Gupta', the latter part of the king's name is written below, to right. See the Coins of Didda, Fig. 13.
21. D.C. Sircar, *Society and Administration in Ancient and Medieval India,* I, Calcutta, 1967; See also A. Cunningham, *Coins of Medieval India from seventh Century down to the Mohammedan Conquests,* Varanasi, 1967, p. 45.
22. Catalogue of the Gupta coins in the Bayana Hoard, p. CXIII, pl. XXXI. 14. See Coins nos. 1&2.
23. *RT.*, verse 196, p. 246, the custom of sati was in vogue in Kashmir from early times. In the stories of *Kathasaritsagara,* which was composed in the valley in C. 11th C. AD, the custom appears to be quite common. About the historical cases of the widow burning themselves at the funeral pyres of their husbands, we have a number of instances in Kalhana's chronicles. After the death of their husband Samkaravarman, Surendravati and two other queens cremated themselves along with him (*RT,* VII, 103). Queen Suryamati burnt herself in the company with her dead husband Ananta (*RT,* VII, 477-79). Mammanika and six other queens accompanied king Kalasa into death (*RT,* VII, 1486). When the body of the deceased was available, the widows burnt themselves along with their dead husband. When it was not available, she ascended a separate pyre. Thus, Jayamati burnt herself separately a few days after Ucchala's body was cremated. (*RT,* VIII, 368). The system of Sati was not confined to royal family alone. Malla, the wife of Bhogasena, the chief justice of Ucchala, followed her husband to death. (*RT,* VIII, 445). Sometimes, courtesans accompanied their masters into fire. Jayamati, a harlot of king Kalasa (*RT,* VII, 724) and Sahaja, a concubine of king Utkarsha (*RT,* VII, 858) entered the pyre of their masters. Sometimes, even the mothers and sisters and other relatives burnt themselves with their beloved deceased. Gajra cremated herself with her son Amanda (*RT,* VII, 1380), Vallabha with her brother-in-law, Malla (VII, 1486) and the sister of Dilhabhattaraka with her brother (*RT,* VIII, 448). 'The custom of sati is not sanctioned by *Dharmashastra* or by the *Smritis.* Manu and Yajnavalkya are reticent about it, though Vishnu seems to condemn it in its passage, which are regarded by many as later interpolations (see R.C. Majumdar (ed.), *The Age of*

Imperial Unity, Bombay, 1960, p. 568). Discussing the general prevalence of this custom in warrior tribes, Altekar is of the opinion that fighting races were very possessive of their women and often preferred to kill them rather than take the risk of their going astray after their husband's death. There was also a general belief that the warrior would require in his next life all the things which were near and dear to him in the present existence (A.S. Altekar, *Position of Women in Ancient India*, Delhi, 1962, p. 116). Contrary to this, the custom of sati was not a regular practice at many instances. The *Nilamata Purana* makes no reference to sati. The custom occurred more frequently after the Lohara Dynasty. But every widow was not required to commit sati. The Tamara widows, in general, did not commit sati, though Kalama testifies that the wife of Tamara Kithara entered fire at the news of her husband's imprisonment and thus, became a sati. (*RT*, VIII, 2334).

24. G.M. Rabani, *Ancient Kashmir: A Historical Perspective*, Srinagar, 1981, p. 160.
25. Cynthia Talbot, "Rudrama Devi, the Female King: Gender and Political Authority in Medieval India", in David Shulman (ed.), *Syllables of Sky, Studies in South Indian Civilization in Honour of Velcharu Narayan Rao*, Delhi, 1995, p. 408.
26. Hansen Kathryn, "The Virangana in North Indian History: Myth and Popular Culture", *Economic and Political Weekly*, April, 30, 1988, pp. 25-33.
27. Kumkum Roy and Uma Chakrabarti, "In Search of Our Past: A Review of Limitations and Possibilities of the Historiography of Women in Early India", *Economic and Political Weekly*, April, 30: 1988, pp. 2-10.
28. *RT.*, VII, 726-28.
29. *RT.*, VII, 850-59.
30. *RT.*, VII, 23-36.
31. *RT.*, VI, 260.
32. G.M. Rabbani, *Ancient Kashmir: A Historical Perspective*, Srinagar, 1981, p. 161.
33. Rajanaka is modern Razdan, added as surname among Pundits today.
34. F.M. Hussnain, *Hindu Kashmir*, Delhi, 1977, p. 176.
35. *Ibid.*, p. 176.
36. *RT.*, VI, 294, p. 254.
37. The ruins of the structure are still visible. The area is now renamed as Khan-Kah Sokhta. Situated on the high plinth, the outer walls of the building consisting of huge blocks of stones and the long series of steps are even now noticeable. S.L. Sali, *Kashmir: History and Archaeology through the Period*, Delhi, 1993, p. 178.
38. *RT.*, VI, 295, p. 254.
39. *RT.*, VI, 296, p. 254.
40. *RT.*, VI, 297, p. 254.
41. *RT.*, VI, 299, p. 254.
42. *RT.*, VI, 300, p. 254.
43. *RT.*, VI, 301, p. 254.

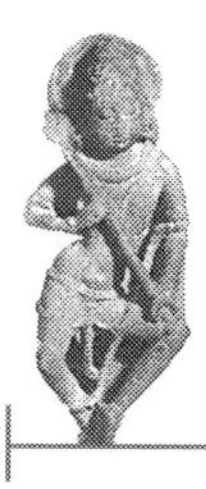

44. *RT.*, VI, 302, p. 255.
45. *RT.*, VI, 303, p. 255.
46. *RT.*, VI, 304, p. 255.
47. *RT.*, VI, 305, p. 255.
48. *RT.*, VI, 178.
49. S.L. Sali, *Kashmir: History and Archaeology through the Period,* Delhi, 1993, p. 178. This temple is presumed to be Mandapa type, i.e. open on all the sides as we find in similar shrines like the temple at Pandrethan or at Srinagar. It is now the Zairat of Baba Bamadin Sahib, a converted Hindu saint. (Stein, *Rajatarangini,* V. II, p. 465.
50. *RT.*, VI, 306, p. 255.
51. *RT.*, VI, 307, p. 255
52. G.M. Rabani, *Ancient Kashmir: A Historical Perspective,* Srinagar, 1981, p. 162.
53. Donations from queens and women of royal family are of course known from the early phases of a few Buddhist sites. We have evidence of donation being made by chief queen of satrap regularly in association with the family of prince Karachi and other sons Aodasa (Satrap), Khalama (Kumara), Maja (Kanistha) along with five other princely persons, a friendly satrap and a Buddhist acharya—Buddila. The queen Abuhola is referred to here also as a daughter and mother donating together with her mother and parental grandmother. Here this inscription clearly describes the structure of the royal family where the chief queen, the donor, occupies a higher social status than the crown prince and Kumaras in performing religious functions i.e. a relic was deposited in a Stupa and the Stupa and monastery were constructed for the acceptance of the universal Samgha of the Sarvastivadins. At another Buddhist site, Ganesra mound at Mathura, a female relative of Ksatapa Ksaharatta Ghataka made donation for the erection of Stupa. Since it had to include more than one single religious sect, royal patronage, being in theory about the competition for patronage, it seems that in the early period there was some kind of division along gender lines, where the kings presided over the brahmanical yajnas, and their wives and sisters made donations to Buddhist monuments. *Epigraphia Indica,* XII 1907-10, pp. 135-47; Romila Thapar, *Tradition and Patronage,* p. 30. Also see Clark, Elizabeth A. 1990, *Patrons and Priests: Gender and Power in late Ancient Christianity, Gender and History,* 2.3: 253-73. It deals with religious patronage by women in the late Roman Society.
54. *RT.*,Verse 309, p. 255.
55. M.K. Dhar, *Royal Life in Ancient India,* Delhi, 1991, pp. 44-45.
56. *RT.*,Verse 322, p. 256.
57. *RT.*, p. 257 fn.
58. *RT.*, 316, p. 236.
59. Kumkum Roy, *Turbulent Waves: Construction of Gender Relations in The Rajtarangini of Kalhana,* IHC Proceedings, 1999.

60. Tunga was a buffalo herdsman with whom she fell in love. He had come to Kashmir from Poonch and who had obtained service as a letter carrier.
61. Shalini Shah, "Gender and Sexuality in Ancient Punjab: A Case Study of Karna Parva in the Mahabharata", in Aparna Basu and Anup Taneja (eds.), *Breaking Out of Invisibility: Women in Indian History,* New Delhi, 2002, pp. 29-30.
62. *RT.*, VI, 338-347, p. 258.
63. *RT.*, VI, 335-336, p. 258.
64. See Devika Rangachari, Constructing Society and Polity in Early Medieval North India, 7th C.-13 th C. AD, Ph.D. Thesis, 2005, p. 144.
65. *RT.*, VI, 349-51, p. 259.
66. *RT.*, VI, 352-54, p. 259.
67. H.C. Ray, *Early History and Culture of Kashmir,* Delhi, 1970, pp. 67-68. M.L. Kapur, *in Eminent Rulers of Ancient Kashmir,* Delhi, 1975, p. 18.
68. H.C. Banerjee, *Cultural Heritage of Kashmir,* Calcutta, 1965.
69. M.L. Kapur, *Eminent Rulers of Ancient Kashmir,* Delhi, 1975, p. 18.
70. *RT.*, VI, 356-65, pp. 259-60.
71. *RT.*, VI, 356, pp. 259-60.
72. *RT.*, VI, 360, p. 259.
73. M.L. Kapur, *History and Culture of Kashmir,* p. 59.
74. See Thomas Trautman, 'When a woman marries, her husband's patrilineal ancestors become hers' and she is cut off from the natal ancestors and kins in *Dravidian Kinships,* Cambridge, 1981, p. 272.
75. M.A. Stein completely ignores this sovereign in his genealogical table of Kashmir dynasties. She is represented, not as a ruler, but as Kshemagupta's wife. See *Rajtarangini,* Vol. III.
76. Vina Mathur, *The Role and Position of Women in the Social, Cultural and Political Life of Kashmir-7th century-16th century AD,* Jammu, 1985.
77. G.M. Rabani, *Ancient Kashmir A Historical Perspective,* p. 171.
78. M.L. Kapur, *Kingdom of Kashmir, Political and Cultural History of Kashmir from the Earliest Times to 1586 AD,* Jammu, 1983.
79. H.C. Ray quotes 'Didda was gifted with energy and statesmanship of a high order' in *Dynastic History of Northern India,* 2nd edn., Delhi, 1973, p. 135.
80. *RT.*, VIII, 419.
81. Cynthia Talbot, "Rudrama-devi, the Female King: Gender and Political Authority in Medieval India", in David Shulman (ed.), *Syllables of Sky, Studies in South Indian Civilization in Honour of Velcharu Narayana Rao,* OUP, Delhi, 1995.
82. *Mahabharata,* 5.40; van Buitenen, J.A.B. (trans. and ed.), *The Mahabharata*: IV. *The Book of Virata* and V. *The Book of the Effort,* Chicago, 1978, p. 129.
83. Yadava always alludes to the caste system in this regard; he also talks of the frustration among conformism and reality. This could be very well applied to women who broke gender norms. See Devika Rangachari, Constructing Society and Polity in Early Medieval North India, 7th C.-13th C. AD, Ph.D. Thesis, p. 210.

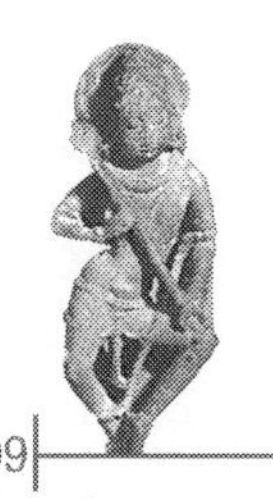

84. See Devika Rangachari, Constructing Society and Polity in Early Medieval North India, 7th C.-13th C. AD, Ph.D. Thesis, p. 210.
85. Saroj Gulati, *Women and Society-Northern India in the 11th and 12th centuries,* Delhi, 1985, p. 28.
86. K.N. Sastri, "Srinagar Inscription of Queen Didda", *EI,* XXXVII, no. 26, 1947-48, pp. 153-55. This inscription has been found in Srinagar. The script of the inscription is Sarada and the language is Sanskrit.
87. B.N. Kaul Deambi, *Corpus of Sarada Inscription of Kashmir,* Delhi, 1982, pp. 97-98.
88. B.N. Kaul Deambi, *Ibid.*, pp. 97-98.
89. Devika Rangachari, "Kalhana's Rajtarangini, A Gender Perspective", *Medieval History Journal,* 5,1, 2002, Delhi, p. 44.
90. Cynthia Talbot, "Rudrama-devi, the Female King: Gender and Political authority in Medieval India", in David Shulman (ed.), *Syllables of Sky, Studies in South Indian Civilization in Honour of Velcharu Narayana Rao,* OUP, Delhi, 1995, p. 414.
91. Ross Balzaretti, Theodilenda, "Most Glorious Queen: Gender and Power in Lombard Italy", *The Medieval History Journal,* 2, 2, 1999, pp. 184-207.
92. Elizabeth van Houts, *Memory and Gender in Medieval Europe, 900-1200,* London, 1999, pp. 11-14.
93. Ross Balzaretti, "Theodilenda, Most Glorious Queen: Gender and Power in Lombard Italy", *The Medieval History Journal,* 2, 2, 1999, pp. 184-207.
94. Ross Balzaretti, *Ibid.*
95. Kumkum Roy, "Gender Relations during the First Millennium: An Overview", in B.D. Chattopadhyaya (ed.), *A Social History of India, History of Science, Philosophy and Culture in Indian Civilization,* Gen. Ed. D.P. Chattopadhyaya, Delhi, 2009, pp. 226.
96. Uma Chakravarti, "Conceptualizing Brahmanical Patriarchy in Early India—Gender, Caste, Class, and State", *Economic and Political Weekly,* April 3, 1993, p. 582.

Chapter V

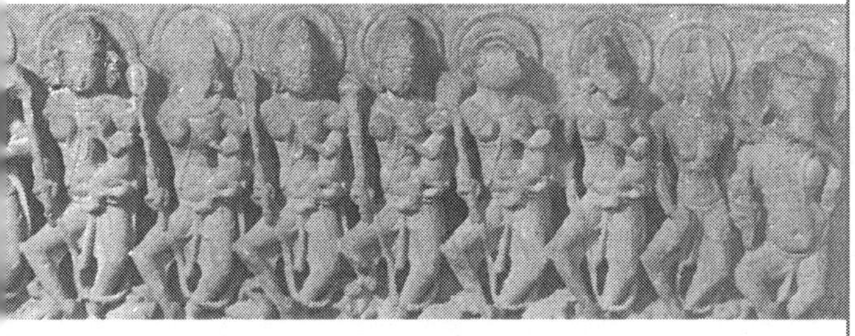

Gender in Inscriptions

The early Indian literary texts (*Dharmashastras* and the epics) are taken to represent the great tradition of the orthodox brahmanical society and historical interpretation of Indian tradition has largely been confined to and conditioned by it. Likewise, the emphasis with respect to heterodox faiths (Buddhism and Jainism) is on their canonical literature. Early Indian inscriptions, till recent times, are rarely taken to be sources of Indian traditions. It needs to be underlined that whereas the texts create and conserve the norm, the epigraphic records contain the norm as well as the variation and deviation from it. As a documentary source of contemporary traditions, they are no less authentic and authoritative. The inscriptions are the true repository of great as well as little traditions of the said periods. The nature, purpose and content of epigraphic records being radically different from literature, we find deviations and variations, which may be treated as a part of historical reality. The study of inscriptions, sometimes, leads to specificity and corrective to textual sources.[1]

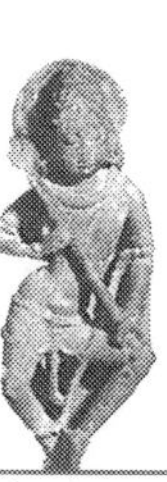

A. WOMEN AND GENDER IN INSCRIPTIONS

MAURYAN INSCRIPTIONS[2] (MAP)

The first and the only inscription talking about the Mauryan queen is the Edict of Ashoka on the Public Benefaction of Queen Karuvaki's Ashokan Pillar Inscription at Allahabad, it is famously known as 'Queen's Pillar Edict'. King Ashoka gives command to his mahamatras as such:

> *Devanampiyasa vacanena savata mahamata*
> *Vataviya(ii) Ye heta dutiyaye deviye dane(i)*
> *Ambavadika va alame va danagahe va(i) ye va pi amne*
> *Kimci gamyati taye deviye(i) se nani (pre.tani) hevain ganaye (pre.ganeyatha)*
> *Dutiyaye deviye'ti(i) Tivalamatu Kaluvakiye(ii)*[3]*

At the word of Devanampriya, the mahamatras everywhere have to be told (this). What gifts (have been made) here by the second queen (viz.) either mango grooves or gardens, or alms houses, or whatever else, these (shall) be registered (in the name) of that queen. This is (the request) of the second Queen, the mother of Tivara, the Karuvaki.[4]

The inscription throws light on the following facts:

(a) it is a command from the king to his mahamatras,
(b) document was drafted by the emperor himself who constituted his own identity by merely a title, Devanampriya or the beloved of Gods,
(c) the king constituted the identity of her royal majesty using the term devi,
(d) initially she figures as 'second Queen' but later also as the mother of Tivara, the Kaluvaki (Karuvaki),
(e) The Queen's Edict suggests that Karuvaki had her residence in Kausambi.

Romila Thapar[5] attributes Karuvaki as the personal name of Queen Tissarakkha, who figures in literary sources along with Asandhimitta and Padmavati, as the other queens of Ashoka. The chief queen was Asandhimitta, and on her death, Tissarakkha was elevated to the rank of the chief queen. Karuvaki seems to be the brahamanic patronym which Ashoka preferred to use for official and public purposes rather than her personal name Tissarakkha. The reference to a matrimonial connection with the brahmana family had its own significance in the contemporary scheme of social identity as Mauryas, who did not belong to either of the two upper varnas might have felt elevated by the exposition of this fact.[6]

The Pillar Edict VII[7] says *"ete ca amne ca bahuka mukha danavisagasi viyapata, se mama c=eva devinam ca"*

Translation: These and many other mukhyas (chiefs or heads of departments) are engaged in the distribution of charities and this too on my own behalf and that of my queens".[8]

We learn that the Mauryan queens were addressed by the epithet Devi and had their private funds to make charity on their own accounts.

Pillar Edict VII states, "In all my harems, they became acquainted in many ways in all the proper objects where satisfaction is to be arranged, here (in the capital) and in different quarters (of the country).[9] This is indicative of the fact that polygamy was the rule and many of the queens did not live with Ashoka at Patliputra but resided at other places. One such example is Karuvaki, which is mentioned above.

No information about Mauryan period would be complete without a reference to Kautilya's *Arthashastra.* In contrast to the above mentioned role of the queen Karuvaki, the text reflects the patriarchal control over the queens in the Mauryan period. Kautilya lays down that "the queens should be kept under strict vigil. He says that he should forbid the queens' contact with the ascetics with shaven heads and matted hair and with jugglers as well as the female slaves from outside. No member of the family should visit these queens except in establishment for maternity and sickness". In these circumstances, the queens, as envisaged by Kautilya, hardly enjoyed any scope to participate in public life and administration. But at the same time, we have inscription recording Ithijhaka Mahamatyas[10], who undoubtedly correspond to the *Stryadhyaska Mahamattas* who were, in all probability, appointed to look after matters concerning women of the palace. B.M. Barua is of the opinion that the *Strayadhyaksha Mahamattas* were instituted to guard the interest of the women, in general, not excluding courtesans, prostitutes, actresses and the like.[11] D.K. Ganguly[12] identifies them with the *Antavamsikas, Antahpuradhyakshas and Antahpuravergades,* mentioned in the contemporary and later documents, as officers connected with the harem of the king. How far is it correct that women's participation in public life was prevalent during the period of Mauryas is not brought out clearly in the Ashokan inscriptions as well as the *Arthashastra* of Kautilya.

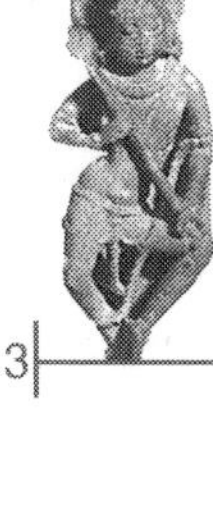

Saka-Kushana Period

The period from the 3rd century BC to the early centuries of Christian era was very important from the point of gendered history of Buddhist/Jaina sites in north India, the testimony of which is seen in the epigraphic data. Hundreds of inscriptions are found at the sites of Mathura[13], Sanchi, Bharhut (we have selected only Mathura for our discussion).

One of the significant aspects of the Mathura society is represented by religious donations by female donors. These donors are also of two categories: (I) queens and women of royal family, (ii) ordinary women. Donations from queens and women of royal family are, of course, known from the early phases of a few Buddhist sites.

Mathura Lion Capital Inscription reads:

"By the Chief Queen (*agramahisi*) of the great satrap (*mahaksatrapa*), daughter (*dhita*) of Ayasi Komusa, mother (*mata*) Abuloha, her parental grandmother (*pitamahi*) Pispasi, her brother (*bhrata*) Hayura, her daughter (*dhita*) Hana, her household and court of horakas...."

Here the donation is being made by chief queen of Satrap Rajula in association with the family of Rajula, prince Kharastha and other sons Aodasa (Satrap), Khalama (Kumara), Maja (Kanistha), along with five other princely persons, a friendly satrap and a Buddhist acharya—Buddila.[14] Here her official status as *agramahisi* (chief queen) is established. The queen Nandasi Akasa is referred to here also as a daughter and mother (of crown prince) donating together with her mother and parental grandmother. The fact that the father and the brother of Nandasi Akasa are mentioned without any title, royal or feudatory, point to the fact that they belong to non-royal family, whose names are not considered important enough to be mentioned in the inscription. Even then she acquired the position of the chief queen. It appears from the content of the inscription that the instructions must have been issued by the queen herself rather than the king. Here this inscription clearly describes the structure of the royal family where the chief queen, the donor, occupies a higher social status than the crown prince and Kumaras in performing religious function, the Stupa and monastery were constructed for the acceptance of the universal *samgha* of the Sarvastivadins and a relic was deposited in a Stupa.

At another Buddhist site, Ganesra mound at Mathura, a female relative of Ksatapa Ksaharatta Ghataka made donation for the erection of Stupa.

Since it had to include more than one single religious sect, royal patronage being in theory about the competition for patronage, it seems that in the early period, there was some kind of division along gender lines, where the kings presided over the brahmanical yajnas, and their wives and sisters made donations to Buddhist monuments.

What are, however, far more notable are the donations of ordinary women for the purpose of making of images and adornment of stupas and chaityas. In the category of Buddhist female donors were:

(a) daughter of lord of a Buddhist Vihara[15] found in Kanishka's reign (Yr. 23)

(b) wives and daughters of professionals, viz. wife of a *pravarika* set up an image of Buddha.[16] In another case the wife of a *sovanikara* (goldsmith) named Nagapriya set up an image of bodhisattva in her own *chaityakuti* for the acceptance of Dharmaguptaka teachers.[17]

Several *bhikkhunis* are mentioned among the donors; among whom two are most important. One is found in the Sarnath image inscription of the 3rd year of Kanishka, also from Bodhisattva image of Mathura and Kosam inscription of Kanishka dated 2nd year of Maharaja Kanishka.[18] *Bhikkhuni* Buddhamitra erected Bodhisattva statue. She is also mentioned as well versed in the *Tripitaka*. She was a female pupil of the monk Bala, who knew *Tripitaka* (Sarnath and Mathura inscriptions). It appears that she was a very well-known lady. It appears from the fact that the nun Dhanavati, donor of Bodhisattva image at Mathura, introduces herself as the sister's daughter of bhikkuni Buddhamitra.

Bhikkhuni Dhanavati of Huvishka's reign (Yr. 33) knew the *Tripitakas*. She set up an image of Bodhisattva at Madhuravanaka, together with her mother and father.[19]

(c) several other lay worshippers:[20]

Among the donors, at least one-third of the Buddhist population consisted of female donors.[21] So the ratio from the available records for female to male donors would be 1:3.

In the case of Jaina faith too, women donors are seen donating in the capacity of wife, daughter, daughter-in-law, mother etc. of a person. The remarkable feature in the case of Jainism is that the ratio of female to male donors is different from Buddhist sect. Here the ratio from available records is 5.4:1.[22] More women are inscribed offering religious donations.

Probably, women in the Jain sect had comparatively more powers and freedom to work at will than these in the Buddhist sect. The categories of Jaina female donors were:

1. Shishinis (= Shishya or female disciple)
2. Daughters, mothers, and wives of professionals,
3. Professional women such as *Sarthavahinis*

There are at least six inscriptions from a single site of Mathura in which the term Arya (which may have been honorific) appeared with the monastic epithet sisini (one in relation to the teacher). Though the Jaina monastic order conferred the gender neutral honorific title Arya to nuns as well as to the monks (so did the Buddhist Church in central India), but this is not indicative of the nuns enjoying near equality with the monks. Monks nowhere figure as disciples of a nun or as sisini of another nun as well as of a monk.

We have evidence of Dhammasoma, *Sarthavahini* in Yr. 22 donating the image of an Arhat.[23] It is not clear whether she was the wife of a Sarthavaha as Buhler has attributed or the second alternative, which is quite unlikely that she herself was a caravan leader. It is noteworthy that neither husband has figured anywhere in the inscription as an attribute of her wifely identity nor is he associated in her benefaction. Kirit K. Shah has rightly recognized that Buhler seems to have been guided by the fact that the feminine attributes in respect of the professional status are normally used for wives of the men concerned. This might be true in many cases, but it may not be so in all.[24] We do have similar instances where Buddhist tradition mentions a potter's woman of the town of Shravasti, who owned a property with one hundred potters' wheel. Her status is nowhere mentioned, and it may be that she was a widow, for we have seen that some legal schools allowed a widow to inherit when there were no sons.

The object of donations were:

1. Jaina image
2. *Ayagapatas* (Tablets of homage)
3. Erection of torana
4. Small pavallion for image of Vardhamana.

The interesting feature is that none of the women belonging to the brahmanical social order are mentioned as making religious donations. There is absolute withdrawal of Brahmanical women from the epigraphic space. There is no brahmanical counterpart to Buddhist *upasika* and Jaina *sravika.* That the order of nuns was alien to the brahmanical tradition is confirmed by literary evidence as well. In the Buddhist social order almost half of the women who have recorded donations individually are nuns, and indeed even among the male donors, there are a large number of monks. This raises a host of questions. Did these women have right of share in the family property? In the case of a single woman making a donation, was this a part of her *stri-dhana,* the wealth given to her by her mother and over which she, in theory, had complete control? It seems curious that such records are more frequent in Buddhist and Jaina contexts than in other religious faiths.

Though even in Buddhist texts considerable distrust was displayed, i.e. they are incapable of carrying out business or earning a living by any profession because they are perceived as uncontrolled, envious, greedy and stupid.[25] A wide range of restrictions were placed on *bhikkhunis,* who were even required to offer their alms to the monks if they ran into them.[26] No similar obligation was placed on the *bhikkhus.* In some cases the *bhikkhunis* received more severe punishment than the *bhikkhus* for similar offences.[27] Despite the general discrimination against women, which is reflected sharply in their lower status vis-à-vis the *bhikkhus* within the social world of the *samgha,* women did join the organisation in large numbers. More women came into it from *gana* to *samghas,* drawn probably by kinship ties with other entrants, but many others came in order to escape the misery of worldly existence.

The heretical religions, which flourished under the patronage of the Greeks and the Saka-Kushanas allowed more and more freedom to women, specially in religious matters and thus became instrumental in their advancement. According to Manu, a woman is never fit to be independent, her father protects her in childhood, her husband protects her in youth and her son protects her in old age.[28] It has been suggested by Manu[29] that women must particularly be guarded, otherwise they would bring sorrow to the family life. Being attracted by Buddha's Dhamma, women often renounced the world and accepted more rigorous life of the *bhikkhunis.* That the Svetambara order is shown by frequent mention of female lay worshippers in Mathura inscriptions where a sect of women asserted their religious rights by adopting heretical doctrines. We have evidence of other women perceived by society as associated with immoral

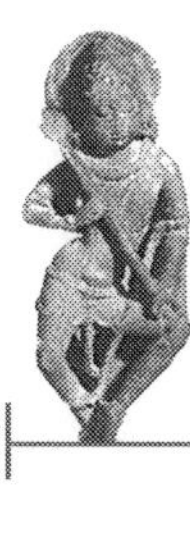

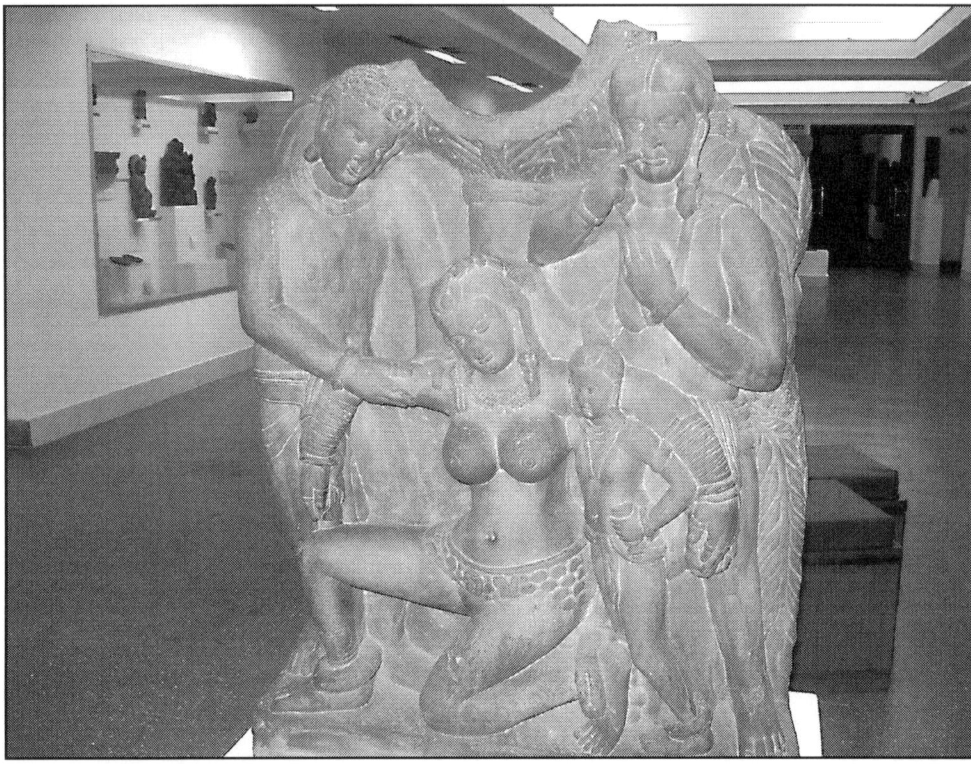

Fig. 14. Vasantasena: Scenes of a courtesan's house, Kushana, 2nd century AD, Mathura.

activities, i.e. *ganikas* (Fig. 14),[30] having the freedom of donating for the religious causes. An early inscription from Mathura[31] records the setting up of a shrine (*devikula*) of Arhat, an *Ayagasabha*, a *Prapa* (reservoir),and *Ayagapata* (stone slab) in the *Arhatayatana* (Arhat temple) of the Nirgranthas by a few *ganikas* who are identified as Nada, Vasa, Danda and Lonashobhika by Bhagwanlal Indraji.[32] This is indicative that the courtesans mentioned in the inscriptions were quite rich, and it is no surprise to find prostitutes taking part in religious affairs. One of the best lay disciples of Buddha, Jivaka Komaravaccha, the physician, was the son of a *ganika*. Her fee per night at Rajagriha was 100 *Kahapanas*.[33] It seems that the *ganikas* mentioned in the above inscription were prominent citizens of Mathura, though the *Divyavadana*[34] mentions *ganikas* as leading a very humiliating life. Overall, it seems that women had distinctly better status in the so-called heterodox sects than in Brahmanism as we do not find women of brahmanical order making large number of donations in

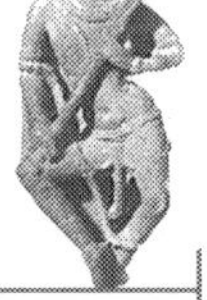

this period. Obviously, the association of women with this kind of donation, suggestive of a particular status, is prevalent during a specific time and in relation to specific objectives.

Royalty and Gender Relations: Gupta Queens in the Inscriptions

The role of women in the political history of ancient India is confined to royal families and the participation of common women, like common men, in the state administration has never been dealt with in contemporary history. Thus, the role of common women cannot be ascertained for want of literary or other data though women in the Saka-Kushana period are noticed making small donations for religious causes (Buddhist, Jaina and Brahamanical), as discussed above. Moreover, the brahmanical social structure, little encouraged public life for women. Owing to the lack of sources and the little impact of the common man on the political history in monarchical times, we may conclude that the role of common women cannot be systematically analysed for want of data.[35] Gupta period highlights certain royal women playing a vital role in the state affairs as:

1. Instruments of political alliance
2. Queen mothers influencing decisions and acquiring crowns for their sons
3. Regent Queens (in the event of the death of their king husbands, when their sons were minors)
4. Queen consorts influencing the king at the helm of political affairs

The history of imperial Guptas extends for more than two centuries over the whole of northern India and their power, accepted by all, from Bay of Bengal in the east to the Arabian Sea in the west, has been assigned initially to the matrimonial alliance between the Guptas and the Lichchhavis.[36] The matrimony augmented the power of Chandragupta to achieve royal status as he assumed the title of *Maharajadhiraja* after his coronation at Patliputra. The political influence of queen Mahadevi Kumaradevi, the daughter of one of the chiefs of *Lichchhavi-gana* is apparent from Gupta epigraphs[37] and Chandragupta-Kumaradevi type of coins.[38] Kumaradevi was instrumental in Gupta Lichchhavi alliance and achieving imperial status for herself and her husband by hiding the low ancestry by which Guptas were known among the Magadhans. R.S. Tripathi claims that Kumaradevi was a very ambitious lady and tried to get all assistance from her parents to achieve imperial status for herself, her husband and progeny. The matrimonial alliance benefited the Guptas.[39] In the Allahabad Pillar inscription[40], Samudragupta is proudly referred to as *Lichchhavi Dauhitra* (the daughter's son of Lichchhavis). By using this title he could link Guptas to *Lichchhavi-gana,* who had enjoyed respectability in the society[41]. Kumaradevi played a pivotal role in influencing her parents for help. For the recognition of this help, the Chandragupta-Kumaradevi type coins were struck (Fig. 15).[42] Further, her name appears in the genealogical part of all the Gupta epigraphs.[43] The importance of this relationship is apparent from extensive and repeated references available in contemporary as well as later epigraphs, coins and literature.[44] R.C. Majumdar states that 'the fact that the Gupta ruler who assumed imperial title of *Maharajadhiraja* was Chandragupta I, who married Kumaradevi, a Lichchhavi princess and that Samudragupta refers himself as *Lichchhavi Dauhitra* and Chandragupta-Kumaradevi type of coins (Fig. 15)[45] with the legend *Lichchhavyah* all go to prove that the rise of the Guptas to an imperial position was largely due to their alliance with the Lichchhavis in which Kumaradevi was instrumental.[46] Chandragupta I ruled not only over Ganga-Yamuna Doab and Saketa but also brought Magadha under his sway.[47] It has been observed that he was greatly assisted by the Lichchhavis of Vaisali in establishing his authority over Magadha and the imperial city of Patliputra and that this assistance was brought by Kumaradevi, the Lichchhavi Princess.[48] It is generally believed that they wanted to keep Chandragupta under their grip, so they got him married to princess Kumaradevi[49], although Altekar[50] finds her politically weak and immature for such a stupendous task. But it may be that after getting herself assimilated with the Guptas—her husband's family, as per Hindu traditions, she became ambitious, dedicated and desired independence for her husband and son as paramount sovereign powers and it may not have proved to be a farsighted policy of the *Lichchhavi-gana*.[51] Mazumdar believes that Kumaradevi was married to Chandragupta-I not due to any compulsion or subordination of Lichchhavis but due to some political strategy agreed upon between the uprising Guptas and revengeful Lichchhavis.[52] Guptas established themselves as an imperial power through this matrimonial alliance with the Lichchhavis, wherein Kumaradevi played a prominent and vital role.

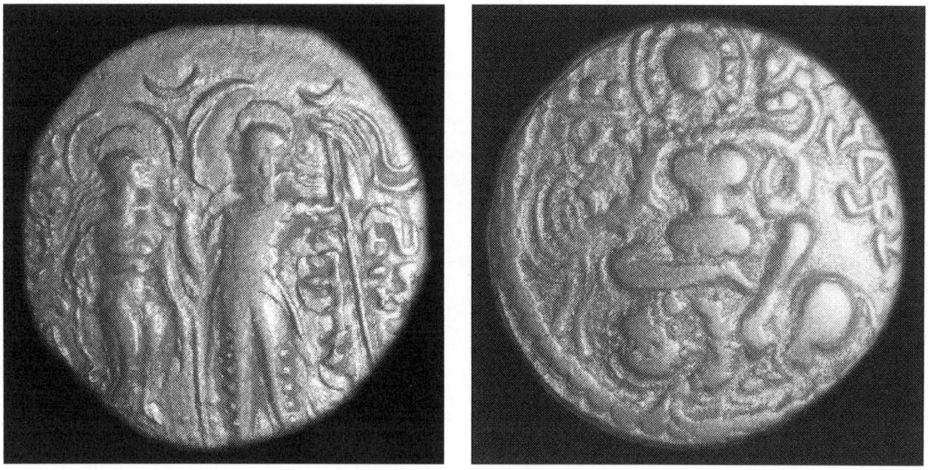

Coin 3—(*Left*) Obverse: Chandragupta-Kumaradevi;
(*Right*) Reverse: Goddess Durga seated on lion

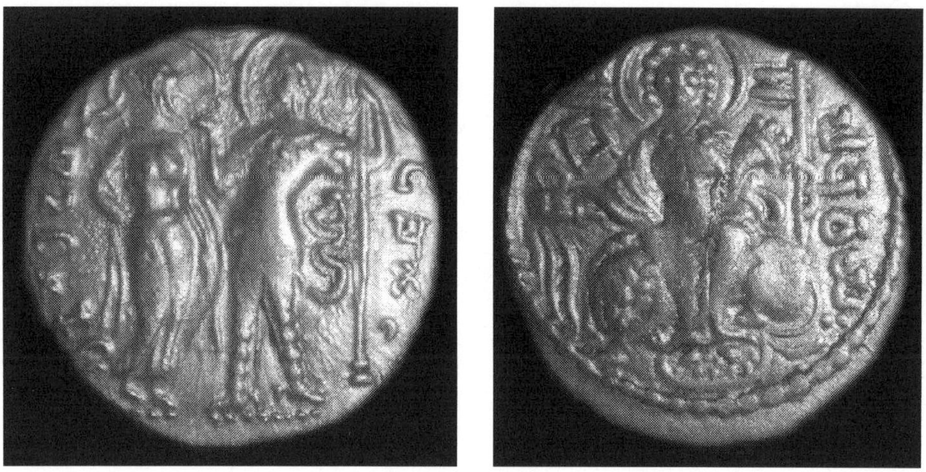

Coin 4—(*Left*) Obverse: Chandragupta-Kumaradevi;
(*Right*) Reverse: Goddess Durga seated on Lion

Fig. 15. Coins, Chandragupta-Kumaradevi type.

Another matrimonial alliance between Samudragupta and the Nagas recorded in the inscription is for Samudragupta's son Chandragupta II and the Naga princess Kubernaga (this is a case of Santana sandhi).[53] There is no direct role of Kubernaga available for political consideration, but for her being mother of Prabhavati, an instrument for matrimonial alliance of the Guptas.

The epigraphic record states that Chandragupta II, son of Samudragupta, came to the throne in c. AD 375-76.[54] He, like his father, was a military genius and led a campaign to the west for the conquest of Malwa and Saurashtra, which were under the Saka rule. The details of his campaign are not available but there are indications that Chandragupta, with his feudatories and ministers had to make a prolonged stay in Malwa without any gain[55]. On the other hand, Vakatakas had enhanced their prestige by capturing Kuntala and Chandragupta wanted a helpful ally on his southern flank, so that he and his army could make a concerted effort in Malwa and Gujarat without any danger. Therefore, he proposed a matrimonial alliance to Prithvisena: for his daughter Prabhavati to be married to Prithvisena's son Rudrasena II (again a case of Santana sandhi).[56] He was so much influenced by his queen Prabhavati that he gave up his ancestral religion Shaivism and became a Vaishnava like the latter.[57] With the deaths of Prithvisena and later Rudrasena II, the queen became regent queen for her minor son.

Mother Queens

Kumaradevi has been mentioned as mother and his maternal grandparents (Lichchhavis) by Samudragupta with great pride. Kumaradevi, being a mother queen, must have exerted to obviate all his rivals, specially seniors, and categorically rejected them in his favour.[58] Her role as queen mother of Samudragupta might have helped him get the throne.

Mathura stone inscription of Chandragupta II refers to the Queen Dattadevi as queen mother of Chandragupta II.[59] The name of Queen Dattadevi, as wife of Samudragupta, has been inferred from the Eran stone inscription.[60] She has also been assigned with the epithet 'Maharani'[61] and 'Mahadevi'[62] in the later inscriptions. But it seems that importance is derived from the epithet queen mother and not Maharani or Mahadevi. The figure of the queen on the *asvamedha* type of coin may have been due to religious necessity. Mentioning Dhruvadevi as chief queen, her son Chandragupta II may have accorded importance to his mother after becoming king. There is a seal recovered from Vaisali[63] describing Dhruvadevi as Mahadevi "Dhruvaswamini".

Inscriptions recording land grants were often engraved on copperplates, held together by a ring, which carried the seal of the donor. Donation of land was statement of power of the ruler.

Poona copperplate of Prabhavati Gupta, the Vakataka queen states:

"Success. Victory has been attained by Bhagavat. From Nandivardhana. There was the Maharaja, the illustrious Ghatotkachchha, the first Gupta King. His excellent son was the maharaja, the illustrious Chandragupta I. His excellent son was Maharaja-adhiraja, the illustrious Samudragupta, who was born of the queen Kumaradevi, who was the daughter's son of the Lichchhavi; who performed several horse sacrifices. His excellent son Maharaja-adiraja Chandragupta II graciously favoured by him; who is the fervent devotee of Bhagvat, who is a matchless warrior on the earth; who has exterminated all kings; whose fame has tasted the water of the four oceans; who has donated many thousands of crores of cows and gold. His daughter, the illustrious Prabhavatigupta of the *dharana* gotra born of the illustrious queen Kubernaga, who was born in the Naga family; who is the fervent devotee of the Bhagvat; who was the chief queen of the illustrious Rudrasena II, the maharaja of the Vakatakas; who is the mother of the heir apparent, the illustrious Divakarasena; having announced her good health, commands the householders of the village, brahmanas and others in the village of Danguna in the ahara of Supratishtha to the east of Vilavanaka, to the south of Sirshagrama, to the west of Kadapinjana, and to the north of Sidivivaraka, as follows: 'Be it known to you that on the twelfth lunar day of the bright fortnight of *karttika*, we have, for augmenting our own religious merit, donated this village with the pouring out of water to the Acharya Chanalasvamin, who is a devotee of Bhagvat as a gift not previously made, after having offered it to the footprints of the Bhagvat. Wherefore you should obey all his commands with proper respect.

And we confer here on him the following exemptions incidental to an *agrahara* granted to the *chaturvidya brahmanas* as approved by former kings; this village is not to be entered by soldiers and policemen; it is exempt from providing grass, hides for seats and charcoal to touring officers; exempt from purchasing alcohol and digging salt; exempt from mines and khadira trees; exempt from supplying flowers and milk; it carries the right to hidden treasures and deposits and major and minor taxes.

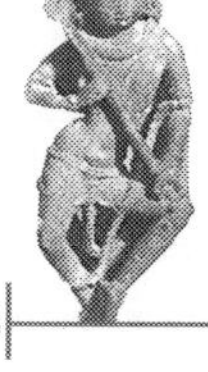

Wherefore this grant should be maintained and augmented by future kings. Whoever disregarded our order will cause obstructions when complained against by the Brahmanas, we will inflict punishment together with a fine...."[64]

The charter has been written in the thirteenth regnal year and engraved by Chakradasa.

Her Poona copper plate seems to imply that following the death of her husband, Prabhavati Gupta assumed the role of a regent, first on behalf of the minor king Divakarasena, and later with his death, for her younger son Damodarsena. A.S. Altekar[65] points out that the period of her regency lasted for about twenty years. Prabhavati may have lived for few more years as her name finds place in Tirodi plates issued in the twenty third year of the reign of her son Pravarasena[66]. The scholars like D.C. Sircar[67] have advanced the view that Prabhavati Gupta ruled the Vakataka kingdom as a *de jure* ruler and not as a regent. This theory, it must be admitted, does not appear to be unlikely, as there are reasons to believe that the Poona plate was dated in her own regnal year.[68] In any case, there was hardly any doubt that Prabhavati Gupta was a dominant personality in the Vakataka Kingdom in the fifth century AD.

The writings of Hiuen Tsang[69] states the existence of Stri-rajyas in the seventh century AD. One of them was called 'Eastern Women's Country', being located in the Kumaon-Garhwal region in the Himalayas.

Post-Gupta Inscriptions

The inscription also throws light on Vardhana-Magadha alliance[70] as suggested by the the appearance of the name of Mahasenagupta, the mother of Prabhakarvardhana[71] as well as the Banskhera[72] and Madhuban copperplate of Harshavardhana.[73] In the literature similar matrimonial alliance is discussed by Bana[74] between Avantivarman's son, Grahavarman and Prabhakarvardhana's daughter Rajyasri, leading to Mukhar-Vardhana alliance. It worked as an eye sore for the Malava king, who was earlier a friend of the Vardhanas. Bana tells through a wise brahmana, named Gambhira, who said to Grahavarman "my son by obtaining you, Rajyasri, has at length united the two brilliant lines of Pushyabhutis and Mukharis, whose worth like that of sun and moon houses is sung by all the world to the gratification of wise men's ears".[75] The Malava king, probably

Devagupta[76] having taken immediate advantage of the death of King Prabhakaravardhana, marched against the Mukhari king, Grahavarmana and put him to death and treated his queen, Rajyasri like a brigand's wife.[77] She was put into prison and was later helped by a Gupta feudatory, who was gauda nobleman, in escaping from the prison and entering into Vindhya forests, along with her attendants. Therefrom her brother, Harshavardhan, rescued her with great difficulty.[78] The passive role played by Rajyasri must have led to the assimilation of Mukhari kingdom into Vardhana empire and it led him to achieve unique imperial political status.

The inscription of the powerful Kadamba ruler Kakutsthavarman of Kuntala, states that their daughters were married to the Guptas and the other royal families.[79] It is not quite certain that whether it was Chandragupta II or his son who married the Kuntala princess. It is clear that women were powerful agents in establishing and augmenting the rule of the imperial Guptas.

Inscriptions of the Post-Gupta Feudatory Chiefs

The prasasti of the temple of Lakha Mandal at Madha in Jaunsar Bhawar[80] composed by Bhatta Kshemasiva, Bhatta Skanda and grandson of Bhatta Kshemasiva, and issued in stone by mason Isvaranaga, son of Nagadatta, records the dedication of a temple of Shiva by a princess Isvara, who is also adorned by the epithet mythological "Savitri", for the spiritual welfare of her deceased husband. Isvara belonged to the royal race of Singhapura. Her husband was Sri Chandragupta, the son of a king of Jallandhara, apparently himself not a reigning king, but either a younger son or possibly an elder son who died during his father's lifetime.

The fact that Isvara was married to a scion of the royal family of Jallandhar. Modern Jallandhar in Punjab makes it very probable that the district over which her ancestors ruled lay in the same province.

Singhapura rajya of the inscription may be identified with the kingdom of Sang-no-pu-lo, i.e. Simhapura, described by Hiuen-Tsang. Dating of the Inscription—AD 600–800.

Dewal Prasati of Lalla the Chhinda dated AD 992-93 records[81] the erection of two temples, dedicated respectively to Shiva and to Parvati and endowing them with some villages, situated in Mayuta of Ahushana, to which he gave the name Devapatti, as well as with a growth of his income. The founders were the provisional chiefs, Lalla of the Chhinda family and his wife Lakshmi, who belonged to the royal race of Chulukisvara. She fed brahmanas everyday in the alms-houses maintained by her and was compassionate towards the distressed, the helpless and the decaying. This eulogy has been written by the son of Vishnuhasi, a Gauda clerk called Takshaditya. It has been incised by Somanatha, the son of Kamadeva, who came from Kanyakubja (Kannauj) and was experienced in the use of chisel.

Inscriptions of Pala Period

We have very little information about the women in Pala period except for one important inscription. Vasantgadh inscription of Purnapala, dated AD 1099[82] records that a queen named Lahimi, the younger sister of Paramara Purnapala and widow of King Vigraharaja, at Vata restored an ancient temple of the sun and restored or founded a tank, apparently the very tank where this record has been found. It is believed that the town of Vata had been found by Sage Vasistha, that it was situated on the river Saravasti, and its inhabitants are described as having been devoted to the worship of the Sun. The inscription indicates two possibilities; one that the women of royalty had certain degree of freedom for making religious benefactions and two, they had certain degree of economic freedom to do so.

Inscriptions of Chedi

Bilhari stone inscriptions of the rulers of Chedi[83] found in Jabalpur district of Central Province of about 11th century AD record that the Queen Nohala, the wife of Chedi ruler Keyuravarsha, erected a temple of Shiva, at which the inscriptions may be supposed to have been put up. She endowed this temple with the villages Dhangatapataka, Pondi, Nagabala, Khailapataka, Vida, Sajjaholi and Gosthapali and she also gave the villages of Nipaviya and Ambipataka to the Sage Isvarasiva, a disciple of Sabdasiva, who again was the disciple of Pavanasiva. Nohala was the daughter of Ananivarman, of the clan of Chalukyas. Her husband, Keyurvarsha, was the son of Prince Musdhatunga who was the son of Kokkalladeva, described as a descendent of Arjuna of the tribe of Haihaiyas, who belonged to the lunar race.

Bhera Ghat stone inscription of Queen Alhanadevi [84] (yr. 907) the Chedi year. Object is to record that the Queen Alhanadevi, the wife (or rather widow) of King Gayakarnadeva and mother of the reigning king Narasinhadeva and his younger brother Jayasimhadeva, founded a Shiva temple with a ma—ha or choister, a hall of study and gardens attached to it; that, probably for the maintenance of these buildings and their occupants. She assigned the income from the two villages of Namaindi, in the Jauli Pattala and of Makarapataka on the right bank of the Narmada in the land adjoining the hills and the management of the whole establishment, to a Pasupata ascetic, named Rudrasi of Lata lineage. The inscription also records that all the buildings etc. aforesaid, at one of which the inscription may be supposed to have been put up, were designed or executed by architect Pithe.

Orissa

Konanda copperplates of Nettabhanja[85] of village Komaça in Orissa open with verses invoking Hara. The grant has been issued from the victorious camp Vanjulvaka by Sri Nettabhanjadeva—abhanjadeva surnamed Kalyanakalara. He is described as son of Rajabhanjadeva, grandson of Saturbhanjadeva and great grandson of Sitabhanjadeva. Object of the inscription is to record the grant of the village Karanjanu, situated in *vishaya* of Saradda, to a brahman named Stambhadeva, belonging to *kamva-sakta*, the *gautam gotra,* the *Autathya pravara* and the *Angirasa.* The *dutaka* of the grant is Bhanja Sumangala. It has been written by Sundhivigrahir̄ Savaraja, incised by Akshasaḷika Durgadeva and sealed by Mamma, which seems to be corruption of Mahamaya or the queen. Bhanja family is dated to 4th century AD. They are only next to Kharvela family of Orissa in antiquity.

The Sanskrit inscription 'Russellkonda Plates of Nettabhanya'[86] (Ganjam distt. Orissa) dated 8th century AD records the king's order issued to the royal officers or the *adhikaranas* of that time as well as the future and to other dependents serving in Kamverala *vishaya.* The officials and subordinates were told that the king had granted the village of Chandutungam as a free gift and revenue free holding in favour of certain brahmanas belonging to the Kausika *gotra.* The grant was actually made on behalf of the queens Kshatridevi and Kaivartadevi and *rajaputri* Meghavalidevi for the easy access of three ladies to heaven. These ladies seem to be the relatives of the king.

Two Sanskrit copperplates of Tribhuvanamahedevi of the Bhaumakara dynasty of Orissa in 9th cent. AD open with the description of the charms of Guhesvarapataka, the capital of the Bhaumakara rulers. Next follows the genealogy of the family. In the Vara dynasty there flourished a powerful king named Unmattasimha. His son was Subhakara, who erected many lofty viharas. His son was Gayada, who was succeeded by Kusumahara. Gosvaminidevi succeeded Kusumahara, who had left no son. The kingdom thrived under her rule, people lived in peace and prosperity. On her grandson, Lonabhara attaining majority, she retired, handing over the charge of the kingdom to him. Lonabhara was blessed with two sons, Kusurahara and Latihara. Two sons succeeded their father, one after another. But of them having died childless, Prithvimahadevi, wife of Kusurahara, ascended the throne. Her parents were Svatahavatunga of Kosala and mother Nrittamahadevi, the daughter of Yasovridddhi. Prithvimahadevi was known to the world by the name of Tribhuvanmahadevi. She is styled Paramabhattarika, Maharajadhuja-Paramesvari and Paramavaishnavi.[87]

She made the following grants in the year of 158 for perpetual offering of obulation, sandal paste, etc. to the deity Umamahesvara, installed in the temple constructed by Sasilekha and named Namesvara after her father, for repairs of the temple, for providing garments and medicines to mendicants, for food and clothing to brahmanas and for the maintenance of the family of the Danapati.

The grant in plate (A) consists of a village named Kottapura, together with the Namesvara talapa—aka in the dist. of Tamalakhanda in Dandabhukhi-mandal situated in Uttara Tosala.[88]

The grant recorded in plate (B) is a plot of land called Utthuka Khandakshetra in the dist. of Dakshinakhada in Dandabhukti mandala of Uttara Tosala.[89]

The queens of Bhanja kingdom are represented in inscriptions as being entrusted with the important task of maintaining the royal seal and scrutinizing the genuineness of documents. Some grants of King Vidyadharabhajna Amogakalasa are known to have been registered with the royal seal by his Queen Jayamahadevi or tri-Kaliga mahadevi.[90]

Two copperplate inscriptions in Sanskrit language of 10th cent. AD mention grants of Bhanja kings of Vanjulvaka (located in the Ganjan region in Orissa) made by the King Nettabhanyadeva in favour of a Brahmin named Bhatta Duuli, registered with a seal by Jivaloka Mahadevi, who seems to have been a queen of Nettabhanja Tribhuvankalasa. [91]

The donation of village or land by the queens raises a question of legal rights of queens over property. K.K. Shah is of the opinion that the donations by queens could only be made if they had personal rights over movable and immovable forms of property.[92]

Kashmir

The inscription engraved on stone slab, dated to the year 68, i.e. AD 992 in the reign of Queen Didda mentions, '*a certain lady whose name is not traceable in the text, gave birth to a son named Dharmanika, lovely as Marana and a great benefactor of cows*'. The second verse of the inscription describes '*Dharmanika as devoted son who gladdened his mother as Kartikeya, Ganapati, Aditya and Krishna gladdened theirs, by charitable diggings which made the lord of Gods and people rejoice*'. The third verse is important as it records the date. It informs that '*in the bright fortnight of the month of suchi, in the year 68 of the Laukika era, corresponding to AD 992 in the reign of queen Didda, he (Dharmanika) honoured his mother with utmost devotion (by dedicating some charitable works to perpetuate her memory)*'.[93] Dharmanika, the donor of the record, does not seem to be a prominent personality. However, the chronicle mentions Dharmanika, who was official under Tunga and well known prime minister of the queen and her successor Sangramaraja. The other inscriptions mention Didda by masculine appellation of Deva rather than Devi (Diddadeva rajye)[94] for which Deambi provides an interesting explanation—"Didda's energy, political acumen and essentially masculine traits of character caused people to view her more as a powerful king than as a mere queen"[95].

Earlier views that women were largely powerless have thus been revised in the light of new interpretations and evidences. Devika Rangachari correctly suggests, "Didda represents the female power at its vibrant peak in the *Rajatarangini*. Her rule of nearly 50 years spanned her husband's Kshemagupta's lifetime, the period of her regency, and her actual accession to the throne as formal ruler of Kashmir (AD 980/1). The tenacity of Didda's rule witnessing a consistent overcoming of obstacles is a striking feature of Kalhana's account".[96] The ideological barrier against ruling queen was breached on several occasions such as

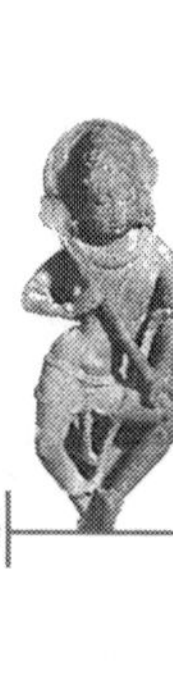

in the case of Didda, Rudrama Devi of Kakatiya dynasty in the thirteenth century, Raziah Sultan of Delhi, etc. Cynthia Talbot observes[97] "The historical records from medieval Andhra, Orissa and Kashmir indicate that women were allowed to exercise supreme political authority on a number of occasions, as the only option that would ensure the retention of a throne or chieftaincy within the immediate kin group. I would argue, therefore, that the centrality of family in certain political cultures of Indian middle ages is the main explanation for the phenomenon of the ruling queens. By family, I mean a small unit including male and female kin both by birth (consanguine) and by marriage (affine). This thesis, that the immediate kindred, including women, took precedence over the patrilineage, contradicts the patrilineal kinship models of the brahmanical law books, which scholars of pre-modern India have tended to regard as hegemonic in their influence, at least among elites".

Mother Goddesses in the Inscriptions

Goddesses supposedly performed the duties of guardian deities in early historical periods. An inscription of the early Kushana period from Mathura engraved on a stone sculpture suggests the cult of village goddess[98] prevailing in that region.[99] Luders reads the concluding portion of the records as *Priyatam devi gramasya* (may goddess of the village be pleased).[100] In literature, we have little evidence of the *grama-devata* (devi), a term frequently used for village goddesses, except for the Devi Bhagvata Purana, which speaks for various forms of goddesses as *grama devis* and refers to their worship in villages and cities.[101] On the other hand, there is adequate literary evidence for *nagar devata*, feminine divinities as guardians of the cities.[102]

We observe from the inscriptional records that goddess of the pot, (*Ghatavasini*), goddess of tree (*Vatayakshini*) or elsewhere goddess of post (*Stambheshwari*)[103] and goddess of speech (*Vakdevi*)[104] or the goddess of eloquence (*Vani*)[105], etc. seem to suggest that the ways through which different goddesses became visible in written records have to be considered in terms of the convergence of several interrelated historical phenomena.[106]

Allahabad Museum Inscriptions of the year 87[107], dated to AD 406 record the setting up of two slabs as a seat, at a pond, for the holy noble devi for the increase of their merit (a) by the son and daugther of the

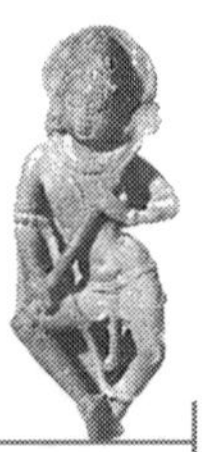

Saddler Saphara, the brother and sister born from the same womb, b) the son and daughter of Madgali, Sanika and Shandhaka. Alphabet is early Gupta or pre-Gupta of cistern variety. Language is mixed Sanskrit.

The inscription of the reign of King Bhulunda dated in the yr. 50 (AD 369-70 i.e. Gupta Era) records the installation of *(pratisthapita)* Mother goddess (*Bhagavatinam....Navatataka matrikanam*, elsewhere also called mahamatranam or great mothers) at a place called Navatataka, by Maharaja Bhulunda[108] The villages of Dubhedika and Dharmanaka, entrusted with a brahmin called Mulasarman and a plot of land in a locality called Arjunapamtika, entrusted with someone with the designation *bhutabhojaka*,were granted by King Bhulunda for the performance of *bali, charu and satra* rites of the mothers and to provide for the perfume, incense, and garlands (*ganghika, dhupa and malyopayogadisu*). The record further stipulates "from now onwards our agents (*ayuktas*) and temple servants (*deva-karminah*) who are engaged in performing the duties of *bali, charu* and *satra* rites and providing *gandha,* etc. and all our partisans, kinsmen, police magistrates, messengers, soldiers and royal heralds should endorse this grant." B.D. Chattopadhyaya points out that the significance of this inscription lies in the term used, *mahamatrika* (the great mothers would again imply contrast with the little mothers (*matrikas*) whose cult assumed importance gradually),[109] and the sacrifice *bali, charu and satra* being three of the five great sacrifices (*pancamahayajna*), which was essentially the ritual of worship of the image.[110] Third, a sacred space is assigned to the great mothers and officials are appointed such as *ayuktas, devakarmi bhutabhojaka* to perform the rituals and look after the sacred space. In the peripheral areas such as Bundelkhand- Baghelkhand region of Madhya Pradesh, *Shakti* is manifest in unique cult of local mother goddesses. We notice from the inscriptions that Divinity in female form (*Shakti*) had started appearing from Gupta period onwards, which is well supported by the literature.[111]

Another inscription is the Khoh copperplate inscription of Maharaja Samksobha of the Parirajaka-Maharaja family of rulers of Dabhalarajya, dated in 528-29[112], which records that the king at the request of Chodugomin, gifted by a copper-plate character (*tamra-sasanena*) half of the village of Opani, located in a territorial division called Maninagapetha to the goddess Pistapuri, whose temple was created by him (*bhagavatyah Pistapuryah karitaka devakulye*). The gift was given to perform *bali*, *charu* and *satra* rites as in the context of mother goddess of Bagh plate. Another Khoh plate issued by Maharaja Sarvanatha, belonging to the family of Ucchakalpa-Maharajas[113], records the donation of village, Dhavasandika as *devagraha* to be shared by Bhagvati Pistapurikadevi and Bhagvat (male deity). It is recorded, it is agreed by him and me that it is granted for the purpose of repairs..... of whatever may become broken or torn, belonging to the Bhagvati Pistapurikadevi, and for the maintenance of *bali*, *charu* and *satra*. The third Khoh copperplate inscription, also of Ucchakalpa-Maharaja Sarvanatha, dated AD 534[114] mentions that the two villages Vyagrahapallika and Kacharapallika, also located in the territorial division of Maninapetha, previously given to Pulindabhata, are now granted by the king to Kumaraswamin and his successors for the purpose of worship of the divine Goddess Pistapurikadevi at the temple (*devakula*), which had been built at Manapura.[115]

B.D. Chattopadhyaya[116] infers that Pistapuri or Pistapurika, as she is otherwise known, which is most likely to be represented by the local deity Patainidevi, must have become, by sixth century, quite a prominent deity in the Bundelkhand region[117]. He also notices in the context of second inscription that the juxtaposion of Bhagvat and Bhagvati Pistapurikadevi, the female deity, is a religious motif. Third, it would appear that the *devakula* of the deity, constructed at Manapura, was different from the one mentioned in the copperplates of Parivrajaka ruler Samksobha; this would not only suggest that more than one newly formed royal families, in a predominantly tribal area, sought affiliation with the cult of Pistapuri, but also the domain of the deity expanded through creation of new temples or sacred centres associated with her.

The two inscriptions from the time of Guhila rulers of Mewar:

Samoli inscription of the time of Siladitya of AD 646 (from the Marwar area of Rajasthan)[118] records the gift or act of religious benefaction by a community of mahajanas, headed by *pramukh mahattaka*, constructed a temple (*devakula*) of the goddess *Aranyavasini* (literally the resident of forest) called Chandika at a place called Aranyakupagiri. Goddess's two feet are invoked at the beginning of the inscription by offering obeisance to her and who also is paired with Hara and Shiva. B.D. Chattopadhyaya takes it as an attempt at universalization of the local goddess and also at juxtaposition of the god and the goddess.[119]

Another inscription, Dabok inscription of the time of Dhavalappadeva: {Harsha} samvat 207[120], records the religious benefaction in the form of *akshyanivi* or fixed endowment, which constitutes what is called *devadaya* in the record. The endowment was made for two occasions: for the devadroni of Mahadhideva Mahamaheshwara instituted (pratisthapita by the donor Vaidya Giyaka) and for another devadroni, created by former Vaidya Yasodeva, of Sri Durgadevi, who had the name Ghattasvamini (literally meaning female deity of the pots). The grant was made by the donor to the deities for acquisition of merit for himself and his parents and it was also to provide resources to the deities in the form of incense and oil and other purposes (*gugulla-dipatailarthe khandasputitasamaropanarthe*). Here again, I submit to B.D. Chattopadhyaya's[121] opinion that the record points to universalization of the goddess by attributing the character of Durga to the local deity Ghatavasini and also the desired juxtaposition of the goddess with Lord Shiva.

Two Sanskirt inscriptions of 9th cent. AD (AD 878) from Bhilsa records the grant of an *akshayanika* made in favour of the *ayatana* or temple of the illustrious Bhaillasvamin. The two *vithis* were purchased by Hatiaka, who granted them in favour of the mother (mother goddess) for the merit of his parents[122].

Rewah inscription of Malaysimha, in the year 944 opens with an invocation to Manjughosha, the Buddhist deity of learning and mentions Buddha as Bhagvan (God). The inscription refers to the name of Sri Tara, Buddhist deity (consort).[123] Inscription is directed to the family of a feudatory chief named Malaysimha, his chief officers, the composer of the *prasasti* and of the mason. The record refers itself to a king named Vijayasimha, who is mentioned as born of the family of Karna. He is the Chedi king, who ruled in Dahala at least up to AD 1196.

Assam

Parbatiya Plates of Uanamalavarmadeva of Tezpur (Assam)[124] of the 9th cent. AD: The inscription begins with a symbol of siddham and the word svasti and verses of adoration, the first in the honour of Lohitya Sindhu. The inscription introduces the Queen of Hargaravarman, Mangala as an incarnation of Goddess Lakshmi (Mahagauri).

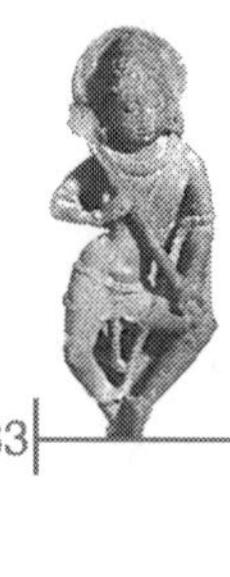

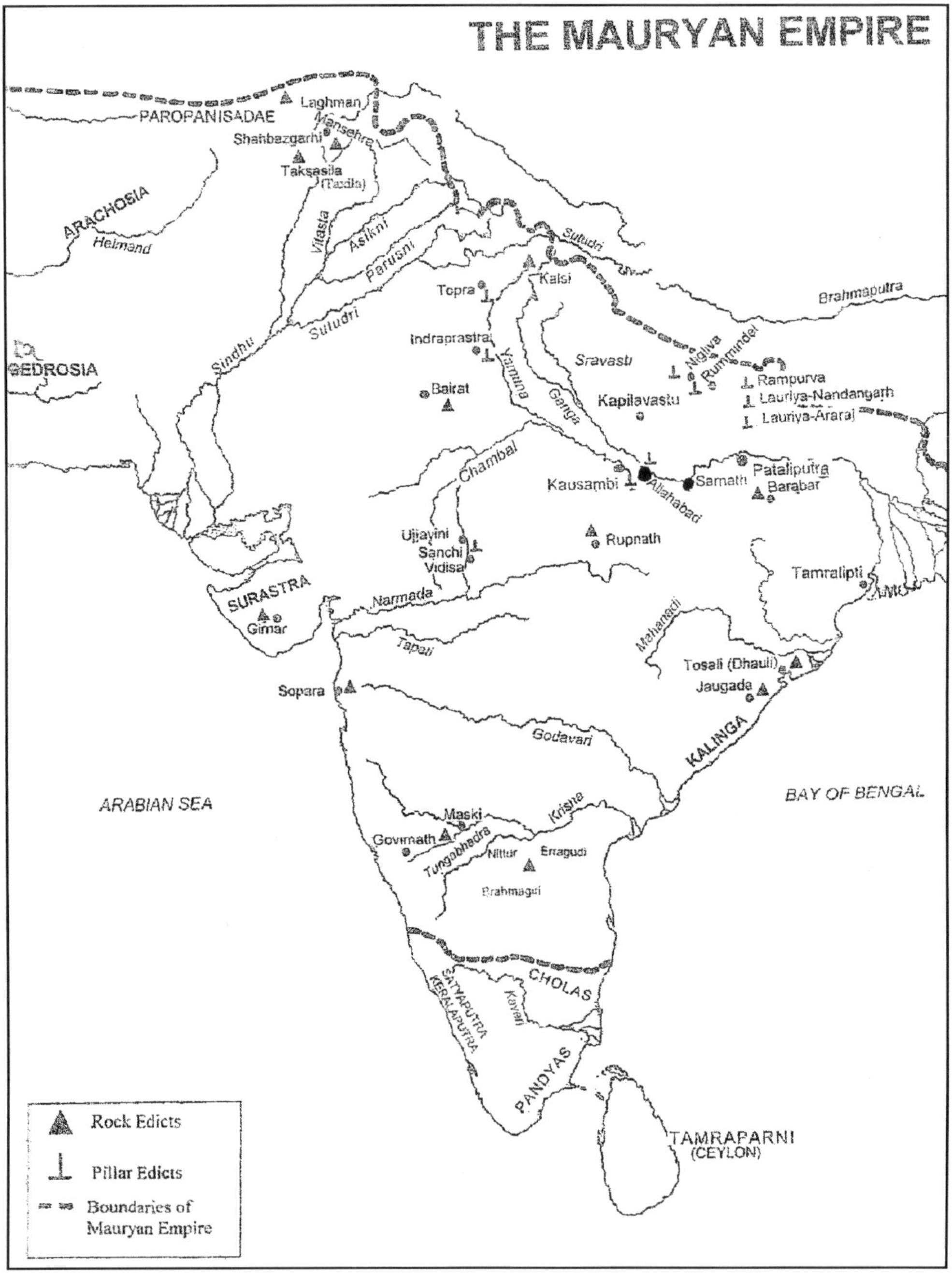

Map 3. Edicts of Ashoka.

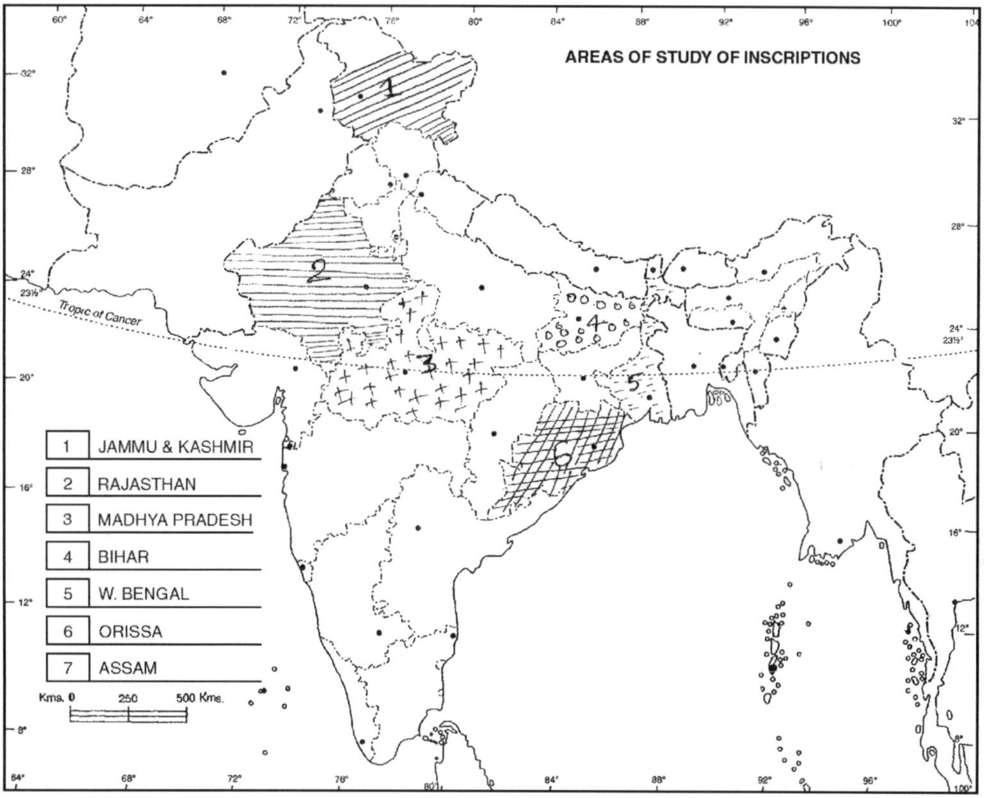

Map 4. Areas of Study of Inscriptions.

The inscription records the grant, which is followed by imprecatory. The king made a gift of the village called Hapssagrama attached to the mandala situated in Uttara-kula and was bounded by Akshidahika, the tank of Chandika (possibly name of the goddess).[125]

B. CONCLUSION

Though the patriarchal tempo of the people has been clearly reflected in the early Indian literature, which generally speaking, decries women's participation in matters concerning economic activities as well as state policies; the inscriptions show variable examples of women participation such as Buddhist and Jaina *bhikkhunis*, lay women and queens of various dynasties. These inscriptions reveal women's visibility in genealogical tables, their kinship ties, their kulas, their relation as mothers, wives, sisters, daughters and so on, sometimes occupational background of the

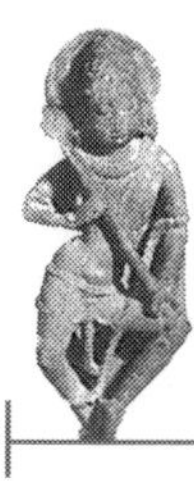

donors in case of common women, place names, court connections. Earlier views on women's invisibility in history have, thus, been revised in the light of new interpretations and evidences.

The epigraphic sources document strategic and politically crucial marriage alliances and power equations between men and women as an aspect of processes of state formation, legal rights to property by the queens to make such big donations and construction activities. Queen's access to resources is undeniable but the degree of control over it and nature of control remains unclear. There is a certain degree of female visibility attested through these grants. Inscriptions delineate goddesses.

NOTES AND REFERENCES

1. See Map no. 3, Area of Study of Inscriptions.
2. See Map no. 4, Edicts of Ashoka.
3. C.D. Chatterji, "Edict of Ashoka on the Public Benefaction of Queen Caruvaki", *Annales of Bhandarkar Oriental Research Institute*, Baroda, Vol. xxxiv, 1953, pp. 30-49.
   * This is corrected version offered by Chatterji, p. 43.
4. *CII,* Vol. I., ii,(VI),(B), p. 159.
5. Romila Thapar, *Ashoka and the Decline of the Mauryas*, Delhi, 1998, p. 30.
6. We have similar examples in case of the Guptas taking pride in their marriage alliance with the Lichchhavis which is discussed later in this chapter.
7. *AI,* pp.107ff.
8. *AI,* p.112.
9. *Ibid.*
10. Hultz, *Corpus Inscriptionum Indicarum,* I, Pillar Edict XII.
11. B.M. Barua, *Ashokan Inscriptions,* Calcutta,1955, p. 183.
12. D.K. Ganguly, *Aspects of Ancient Indian Adminstration,* Delhi, 1979, p. 79 fn.
13. For this we may also refer to my book, *Mathura: The Settlement Pattern and Cultural Profile of an Early Historical City* (Vijaya Laxmi Singh), Delhi, 2005.
14. *Epigraphia Indica,* XII 1907-10, pp. 135-47.
15. H. Luders, *Mathurā Inscriptions,* No. 136.
16. *Epigraphia Indica,* XIX, 1927-2, p. 96; H. Luders, *Mathurā Inscriptions* No. 1, pp. 116-19.
17. *Archeological Survey of India Annual Report,* 1909-10, 2, 1914, p. 65, MI. No. 50, pp. 187-88.
18. "Kosam Inscription of Kanishka", *EI,* XIV, no. 28, p. 210, Luders' *Mathurā' Inscriptions.*

19. *Epigraphia Indica*, VIII, pp. 181-2; H. Luders, *Mathurā Inscriptions*, No. 249, 54-5; *Archaeological Survey of India Annual Report on Indian Epigraphy*, 1972-73, p. 116.
20. For this we may also refer to my book, *Mathura, The Settlement Pattern and Cultural Profile of an Early Historical City* (Vijaya Laxmi Singh), Delhi, 2005.
21. *Ibid.*
22. *Ibid.*
23. *Epigraphia Indica*, II, no. 29, p. 395.
24. Kirit K. Shah, *The Problem of Identity: Women in Early Indian Inscriptions*, Delhi, 2001, p. 161.
25. *Anguttara Nikaya*, II, p. 7.
26. *Cullavagga*, *Suttanipata*, p. 39.
27. I.B.H. Horner, *The Book of Discipline*, Vol. III, p. XXXIX.
28. I.B.H. Horner, *The Book of Discipline*, IX, 3.
29. I.B.H. Horner, *The Book of Discipline*, IX, 4-13.
30. See the photograph of a Ganika Vasantsena in the Kushana period, No. 14.
31. See Actes du sixieme Congres International des Orientalists a Leide, pt. III, pp. 142; cited in A.K. Chatterji, *A Comprehensive History of Jainism*, Vol. I, p. 45.
32. A.K. Chatterjee, *A Comprehensive History of Jainism*, Vol. I, p. 45.
33. *Mahavagga*, p. 380.
34. *Divyavadana*, p. 218.
35. Indra, *The Status of Women in Ancient India*, Delhi, 1955, pp. 245-46.
36. R.C. Majumdar, *The Classical Age*, Bombay, 1954, p. XLI.
37. *CII*, III, 26, 44, 52 nd 257.
38. R.K. Mukherjee, *Gupta Empire*, p. 14, where he suggests the joint rule by the king and queen.
    It has been observed that Chandragupta was greatly assisted by the Lichchhavis of Vaisali in establishing his authority over Magadha and the imperial city of Pataliputra.
39. R.S. Tripathi, *History of Ancient India*, Delhi, 1999, p. 239.
40. *Allahabad Posthumous Stone Pillar Inscription*, *CII*, III, p. 8.
41. H.C. Roychaudhari accords Kumaradevi a vital and prominent role in the Gupta-Lichchhavi alliance. *Political History of Ancient India*, p. 530. The origin of Guptas is still open for debate. In *Skanda Purana* they have been assigned Dharana gotra (Dharmarnya Khanda 2, ch. 39). Others show their origin from Karskaras. The names of some of the officials of Satvahana dynasty and some people in the early Buddhist inscriptions do have Guptas as their ending name. But there is no solid evidence to call them as the predecessors of the imperial Guptas. Therefore, this matrimonial alliance could be beneficial to Guptas to conceal their non-recognized origin. It is due to this that Samudragupta calls himself proudly as *Lichchhavi dauhitra*. See *ABORI*, XII, p. 50; IHQ, XIV, p. 582.

42. For details see, Sudhakar Chattopadhyaya, *Early History of North India*; A.S. Altekar, *Catalogue of Coins of Gupta Dynasty* (introduction), p. XXIX. These coins which were found in Burdwan, Gaya and Ayodhya portray the marriage ceremony showing the husband offering with right hand a ring to his wife. They also bear the legend 'Chandra' on the obverse and 'Kumaradevi' on the reverse and on left, while on reverse and on right there is the significant legend 'Lichchhavyah'. See the coin no. 1 and 2.
43. *CII*, III, pp. 26, 44, 52 and 257.
44. Majumdar and Altekar, *Vakataka-Gupta Age*, p. 122.
45. See coins 1 and 2 (Fig. 13).
46. R.C. Mazumdar (ed.) *Classical Age*, p. 3.
47. The statement in the *Puranas* about the enjoyment by the Guptas of the countries along Ganga, Saketa and Magadha refers to the period of Chandragupta I. See F.E. Pratiger, *The Dynasties of the Kali Age*, pp. 53-54.
48. Sudhakar Chattopadhyaya, Early History of North India, Calcutta, 1958, p. 271.
49. *Indian Historical Quarterly*, XIV, pp. 584-85.
50. A.S. Altekar, *State and Government in Ancient India*, Delhi, 2001, p. 341.
51. JIH, V-VI.
52. R.C. Mazumdar (ed.), *Classical Age*, p. 3.
53. Tripat Sharma refers to this terminology, in *Women in Ancient India, From AD 320 to AD 1200.*
54. *EI*, XXI, p. 1ff.
55. *CII*, III, pp. 35-36.
56. See Tripat Sharma, *Women in Ancient India, From AD 320 to AD 1200.*
57. D.C. Sircar, *Studies in the Society and Administration of Ancient and Medieval India,* Calcutta, 1967, pp. 411-15.
58. *CII*, III, p. 6.
59. *CII*, III, pp. 43-44.
60. *CII*, III, pp. 21. fn 3, p. 27; Radhakund Mookerji, while describing the aswamedha type of coin of Samudragupta, observes that on the obverse of such coins is standing the chief quuen (agramahisi) wearing loose robe and jewellery, holding chawry over right shoulder in right hand hanging by her side, on left is a sacrificial spear bound with fillet and on some specimen garuda at feet with legend Asvamedha parakramah. He identifies this figure of Mahisi with queen Datta-Dattadevi, mother of Chandragupta II, as mentioned in Eran Pillar inscription of Samudragupta. See R.K. Mookerji, *The Gupta Empire*, p. 39.
61. "Bilsad Stone Inscription of Kumaragupta"; *CII III*, pp. 43-44.
62. "Bihar Stone Pillar Inscription", *Ibid.*, p. 47-52; Bhitari Stone pillar inscription, pp. 52-55.
63. *ASIR*, 1903-04, p. 207, K.K. Thapliyal, *Seals and Sealings....*, p. 47.
64. "Poona Copper Plate of Prabhavati Gupta" in V.V. Mirashi (ed.), *Inscriptions of Vakatakas*, II, V, p. 5ff.

65. R.C. Majumdar, *Vakataka Gupta Age*, Lahore, 1946, p. 104.
66. *EI*, XXXII, pp. 167 ff.
67. D.C. Sircar, *SSAAMI*, I, pp. 234-35.
68. D.K. Ganguly, *Aspects of Ancient Indian Administration*, Delhi, 1979.
69. T. Watters, *On Yuan Chawang's Travels in India*, I, p. 330.
70. B.P. Sinha, *Decline of the Kingdom of Magadha*, Patna, 1954, p. 275, fn. 3.
71. *CII*, III, p. 205ff.
72. *EI*, IV, p. 208.
73. *EI*, IV, pp. 208-11.
74. D. Devahuti, *Harsha: A Political History*, p. 68.
75. D. Devahuti, *Harsha: A Political History*, p. 129.
76. *EI*, I, p. 77.
77. R.S. Tripathi, *History of Kanauj*, Banaras, 1937, p. 51.
78. D. Devahuti, *Harsha: A Political History*, p. 78.
79. D. Devahuti, *Harsha: A Political History*, p. 478.
80. "The Prasasti of the Temple of Lakha Mandal at Madha in Jaunsar Bhawar", *Epigraphia Indica*, Vol. I, no. 2, p. 10.
81. "Dewal Prasati of Lalla the Chhinda", *EI*, I, no. 12, p. 75.
82. EI, IX, no. 2, p. 10.
83. EI, I, no. XXXI, p. 251.
84. "Bhera Ghat Stone Inscription of the Queen Alhandevi (yr. 907), the Chedi Year", *EI*, II, no. 2, p. 7.
85. "Konanda Copper Plates of Nettabhanja", *EI*, XIV, No. 23, p. 172.
86. "Russellkonda Plates of Nettabhanya", *EI*, XVIII, No. 41, p. 259.
87. "Two Copper Plates of Tribhuvanamahedevi of the Bhauma-kara dynasty of Orissa", *EI*, XXIX, no. 30, p. 210, also B. Misra, Orissa Under the Bhauma Kings, *JBORS*, Vol. 2, pp. 419-22.
88. *Ibid.*
89. *Ibid.*
90. D.C. Sircar is of the opinion that Tri-Kaliga mahadevi is the secondary name of the queen of Ranaka Jayavarman, who was endowed by the king with an amount of administrative power. Epigraphic Notes, *EI*, XVIII, p. 335.
91. "Two Grants of Bhanja Kings of Vanjulvaka", *EI*, VIII, No. 44, p. 272.
92. K.K. Shah, "Legal Rights of Woman to Landed Wealth: A Case Study of Chandella Queens" in Kiran Pawar (ed.), *Women in Indian History-Social, Economic, Political and Cultural Perspectives*, Delhi, 1996, pp. 68-84.
93. K.N. Sastri, "Srinagar Inscription of Queen Didda", *EI*, XXXVII, no. 26, 1947-48, pp. 153-55. This inscription has been found in Srinagar. The script of the inscription is Sarada and the language is Sanskrit.
94. B.N. Kaul Deambi, *Corpus of Sarada Inscription of Kashmir*, Delhi, 1982, pp. 97-98.
95. B.N. Kaul Deambi, *Corpus of Sarada Inscription of Kashmir*, pp. 97-98.

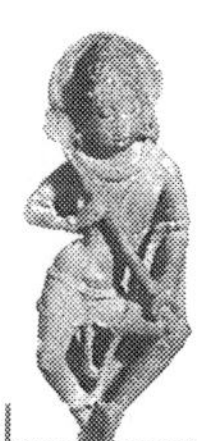

96. Devika Rangachari, "Kalhana's Rajtarangini, A Gender Perspective", *Mediaval History Journal*, 5, 1, 2002 Delhi, p. 44.
97. Cynthia Talbot, "Rudrama-devi, the Female King: Gender and Political authority in Medieval India", in David Shulman (ed.), *Syllables of Sky, Studies in South Indian Civilization in Honour of Velcharu Narayan Rao,* OUP, Delhi, 1995, p. 414.
98. The term mother goddess or village goddess or goddess are used here for all female figurines whose attributes suggest cultic or ritualistic significance. Importance of the worship of images of early historical Mathura is represented in an abundance of carved ring stones and disc stones, terracotta images and plaques. A number of mother goddess figurines have been discovered in stratified contexts in the course of Mathura excavations. See Joshi and Margbandhu, 1976-77.
99. Also we have sculpture of seven Matrikas from Mathura, see photograph no. 10.
100. Luders, *Mathura Inscriptions*, p. 209; D.C. Sircar, *Select Inscriptions*, I, p. 133.
101. P. IX. 1.137a; v.158a.
102. See the survey of literature on this in J.N. Tiwari, *Goddesses Cult in Ancient India*, Delhi, pp. 33-34.
103. D.C. Sircar, *Select Inscriptions,* pp. 287-89. "Puri Plate of Kulastambha", *EI*, XXIX, no. 22, p. 164.
104. Bijholi Rock Inscription of Chahamana Somesvara, V.S. 1226, Vol. XVI, no. 9, p. 84.
105. *EI,* IX, no. 2, p. 2.
106. B.D. Chattopadhyaya, *Studying Early India*, Delhi, 2005, p. 181. Chattopadhyaya feels that it is necessary to recognize these phenomena because while we notice the movement of certain cults from obscurity to their visibility in historical records. It must have been a continuing process in Indian religious history.
107. "Allahabad Museum Inscriptions of the Year 87", *EI.* XIII, No. 39, p. 245.
108. The name Bhulunda represents a tribal (non-Sanskritic) name, which was later replaced by sanskritized name of his successors as Swamidasa, Rudradasa, Bhattaraka and Nagabhatta; they all ruled in succession as members of the same family of rulers from Balkha (Bagh in the Dhar district of Madhya Pradesh. K.V. Ramesh and S.P. Tiwari, "A Copperplate hoard of Gupta period from Bagh", ASI, 1990, pp. 4-6; also see B.D. Chattopadhyaya, *Studying Early India, Archaeology Texts And Historical Issues*, Delhi, 2005, p. 176.
109. Thomas Coburn, *Devi Mahatmya: Crystallization of the Goddess Tradition,* Delhi, 1984, Appendix A.
110. B.D. Chattopadhyaya, *Studying Early India*, p. 182.
111. Thomas Coburn, *Devi Mahatmya: Crystallization of the Goddess Tradition,* Delhi, 1984; David Kinsley, *Hindu Goddesses: Vision of the Divine Feminine in the Hindu Religious Tradition,* Delhi, 1987; J.N. Tiwari, *Goddess Cult in Ancient India,* Delhi, 1985.

112. J.F. Fleet, *Corpus Inscriptionum Indicarum*, Vol. 3, Inscriptions of Early Gupta Kings and Their Successors, reprint, 1970, pp. 112-16.
113. J.F. Fleet, *CII,* III, pp. 121-25.
114. J.F. Fleet, *CII,* III, pp. 135-38.
115. "*Tenapi Manapur karitaka devakule bhagavatyahPistapurikadevyah pujanimittam khanda-sphutitapratisamskaranay*".
116. B.D. Chattopadhyaya, *Studying Early India,* p. 178.
117. B.D. Chattopadhyaya ignores Fleet's identification of Pistapura located in Andhra (*CII,* III, p. 113, fn 2) and follows Cunningham's identification of the place on the basis of his description of the temple of Pataindevi: "Eight miles to the north of Uchahara and four miles to the east of Pithaora, the temple of Patainidevi forms a conspicuous object in the treeless landscape, standing out boldly on a low projecting spur of the lofty hill quarries, which furnished the stones of the Bhahut sculptures. The temple itself is a very small one... but it is remarkable for its massive stones, and more particularly for its flat roof, which is formed of a single slab... after the manner of the early Gupta temple". Alexander Cunningham, *Report of a Tour in the Central provinces in 1873-74 and 1874-75 (Vol. 9),* Calcutta, 1879, pp. 31-33.
118. R.R. Halder, "Samoli Inscription of the Time of Siladitya {Vikram Samvat} 703", *Epigraphia Indica,* Vol. 20, reprinted by ASI, 1983, pp. 97-99. The record of gift is not from any royal family, but the text of the inscription does record the royal context by using the expression deva-dvijagurujananandi, i.e. one who gladdened the gods, the brahmanas and the preceptors.
119. B.D. Chattopadhyaya, *Studying Early India,* p. 179.
120. R.R. Halder, *EI,* 20, pp. 122-5; also see D.C. Sircar, "Date of Dhabok Inscription", *EI,* 35, part, 2 Delhi, 1963, pp. 100-2.
121. B.D. Chattopadhyaya, *Studying Early India,* p. 179.
122. "Two inscriptions from Bhilsa", *EI.* XXX, no. 36, p. 210.
123. "The Rewah Inscription of Malaysimha, in the year 944", *EI,* Vol. XIX, no. 53, p. 295.
124. "Parbatiya Plates of Uanamalavarmadeva", *EI,* Vol. XXIX, no. 20, p. 145.
125. The inscription mentions number of geographical names. The names of the hill Kamakuta and the god Kamsvara would suggest that the goddess Mahagauri was no other than Kamesvari/Kamakhya.

* Progijyotisha, heart of which lay in Guwahati of Assam from 4th cent. BC. Sometimes the name of the country is also given as Kamarupa, a designation possibly associated with that of the goddess Kamakhya.

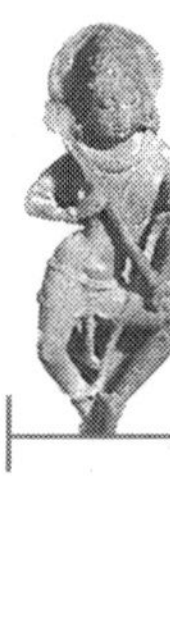

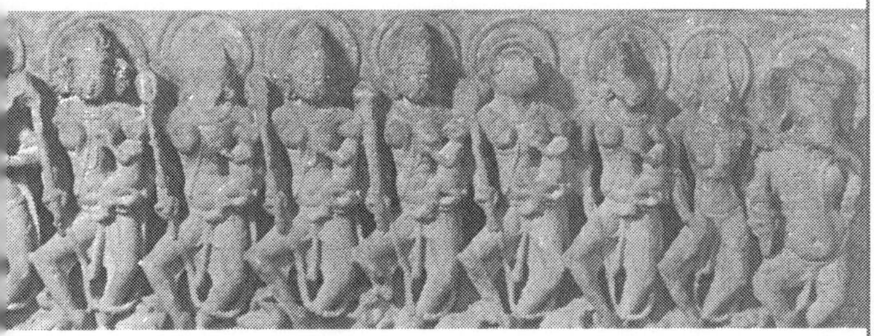

Epilogue

Looking at women through multiple lenses, multiple voices and sources brought to bear on a particular argument – drawing out alternative positions – sometimes subtle, at other times unpopular – is more than just an academic exercise; it has political implications as well. This study is relevant and consequential for contemporary Indian women who are exploring gender justice which is a significant concern of the day.

We have tried to discuss the phenomenon of women in relation to men. There is endless scope for educating ourselves on this subject. This book is a mere sketch in the contours of knowledge on gendered relations. Are women victims of patriarchal system or are they partial collaborators? Instead of viewing patriarchal power as merely limiting and restrictive, we understand that this power is productive too. It has created familial, social worlds that we know and are familiar with and which shape our selfhood.

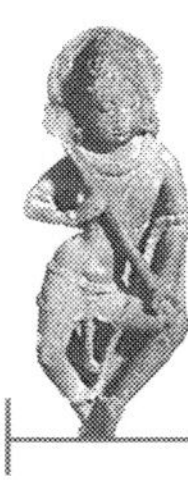

In conclusion, we have achieved the objectives of:

1. Defining gender and placing women's diverse identities in history.
2. Critical evaluation of the source materials taking into account the silence of women's history from the texts.
3. Recovering the lives of women from the neglect of historians.
4. Charting female agency, recognizing women's strategies, accommodations and negotiations in a male dominated world.

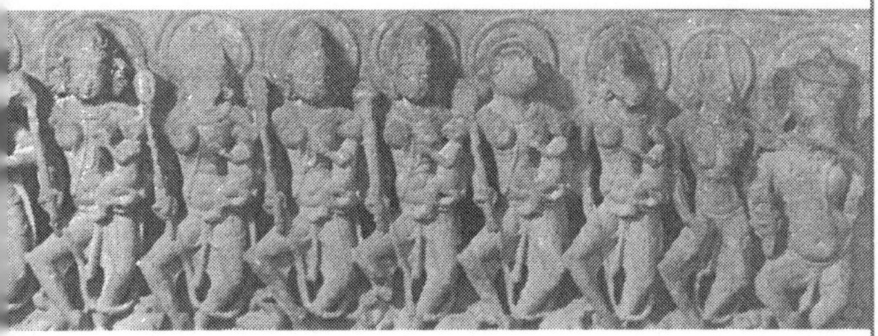

Glossary

Aberrant	Straying from the right or normal way.
Ajivkas	Ancient religious sect, associated with Makkhali Gosasla.
Albeit	To introduce a fact or comment which adds more detail to what you have just said.
Almsgiver	A giver of alms.
Amavasya day	Amavasya is the Indic name for the new moon.
Anarchists	Anarchism is a political philosophy encompassing theories and attitudes which considers the state as compulsory and government as unnecessary, harmful and/or undesirable.
Androcentrism	Centred or focussed on men, often to the neglect or exclusion of women.

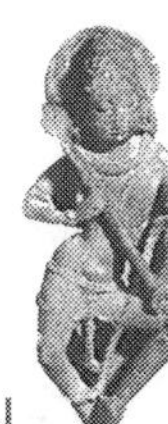

Annales school — The *Annales d'histoire économique et sociale* was founded by Marc Bloch and Lucien Febvre in 1928. Its main innovation was to shift the focus on writing problem-oriented analytical history and looking at human activity comprehensively. Peter Burke divides the movement in three phases or generations.

Annihilate — To cause to be of no effect.

Anomalous — Of uncertain nature or classification.

Appellation — Identifying word or words by which someone or something is called and classified or distinguished from others.

Archaeological artefacts — In archaeology, an artifact or artefact is any object made or modified by a human culture, and often one later recovered by some archaeological endeavour.

Arhats — In the shramanic traditions of Ancient India, arhat (Sanskrit) or arahant (Pali) signified a spiritual practitioner who had to use an expression common in the Tripitaka "laid down the burden" and realised the goal of nirvana, the culmination of the spiritual life.

Artefact — In archaeology, an artifact or artefact is any object made or modified by a human culture, and often one later recovered by some archaeological endeavour. Examples include stone tools such as projectile points, pottery vessels, metal objects such as buttons or guns, and items of personal adornment such as jewellery and clothing. Other examples include bones that show signs of human modification, fire cracked rocks from a hearth or plant material used for food.

Asuras — Demons.

Asvamedha — Grandest of the Vedic religious rites of ancient India, performed by a king to celebrate his paramountcy. The ceremony is described in detail in various Vedic writings, particularly the *Satapatha Brahmana*. An especially fine stallion was selected and was allowed to roam freely for a year under the protection of a royal guard. If the horse entered a foreign country, its ruler had either to fight or to submit. If the horse was not captured during the year, it was victoriously brought back to the capital accompanied by the rulers of the lands it entered, and then sacrificed at a great public ceremony, which was accompanied by much feasting and celebration. The wandering horse was said to symbolize the Sun in its journey over the world and, consequently, the power of the king over the whole Earth. On successfully carrying out a horse sacrifice, the king could assume the title of *Chakravartin* (universal monarch). The rite served not only to glorify the king but also to ensure the prosperity and fertility of the entire kingdom.

Barons — Baron is a title of nobility.

Benevolent — Kind, helpful and tolerant.

Biography — A 'biography' is a description of someone's life, usually published in the form of a book or essay, or in some other form, such as a film.

Bourgeoisie — Middle class.

Brahma — Sacerdotal power. Ahimsa: Non-injury, non-violence.

Brahmanism — Religion of early India which came to prominence in the Vedic period, and is effectively to be identified with Vedic religion and its continuity. It emphasized sacrifice and ritual under the control of the brahmanas as those who have access to the rituals and control of them.

Capitalism — It is an economic system in which wealth, and the means of producing wealth, are privately owned and controlled rather than being state owned and controlled.

Celestial — Supernatural beings living in heaven, such as divinities and angels.

Civil and Political Rights — A class of rights and freedoms that protects individuals from the government and state power, and assures their ability to participate in the civic and political life of the state.

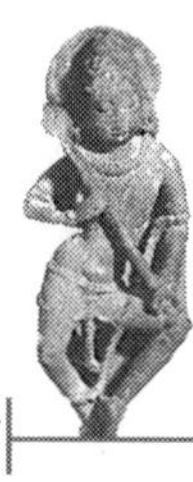

Clan	A clan is a group of people united by kinship and descent.
Clergy	Clergy is the generic term used to describe the formal religious leadership within a given religion.
Commentaries	Description of an event.
Coronation	Coronation is a ceremony marking the investiture of a monarch with regal power, specifically involving the placement of a crown upon his or her head, and the presentation of other items of regalia.
Courtesan	Originally a woman courtier, or a person who attends the court of a monarch or other powerful person.
Dana	Ritual giving.
Dharmashastra	All legal texts and commentaries (*bhashyas*) and digests (*nibandhas*) written in Sanskrit. The word Dharmashastra is used in connection with the works of Apastamba, Gautama, Vasistha and Baudhayana as well as Smritis and their commentaries and digests too.
Dichotomy	The process or practice of making such a division.
Dilapidation	Dilapidation is a term meaning in general falling into decay.
Doab	Fertile land between two rivers.
Dogma	Something held as an established opinion.
Dauhitra	Daughter.
Egalitarian Societies	Generally, it applies to being held equal under the law and society at large. In actual practice, one may be considered an egalitarian in most areas listed below, even if not subscribing to equality in every possible area of individual difference.
Emblem	An emblem is a pictorial image, abstract or representational, that epitomizes a concept.
Enlightenment	Knowledge.
Ethnographic	It is a methodological strategy used to provide descriptions of human societies.
Fecundity	Fruitful in offspring or vegetation.

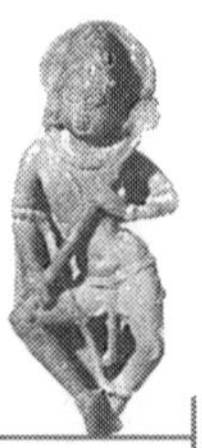

Feminist Agenda Coalition of feminist women committed to working with like-minded others to create a new and fairer global agenda, with women's voices at its centre.

Feudatories A person who holds lands by feudal tenure; a feudal vassal.

Forbearance Abstaining from the enforcement of a right.

Foreshadowing It is the use of hints or clues to suggest what will happen later in literature.

Gana A word which has many meanings, including an oligarchy.

Gender Refers to the socially constructed roles, behaviour, activities and attributes that a particular society considers appropriate for men and women.

Harem Refers to the sphere of women in a usually polygynous household and their quarters which are enclosed and forbidden to men.

Hermitage Although its modern meaning is usually a place where a hermit lives in seclusion from the world, hermitage was more commonly used to mean a settlement where a person or a group of people lived religiously, in seclusion.

Heterodox As an adjective, heterodox is used to describe an opinion, theory, or person that departs from accepted beliefs or standards. The noun heterodoxy is synonymous with unorthodoxy, while the adjective heterodox is synonymous with dissident. Heterodox can also be synonymous with heresy, although it is often a less harsh term, sometimes implying an unorthodox opinion held in ignorance.

Heuristically Of or relating to a usually speculative formulation serving as a guide in the investigation or solution of a problem.

Hierarchy Any system of persons or things ranked one above another.

Historical Revisionism Within historiography, that is the academic field of history, historical revisionism is the reinterpretation

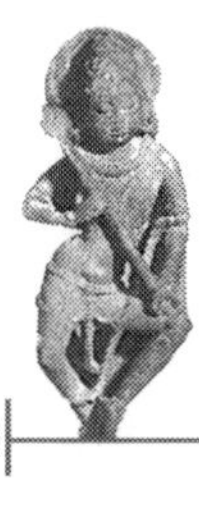

of orthodox views on evidence, motivations and decision-making processes surrounding historical event. The assumption of the revisionist is that the interpretation of a historical event or period, as it is accepted by the majority of scholars, needs a significant change.

Hominid — Species similar to humans.

Industrial Revolution — The Industrial Revolution was a period in the late 18th and early 19th centuries when major changes in agriculture, manufacturing, mining and transportation had a profound effect on the socioeconomic and cultural conditions in Britain.

Inestimable — Incapable of being estimated.

Intellectual Movements — These movements brought great advancement in human rights, technology and political freedom. They also brought about great destruction, war and revolution.

Jatakas — One of the 15 books of the Khuddaka Nikaya, containing stories of the previous births of the Buddha. Jataka signifies the birth stories of the historical Buddha, of the anecdotes of his present and past lives. By the beginning of fifth century AD, the total anecdotes of the past came to be 550 in number. A complete translation of Jataka was initiated by late Prof. Cowell, and executed by Dr. W.H.D. Rouse and other scholars. It has been published in England from Cambridge (1895–1907). The *Jataka* commentary edited by Fousboll was somewhat later version of the earlier works in Sinhalese and Pali.

Language — Spoken symbols of communication.

Mahamatras — High officials in the Mauryan state.

Malevolent — Showing a desire to harm other people.

Masculine — A person who possesses the characteristic traits of a man.

Masculinity — Masculinity is manly character. It specifically describes men and boys, that is personal and human, unlike *male* which can also be used to describe animals, or *masculine* which can also be used to describe noun classes.

Maṭha — It is a term for monastic and similar religious establishments of the Hindu, Buddhist and Jain traditions.

Matriarchy — Hypothetical social system in which the mother or a female elder has absolute authority over the family group; by extension, one or more women (as in a council) exert a similar level of authority over the community as a whole.

Mesolithic Period — The term "Mesolithic" was introduced by John Lubbock in his work *Pre-historic Times*, published in 1865. The term was, however, not much used until V. Gordon Childe popularized it in his book *The Dawn of Europe* (1947).The Mesolithic or Middle Stone Age was a period in the development of human technology in between the Paleolithic or Old Stone Age and the Neolithic or New Stone Age.

Methodology — The analysis of the principles of methods, rules, and postulates employed by a discipline.

Misogyny — Mistrust of women.

Moksha — Liberation from the cycle of birth and death.

Narrative — A narrative is a story that is created in a constructive format and describes a sequence of fictional or non-fictional events.

Nibbana — Final liberation.

Niyoga — Levirate; the ancient custom of a widow cohabiting with her brother-in-law or another man in order to produce sons.

Nobility — Is a government-privileged title which may be either hereditary or for a lifetime.

Normative Texts — Normative texts are meant to be highly impersonal and decontextualised, yet at the same time they also deal with a range of human behaviour that is difficult to predict, which means they have to have a very high degree of determinacy on one hand, and all-inclusiveness on the other.

Obnoxious Exposed to something unpleasant or harmful.

Oral tradition Oral tradition, oral culture and oral lore are messages or testimony transmitted orally from one generation to another.

Ostentation Pretentious display meant to impress others; boastful showiness.

Ostracism Exclusion by general consent from common privileges or social acceptance.

Pantheon Group of important people.

Patriarchy It is an important concept in feminism. Although the narrowest definition of patriarchy is "father-rule", this leaves out the far-reaching social consequences of the way of thinking that underlies this social practice. Patriarchy is most likely a reflection of deeper expectations of formal male dominance in a wide range of social relationships.

Patrilineage Line of descent traced through the paternal side of the family.

Patronage Patronage is support, encouragement, privilege.

Plaque Plate.

Plural Society A plural society is defined as a society combining ethnic contrasts: the economic interdependence of those groups, and the ecological specialization.

Political Movements A political movement is a social movement working in the area of politics.

Polyandry Polyandry refers to a form of polygamy, or other sexual union, in which a woman is married to two or more husbands at the same time. Polygyny, on the other hand, refers to polygamy in which one man is married to two or more wives.

Polygamous Having more than one mate at a time; used of relationships and individuals.

Prakrit — An ancient language belonging to the Indo-European family of languages, with various dialects such as Maharashtri, Shauraseni, and Magadhi.

Preceptor — A teacher; an instructor.

Prejudice — The word prejudice refers to prejudgment: making a decision about, before becoming aware of the relevant facts of a case or event.

Procession — A procession is, in general, an organized body of people advancing in a formal or ceremonial manner.

Protracted — To draw out or lengthen in time; prolong.

Quantitative Analysis — The process of determining the value of a security by examining its numerical, measurable such as revenues, earnings, margins, and market share.

Queer Theory — A term representing the diverse body of theory that takes as its starting point the definition of queer as an identity that acquires meaning from its opposition to the norm. Queer is used to represent alternative positions to age difference, sexuality, etc.

Radical — Historically, early radical aims of liberty and electoral reforms in Great Britain widened with the American Revolution and French Revolution so that some *radicals* sought republicanism, abolition of titles, redistribution of property and freedom of the press.

Rati — Sexual pleasure.

Regent Queen — A queen who serves as ruler when the king dies.

Reinvigorate — To give new life or energy to.

Renunciation — In Buddhism, the Pali word for "renunciation" is *nekkhamma.*

Reproach — To express disapproval of, criticism of, or disappointment in (someone).

Royal Patronage — Power to give a favoured appointment to an office or position in politics, business, or the church.

Salvation — In religion, salvation is the concept that God "saves" humanity from death, as part of His plan to provide for them an eternal life.

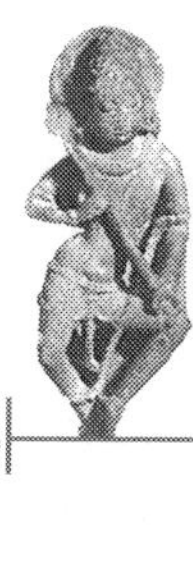

Samgha	Samgha is a word in Pali or Sanskrit that can be translated roughly as "association" or "assembly," "company" or "community" with common goal, vision or purpose.
Sannyasis	Sannyas is formal renunciation of worldly life, traditionally adopted only by men, as the final stage in the Hindu social cycle. The sannyasi wears saffron clothes and are forbidden the company of women, particularly his former wife. He may travel as a teacher, or train disciples in an ashram or monastic hermitage. He is expected to live an ascetic life studying the scriptures.
Satrap	Satrap was the name given to the governors of the provinces of ancient Median and Persian empires.
Savour	To enjoy (a pleasure) for as long as possible.
Scramble	Partition.
Smriti Literature	An important branch of ancient Sanskrit literature, dealing with every aspect of Indian life. Important Smritis are *Manusmriti* (a legal code), *Yajnavalkya Smriti, Narada Smriti, Brihaspati Smriti* and *Katyayana Smriti* (formal law and legal procedure).
Sociability	The quality or state of being sociable, the act or an instance of being sociable.
Stupas	A stupa is a mound-like structure containing Buddhist relics, once thought to be places of Buddhist worship, typically the remains of a Buddha or saint.
Subservience	Subordinate in capacity or function.
Theology	Theology is the study of the existence or attributes of a god or gods, and of how that god or those gods relate to the world and especially to human existence; more generally, it is the study of religious faith, practice and experience, or of spirituality.
Tranquility	It is a situation of calmness and stability.
Valorized	To give or assign a value to.
Vedanga	Literally 'Limbs of the Veda', auxiliary texts associated with the Vedas.

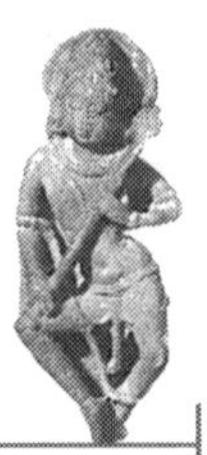

Vedas	Four ancient Sanskrit texts, namely the *Rig Veda*, *Yajur Veda*, *Sama Veda*, and *Atharva Veda*.
Verses	One of the parts into which a poem or song is divided.
Vihara	Vihara is Sanskrit or Pali for monastery. Vihara is a place of worship for followers of Buddhism.
Virtue	Moral excellence; goodness; righteousness; conformity of one's life and conduct to moral and ethical principles; uprightness; rectitude.
Witchcraft	In various historical, anthropological, religious and mythological contexts, it is the use of certain kinds of supernatural or magical powers.
Yajna	Sacrifice.

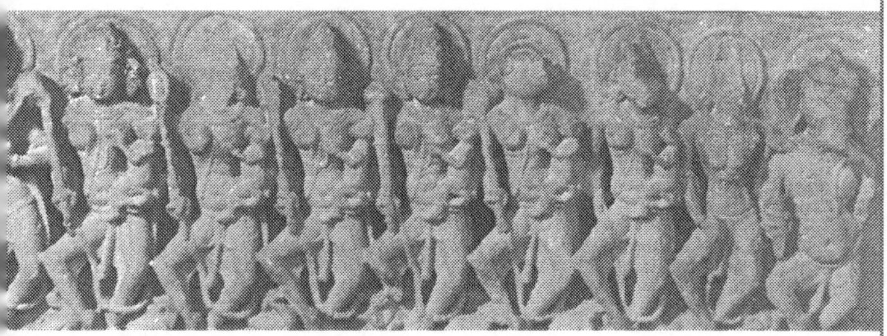

Bibliography

Aaron, Jane and Sylviya Walby (eds.), *Out of Margins: Women studies in the Nineties,* London,1991.

Agrawala, V.S., *Devi-Mahatmyam, The Glorification of the Great Goddess,* Varanasi, 1963.

Aiyar, Indira S., *Durga as Mahishasurmardini: A Dynamic Myth of Goddess,* Delhi, 2005.

Altekar, A.S., *Education in Ancient India,* Benares,1934.

——, *State and Government in Ancient India,* Delhi, Motilal Banarsidass, 1958.

——, *The Position of Women in Hindu Civilization: From Prehistoric Times to the Present day,* Delhi, Motilal Banarsidass.

Apte, V.S., *Sanskrit-English Dictionary* (reprint), Delhi, Motilal Banarsidass, 1976.

Babb, L.A., *Divine Hierarchy: Popular Hinduism in Central India,* New York, 1975.

Bachofen, Johan, *Mutterr Echt,* 1967 (English trans. Myth religion and Mother's Right tr. R. Manheim, Princeton, NJ).

Bader, C., *Women in Ancient India,* London, 1930.

Bailey, Joanne, "Is the Rise of Gender History 'Hiding' Women from History Once Again?" *History in Focus,* New Hall, Cambridge.

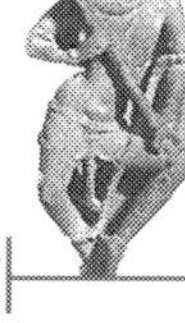

Banerjee, H.C., *Cultural Heritage of Kashmir*, Calcutta, 1965.

Barta, Peter I. (ed.), *Gender and Sexuality in Russian Civilization*, New York, 2001.

Barua, B.M., *Ashokan Inscriptions*, Calcutta, 1955.

——, *Old Brahmi Inscriptions*, Calcutta, 1929.

Basham, A.L., *The Wonder That Was India*, Calcutta, 1974.

——, *A Cultural History of India*, Calcutta, 1975.

Beauvoir, S. de., *The Second Sex*, trans. and edited by H.M. Parshley, New York, 1952.

Bela, Vivante (ed.), *Women's Role in Ancient Civilization: A Reference Guide*, London, 1999.

Bhattacharji, Sukumari, "Economic Rights of Ancient Indian Women", *Economic and Political Weekly*, Vol. XXIV, no. 9-10, March 2-9, 1991.

Bhattacharji, Sukumari, *Women and Society in Ancient India*, Calcutta, 1994.

Bhattacharya, N.N., *Proprietary Rights of Women in Ancient India*, 2001.

——, *History of Shakta Religion*, New Delhi, 1996.

Bisnoi, Savita, *Economic Status of Women in Ancient India*, Meerut, 1988.

Blackstone, Kathryn, *Women in the Footsteps of Buddha: The Struggle for Liberation in the Therigatha*, Curzon Surrey, 1998.

Boulding, Elice, *The Underside of History: A View of Women Through Time*, Boulder, Colorado, 1976.

Brokington, John, *The Sanskrit Epics*, Brill, 1998.

Buhler, G. (ed.), *Dharmasūtra*, Bombay, 1894, tr. G. Buhler, *Sacred Book of the East*, Vol. II, London, 1879.

Burgess, J. (ed.), *Epigraphia Indica*, Vols. I to XLII (reprint), Delhi.

Cadavers, Charming, *Horrific Figurations of the Feminine in Indian Buddhist Hagiographic Literature*, Chicago, 1996.

Cameron, Averil and Amelie Kuhrt (eds.), *Images of Women in Antiquity*, London Croom Helm., 1993.

Chakladar, H.C., *Social Life in Ancient India: Studies in Vatsyana Kamasutra*, Calcutta, 1929.

Chakrabarti, Uma and Kumkum Roy, "In Search of Our Past: A Review of the Limitations and Possibilities of the Historiography of Women in Early India", *Economic and Political Weekly*, 23: WS 2-10, 1988.

Chakrabarti, Uma, "The Family in Ancient India: Ideal and Reality", *Social Change*, 26: 26-33, 1996.

——, *Social Dimensions of Early Buddhism*, Delhi, 1987.

——, "Conceptualizing Brahmanical Patriarchy in Early India: Gender, Caste, Class And State", *Economic and Political Weekly*, April, 3, 1993.

——, "The Rise of Buddhism as Experienced by Women", *Manushi*, 8: 6-10.

——, *Gendering Caste Through a Feminist Lens*, Stree, Delhi, 2003.

——, "Beyond the Altekarian Paradigm: Towards a New Understanding of Gender Relations in Early Indian History", p. 77, in Kumkum Roy (ed.), *Women in Early Indian Societies*, Delhi, rept., 2001.

Chandra, Moti, *World of Courtesan*, Delhi, 1973.

Charles, N. and Felicia Hughes Freeland (ed.), *Practicing Feminism Identity Difference Power*, London, 1996.

Chatterjee, A.K., *A Comprehensive History of Jainism,* Vol. I, Delhi, 2003.

Chatterji, C.D., "Edict of Ashoka on the Public Benefaction of Queen Karuvaki", *Annales of Bhandarkar Oriental Research Institute Baroda,* Vol. XXXIV, 1953.

Chattopadhyaya, B.D., *Studying Early India: Archaeology, Texts and Historical Issues,* Delhi, 2005.

Chattopadhyaya, Sudhakar, *Early History of North India,* Calcutta, 1958.

Chauhan, Kamla, *Cultural History of Northern India*, Delhi, 1988.

Coburn, Thomas, *Devi Mahatmya: Crystallization of the Goddess Tradition*, Delhi, 1984.

Collier, J.f. and J.Y. Sylvia (eds.), *Gender and Kingship: Essays Towards a Unified Analysis*, Standford: Standford Univ. Press, 1987.

Connell, R.W., *Gender and Power: Society, The Person and Sexual Politics,* Cambridge, Polity Press, 1987.

Coontz and Henderson (eds.), *Women's Work, Men's Property: The Origin of Gender and Class*, London, Verso, 1986.

Cowell, E.B. and F.A. Neil, *Divyavadāna,* (ed.), Cambridge, 1866.

Crook, J.A., *The Law and Life of Rome*, London, 1967.

Das, R.M., *Women in Manu and His Seven Commentators*, Varanasi, 1962.

Davids, C.A.F. Rhys and K.R. Norman, *Poems of the Early Buddhist Nuns,* 1989.

Davids, C.A.F. Rhys, *Psalms of the Early Buddhists,* (Tr.), Pali Text Society, London, (1st edn. 1909, 1913), 1964.

——, *Therigatha (Psalms of the Sisters).*

Deambi, B.N. Kaul, *Corpus of Sarada Inscription of Kashmir*, Delhi, 1982.

Dhar, M.K., *Royal Life in Ancient India*, Delhi, 1991.

Ditz, T., "The New men's History and the Peculiar Absence of Gendered Power: Some Remedies from Early American Gender History", *Gender and History,* 16.1, 2004.

Dube, Leela, "On the Construction of Gender: Hindu Girls in Patrilineal India", *Economic and Political Weekly,* 23, 1988.

Erndl, Katherine M., *Victory to The Mother*, Oxford, 1993.

Falk, Nancy Auer, "The Case of Vanishing Nuns: The Fruits of Ambivalence in Ancient Indian Buddhism", in Nancy Auer Falk and Rita M. Gross (eds.), *Unspoken Worlds: Women's Religious Lives,* Wadsworth, 1989.

Fanthom, E.H. Foley, N. Kampen, S. Pomeroy and H. Shapiro (ed.), *Women in Classical World*, New York, 1994.

Faure, Bernard, *The Power of Denial-Buddhism Purity and Gender*, New Jersey, 2003.

Fausboll, V., *Jātaka with Commentary,* (ed.), London, 1877-97, tr. E.B. Cowell, Vols. I-VII, Cambridge, 1895-1907.

Fick, R., *The Social Organisation of North East India in Buddha's Time*, Calcutta, 1920.

Flax, Jane, "Postmodernism and Gender Relations in Feminist Theory", *Signs*, University of Chicago Press (Chicago) 12.4, 1987.

Fleet, J.F., *Corpus Inscriptionum Indicarum*, Vol. 3, *Inscriptions of Early Gupta Kings and Their successors*, reprint, 1970.

Foley, Helene P. (ed.), *Reflections on Women in Antiquity,* New York, 1981.

Ganguly, D.K., *Aspects of Ancient Indian Adminstration*, Delhi, 1979.

Gardner Jane, F., *Women in Roman Law And Society*, London, 1986.

Gatewood, Lyn E., *Devi and the Spouse Goddess: Women Sexuality and Marriage within India*, Delhi, 1985.

Geetha, V., *Theorizing Feminism,* Series editor, Matreiyi Krishnaraj, Calcutta, 2002.

Ghadially, Rehana (ed.), *Women in Indian Society*, Delhi, 1988.

Gilchrist, Robert, *Gender and Archaeology, Contesting the Past*, London, 1999.

Goldman, Robert P., *The Ramayana of Valmiki: An Epic of Ancient India, Bāla Kāṇda* (Vol. 1), Introduction, Princeton, 1999.

Gross, Rita M., *Buddhism After Patriarchy*, Oxford University Press, New York, 1993.

Gulati, Saroj, *Women and Society– Northern India in the 11th and 12th centuries*, Delhi, 1985.

Gunew, Sneja (ed.), *Feminist Knowledge: Critique and Construct,* London, 1990.

Halder, R.R., "Samoli Inscription of the Time of Siladitya {Vikram Samvat} 703', *Epigraphia Indica*, Vol. 20, reprinted by ASI, 1983.

Hallett, Judith P., *Fathers and Daughters in Roman Society: Women and the Elite Family*, UK, New Jersey, 1984.

Hartel, H., *Excavations at Sonkh*, 1993.

Hartsock, N.C.H., *Money Sex and Power: Towards a Feminist Historical Materialism*, Longman: New York, 1983.

Horner, I.B., *Women under Primitive Buddhism*, Delhi, Motilal Banarsidass, 1975.

Houts, Elizabeth van, *Memory and Gender in Medieval Europe*, 900-1200, London, 1999.

Hughes, Sister Maeve, *Epic Women East and West*, Calcutta, 1984.

Hultzsch, E., *Baudhayana Dharmasutra*, (ed.) Leipzig, 1884, Kasi Sanskrit Series, Benares, 1895-97.

Hultzsch, E. (ed.), *Inscriptions of Ashoka, Corpus Inscriptionum Indicarum,* Vol. I, Oxford, 1925.

Hussnain, F.M., *Hindu Kashmir*, Delhi, 1977.

Indra, *The Status of Women in Hindu India*, Delhi, 1955.

Jacobi, H., *Acaranga Sutra and Kalpa Sutra,* (trans.) Sacred Books of the East, XXII, Oxford, reprint, Delhi, 1980, Pt. II.

Jain, Devaki (ed.), *Indian Women*, New Delhi, Publication Division, Ministry of Information and Broadcasting, Govt. of India, 1975.

Jaiswal, Suvira, "Women in Early India: Problems and Perspectives", *Proceedings of Indian History Congress,* 42. 54-60. 1981.

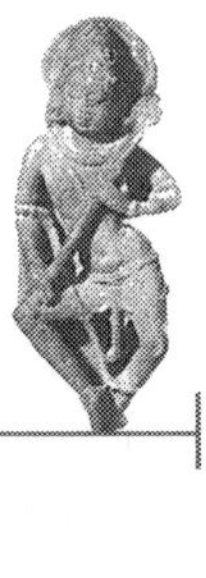

Jamisom, S.W., *Encyclopedia of Religion and Ethics,* 1996.

Jayal, Shakambari, *Status of Women in the Epics,* Delhi, 1966.

Kali, Davadatta, *In Praise of the Goddess: The Devi Mahatmya and Its Meaning,* Nicolas-Hays, Inc., Berwick, Maine, 2003.

Kane, P.V., *History of Dharmaśāstra,* Vol. I-III, Poona, 1930-46; Vols. IV-V, Poona, 1974.

Kangle, R.P. (ed. and tr.), *Arthaśāstra of Kautilya,* Bombay, 1960-65.

Kapur, M.L., *Eminent Rulers of Ancient Kashmir,* Delhi, 1975.

Kathryn, Hansen, "The Virangana in North Indian History: Myth and Popular Culture", *Economic and Political Weekly,* April, 30, 1988.

Keilhorn, F. (ed.), *Vyakarana Mahābhāsya of Patañjali,* 3 vols., Bombay, 1892-1909.

Kelley, Joan, *Women, History and Theory, the Essays of Joan Kelley,* London, 1984.

Kinsely, Darid R., *The Sword and The Flute: Kali and Krisha, Dark Vision of the Terrible and the Sublime Hindu Mythodology,* Berkley and Los Angles University of California Press, 1975.

Kinsley, David, *Hindu Goddesses,* California, 1988.

——, *Hindu Goddesses: Vision of the Divine Feminine in the Hindu Religious Tradition,* Delhi, 1987.

Kishwar, Madhu, "A Horror of Ism: Why I Do Not Call Myself a Feminist" in Maitreye Chaudhuri (ed.), *Feminism in India,* Delhi, 2004.

Konow, S., "Kharosthi Inscriptions with the Exception of Those of Ashoka", *Corpus Inscriptionum Indicarum,* Vol. II, pt. I, Calcutta, 1929.

Kosambi, D.D., *An Introduction to the Study of Indian history,* Bombay, 1975.

——, "Historical Perspective of Women", in H.C. Upadhyaya (ed.), *Status of Women in India,* Delhi, 1991.

——, *Myth and Reality,* Bombay, 1962.

——, *The Culture and Civilisation of Ancient India in Historical Outline,* Delhi, 1975.

Kuhn, Annette and Ann Marie Wolpe (eds.), *Feminism and Materialism, Women and Modes of Production,* London, Routledge and Kegan Paul, 1978.

Kumari, Ved, *Nilmata Purana,* Vol. I, Srinagar-Jammu, 1968.

Law, B.C., *Women in Buddhist Literature,* Varanasi, Indological Book House (first edn. 1927), 1981.

Lefkowitz, Mary and Maureen Fant, *Women's Life in Greece and Rome: A Source Book in Translation,* 2nd edn., Baltimore MD, 1992.

Lerner, Gerda, *The Creation of Patriarchy,* Delhi, 1986.

——, *The Majority Finds the Past,* New York, Oxford Univ. Press, 1987.

Lüders, H., *Mathurā Inscriptions,* K.L. Jenert (ed.), Gottingen, 1961.

——, *Brahmi Inscriptions from Bharhut,* rev. and supplemented.

Majumdar, R.C., *The Classical Age,* Bombay, 1954.

Manna, Sibendu, *Mother Goddess,* Punthi Pustak, Calcutta, India, 1993.

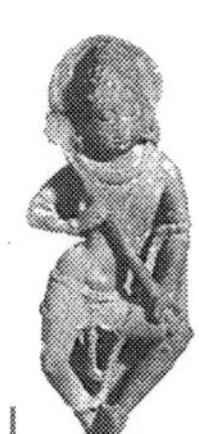

Mathur, Vina, *The Role and Position of Women in the Social, Cultural and Political Life of Kashmir: 7th century-16th century AD*, Jammu, 1985.

Mc Clure, K. Laura (ed.), *Sexuality and Gender in the Classical World: Reading and Sources*, Blackwell, UK, 2002.

Mirashi, V.V. (ed.), "Poona Copper Plate of Prabhavati Gupta" in *Inscriptions of Vakaṭakas*, Vol. II.

Morley, R. and Val Walsh (ed.), *Feminist Academics: Creative Agent For Change*, London, 1995.

Muir, E. and Guido Ruggiero (eds.), *Sex and Gender in Historical Perspective*, Baltimore and London: John Hopkins University Press, 1990.

Muir, J., *Original Sanskrit Texts* (5 vols.) IV, London, 1860-71.

Nath, Vijay, *Dana: Gift System in Ancient India, (600 BC-AD 300): A Socio-Economic Perspective*, Delhi, 1987.

Nelson, Sarah, Millegde, *Gender in Archaeology*, Sage, Delhi, 1997.

Neumann, K.E., *Die Lieder der Monche and Nonnen Gotama Buddhos*, Berlin, 1899.

Neumayer, A., *Pre-Historic Rock Paintings in Central India*, 1983.

Oldenberg and F. Max Muller, *Apastamba Grihya Sutra*, tr. by The Grihya Sutras, S.B.E, Vol. XXX, Delhi, 1965.

Ortner, Sherry B. and H. Whitehead (eds.), *Sexual Meanings: The Cultural Construction of Gender and Senility*, Cambridege: CUP, 1981.

Pandia, Chandrakanta (ed.), *Women in Dharmasastras*, Delhi, 2009.

Patnaik, Usha and Manjari Dingwancy (eds.), *Chains of Servitude: Bondage and Slavery in India*, Delhi, 1985.

Patton, Laurie, *Jewels of Authority, Women and Textual Tradition in Hindu India*, Delhi, 2002.

Paul, Diana Y., *Women in Buddhism: Images of the Feminine in the Mahayana Tradition*, California, London, 1985.

Rabani, G.M., *Ancient Kashmir: A Historical Perspective*, Srinagar, 1981.

Radford, J., "History of Women's Liberation in Britain: A Reflective Personal History", in Gabriele Griffin, *Marianne Hestine*, Shirin Rai and Sasha Roseneil (eds.), *Stirring It: Challenges From Feminism*, London, 1994.

Ramaswamy, Vijaya, *Walking Naked, Women, Society and Spirituality in Ancient India*, Shimla, 1997.

——, "Aspects of Women and Work in Early South India", *Indian Economic and Social History Review*, Jan-March, 1989.

Ray, H.C., *Early History and Culture of Kashmir*, Delhi, 1970.

Rhys Davids, T.W. and J.E. Carpentier, *Digha Nikāya*, ed., 3 vols., London, 1899-1911, tr. T.W. Rhys Davids, 3 vols., *Sacred Book of the East*, London 1899-1921.

Rita, M. Gross (ed.), *Unspoken Words: Women's Religious Lives*, Wadsworth, 1989.

Robbinson, Victoria and Diane Richardson, *Introducing Women's Studies: Feminist Theory and Practice*, London, 1997.

Rosaldo, Michelle Zimbalist, "Women Culture and Society: A Theoretical Overview", in Michelle Zimbalist Rosaldo ad Louise Lamphere (ed.), *Women, Culture and Society*, California, 1974.

Ross Balzaretti, Theodilenda, "'Most Glorious Queen': Gender and Power in Lombard Italy", *The Medieval History Journal*, 2, 2, 1999.

Roy, Kumkum and Uma Chakrabarti. "In Search of Our Past: A Review of Limitations and Possibilities of the Historiography of Women in Early India", *Economic and Political Weekly*, April 30, 1988.

Roy, Kumkum, "Turbulent Waves: Construction of Gender Relations in the *Rajtarangini* of Kalhana", Indian History Congress Proceedings, 1999.

——, "Defining the Household: Some Aspects of Prescription and Practice in Ancient India", *Social Scientists*, 248-49: 3: 18, 1994.

——, "Justice in the Jatakas", *Social Scientist*, 275-77, 23-40, 1996.

——, "Marriage as Communication: An Exploration of Norms and Narratives in Early India", *Studies in History*, 10: 183-98. 1994

——, "Recent writings on Gender Relations in Early India", in Kirit K. Shah (ed.), *History and Gender: Some Explorations*, Delhi, 2005.

——, "Veiling the Kamasutra", *Indian Journal of Gender Studies*, 3, pp. 155-70, 1996.

——, "Towards the History of Reproduction", Indian History Congress Sectional President's address, Kannur, 2008.

——, "Women and Men Donors at Sanchi: A Study of Inscriptional Evidence", in L.K. Tripathi (ed.), *Position and Status of Women in Ancient India*, Varanasi, Vol. I, 1995.

Sali, S.L., *Kashmir: History and Archaeology through the Period*, Delhi, 1993.

Sankalia, H.D., *Ramayana: Myth or Reality*, New Delhi, 1973.

Sankaranarayanan, S., *Glory of the Divine Mother (Devī Māhātmyam)*, India, 2001.

Sarah, Pomeroy, *Goddesses, Whores, Wives and Slaves*, New York, 1975.

Sarao, K.T.S., *Origin and Nature of Ancient Indian Buddhism*, Printed for free distribution of The Corporate Body of The Buddha Educational Foundation, Taipei, Taiwan.

Sarkar, H., "The Nagarjunkonda Phase of the Lower Krishna Valley Art: A Study Based on Epigraphic Data", in Fredrick M. Asher and G.S. Gai (eds.), *Indian Epigraphy: Its Bearing on History of Art*, New Delhi, 1985.

Sastri, K.N., "Srinagar Inscription of Queen Didda", *EI*, XXXVII, no. 26, 1947-48.

Sax, William S., *Mountain Goddess: Gender and Politics in a Himalayan Pilgrimage*, New York, 1991.

Sayers, Janet, Mary Evans and Nanneke Redclift (eds.), Engels *Revisited: New Feminist Essay*, London, Tairstock, 1987.

Schopen, Geregory, "Deaths, Funerals and the Division of Property in a Monastic Code", in Donald Lopez Jr. (ed.), *Buddhism in Practice*, Princeton, 1995.

Scott, J.W., "Gender: A Useful Category of Historical Analysis", in J.W. Scott (ed.), *Feminism and History,* OUP, New York, 1996.

——, *Gender and the Politics of History,* New York, Columbia University Press, 1987.

Shah, Kirit K., *The Problem of Identity: Women in Early Indian Inscriptions,* Delhi, 2001.

Shah, Shalini, "Gender and Sexuality in Ancient Punjab: A Case Study of Karna Parva in the Mahabharata", in Aparna Basu and Anup Taneja (eds.), *Breaking Out of Invisibility, Women in Indian History,* New Delhi, 2002.

Sharma, Tripat, *Women in Ancient India (From AD 320 to 1200),* New Delhi, 1987.

Sharma, R.S., *Perspectives in Social and Economic History of Early India,* Delhi, 1983.

Shastri, Shakuntala Rao, *Women in Vedic Age,* Bombay: Bhavan's Book University, 1952.

Sheridan, Susan, "Feminist Knowledge, Women's Liberation and Women's Studies" in Sneja Gunew (ed.), *Feminist Knowledge: Critique and Construct,* London, 1990.

Shrimali, K.M., How Not to be a Vamana Traversing Gender Constructions of the Domain of Divinities in Kirit K. Shah (ed.), *History and Gender: Some Explanations,* Delhi, 2005.

Silverblatt, Irevs, "Women in States", *Annual Review of Anthropology,* USA, 1998.

Singh, V.L., "Repositioning Women in Ancient India in the Context of Amaravati Inscriptions", *Proceedings of Indian History Congress, 2003.*

——, "Situating Women Donors in Early Historical Urban Mathura" in *Proceedings of Indian History Congress, 2002.*

——, *Mathura: The Settlement Pattern And Cultural Profile of an Early Historical City,* Delhi, 2005.

Singh, A.K., *Women Workers in Ancient India,* Delhi, Radha Publications, 1990.

Singh, U., "Sanchi: The History of the Patronage of an Ancient Buddhist Establishment", *The Indian Economic and Social History Review,* Vol. 33, no. I, 1996.

Sinha, B.P., *Decline of the Kingdom of Magadha,* Patna, 1954.

Sircar, D.C., "Shakti Cult in Western India", in D.C. Sircar (ed.), *The Shakti Cult in Tara* Calcutta, 1967.

——, *Indian Epigraphical Glossary,* Delhi, 1966.

——, *Select Inscriptions Bearing on Indian History and Civilization,* Vol. I, Calcutta, 1965.

Sponberg, Allan, "Attitude towards Women and the Feminine in Early Buddhism", in Jose Ignasio Cabezon (ed.), *Buddhism, Sexuality and Gender,* Sri Satguru Publications, Delhi, 1992, pp. 3-36.

Srinivas, M.N., *The Changing Position of Indian Women,* Bombay, OUP, 1978.

Stearns, Peter N., *Gender in World History,* London, New York, 2000.

Stevan Harrell and Paula Richman (eds.), *Gender and Religion: On the Complexity of Symbols,* Beacon Press, Boston.

Sue, Lees, "Feminist Politics and Women Studies: Struggle not Incorporation", in Jane Aaron and Sylviya Walby (eds.), *Out of Margins: Women Studies in the Nineties,* London, 1991.

Sutherland, S.J.M., "Senior Wives and Elder Sons", in Sally J.M. Sutherland (ed.), *Bridging Worlds: Studies on Women in South Asia,* Delhi, 1992.

Sutherland, Sally J., "Seduction, Counter Seduction and Sexual Role Models in the Sanskrit Epics", *Journal of Indian Philosophy,* 20.

Takakusu, Junjiro, *A Record of the Buddhist Religion as Practiced in India and the Malay Archepelago (AD 671-695) by Itsing,* Delhi, 1966 (1986).

Talbot, Cynthia, "Rudrama Devi, the Female King: Gender and Political Authority in Medieval India", in David Shulman (ed.), *Syllables of Sky, Studies in South Indian Civilization in Honour of Velcharu Narayan Rao,* Delhi, 1995.

Tessa, Bartholomeusz, "The Female Mendicant in Buddhist Sri Lanka", in Cabezon (ed.), *Buddhism Sexuality and Gender,* 1992.

Thapar, Romila, *Ancient Indian Social History: Some Interpretations,* Delhi, 1984.

——, *Ashoka and the Decline of the Mauryas,* Bombay, 1977.

——, *Cultural Pasts,* Delhi, 2000.

——, "Looking Back in History", in Devaki Jain (ed.), *Indian Women,* New Delhi, Publication Division, Ministry of Information and Broadcasting, Govt. of India, 1975.

Thomas, P., *Indian Women through the Ages,* New York, 1964.

Tiwari, J.N., *Goddess Cult in Ancient India,* Delhi, 1985.

Trautman, Thomas, *Dravidian Kinships,* Cambridge, 1981.

Treckner, V. (ed.), *Milindapañho,* London, 1928. (ed. R.D. Vadekar, Bombay, 1940, (trans.), T.W. Rhys Davids, *Sacred Book of the East,* XXXVI, Oxford, 1890-94).

Tripathi, L.K. (ed.), *Position and Status of Women in Ancient India,* Vol. 1, Varanasi, 1988.

Tripathi, R.S., *History of Kanauj,* Banaras, 1937.

——, *History of Ancient India,* Delhi, 1999.

Verma, Chapla, "The Wildering Gloom: Women's Place in Buddhist History", in Mandakranta Bose (ed.), *Faces of Feminine in Ancient, Medieval and Modern India,* Delhi, 2000.

Vishnoi, Savita, *The Economic Status of Women in Ancient India,* Kusumanjali Publication, Meerut, 1987.

Wallach, Scott Joan, *Gender, A Useful Category of Historical Analysis,* Cambridge, 1988.

Wallmans, "The Epistemologies of Sex", in Lionel Tiger and Heather T. Flower (eds.), *Female Hierarchies,* Chicago, 1978.

Walters, J.S., "A Voice from the Silence: The Buddha's Mother's Story", *History of Religion,* 33, 4.

Warwick, Alex and Rosemary Auchmuty, " Women Studies as Feminist Activism" in Gabriele Griffin (ed.), *Feminist Activism in the 1990's,* London, 1995.

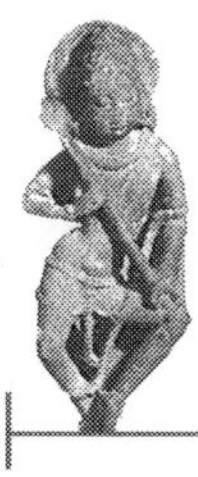

Wiesers, Merry E., *Women and Gender in Early Modern Europe*, 2nd edn., 2000.

Wiesner-Hanks, Merry, "Women's History and World History Course", *Radical History Review*, winter, Vol. 9, 2005.

Wills, J.D., "Nuns and Benefactress: The Role of Women in the Development of Buddhism" in Yvonne Yazbeck Haddad & Ellison Banks (eds.), *Women, Religion and Social Change*, 59-85, Albany New York Press, 1985.

Winternitz, Maurice, *The History of Indian Literature*, Vol. I, Delhi, 1996.

Zimemr, Heinrich, *Myths and Symbols in Indian Art and Civilization*, Princeton, 1946.

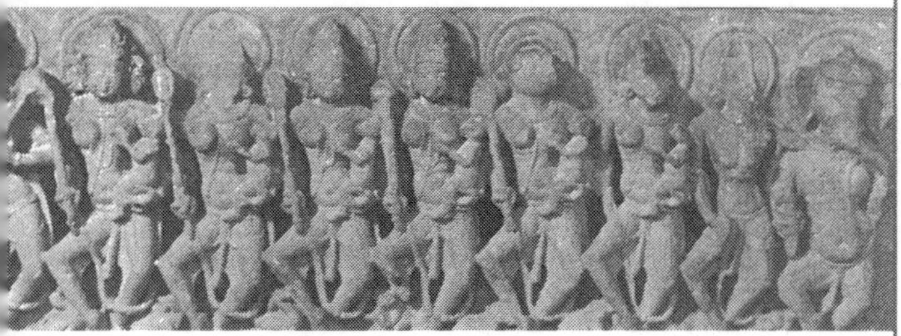

Index

A Social History of Early India 9
Abhimanyu 94, 96
Abhimanyupura 96
Addhikasi 38
Aditya 102, 129
Agni-pariksha 62
Agrahara 98, 123
Agramahisi (chief queen) 114
Agrawala, V.S. 68
Aindri 71
Aiyer, S. 77
Ajatsatru 43
Akos Ostor 80
Allahabad 112, 120, 130
Altekar 5, 8-10, 19-20, 61-62, 124
Ambapali 38, 45
Ambika 72, 77, 82
Amitabha 97
Ananivarman 126
Ananta 73
Ancient Palestine 15
Andhra 101, 103, 130
Androcentric Literature 28
  society 42
  tradition 27
Anga 30, 71
Animal sacrifice 44
Annapurna 65, 81
Antahpuradhyakshas 113
Antahpuravergades 113
Antavamsikas 113
Anti-feminism 42, 46
Archaic Roman law 15
Arhat(s) 23, 29, 32, 34, 37, 39, 116, 118

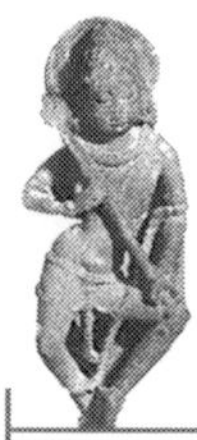

Arjuna 126, 131
Arthashastra 11, 113
Asamanta Jataka 43
Asandhimitta 112
Ashoka 28, 112-13
Assam 65, 81, 133
Astely, Ian 40
Asvamedha 60, 93, 122
Ayodhya 58-59, 61, 63-65
Ayodhya-Kanda 59
Ayagapatas (Tablets of homage) 116
Azam, Mohammad 96

Babb, L.A. 77
Bachofen, Johan 7
Baghelkhand 131
Bajaj, P.N. 100
Bala Kanda 60
Balzaretti, Ross 103
Bana 124
Banerjee, H.C. 99
Banskhera 124
Bartholomeusz 41
Barua, B.M. 113
Bay of Bengal 119
Benaras 81
Bengal 2, 119
Bhadda 30, 37-38
Bhagavat 123
Bhaillasvamin 133
Bharhut 114
Bhatta Duuli 129
Bhattacharji, Sukumari 9
Bhatta Skanda 125
Bhaumakara dynasty 128
Bhera Ghat Stone Inscription 127
Bhikhu Upali 32
Bhikkhuni(s) 28-29, 32, 34-37, 40-41, 115, 117, 135
Bhikkhuni Buddhamitra 115
Bhikkhuni Chanda 32
Bhikkhuni Dhanavati 115
Bhikshuni samgha 41
Bhilsa records 133
Bhima Kesava 97
Bhimbetka 16
Bhrikuti 97
Bhuyya 96, 98
Bilhari Stone Inscriptions 126
Bimbisara 31, 39, 43
Blackstone 29-30
Brahma 69, 71, 73
Brahmabandhu 31
Brahmani 71, 79
Brahmanical rituals 44
Brahmi 68
Bribe and Placation Policy 99
Brihat Samhita 90
Brockington, John 59, 62
Buddha 28, 30-32, 34-35, 37, 41-42, 44-46, 50, 97-98, 115, 118, 133
Buhler 116
Bundelkhand 131-32

Chandika 71-72, 77, 82, 132
Canonical literature 111
Chaityakuti 115
Chakravarman 91, 102
Chakravarti, Uma 18-19, 36, 40
Chalukyas 126
Chamunda 68, 71
Chanda 71
Chandala 91
Chandragupta 77, 119-23
Chandragupta II 121-23
Chandragupta-Kumaradevi 77, 93, 119-20
Chattopadhyaya, B.D. 9, 131-33
Chaturvidya brahmanas 123
Chedi 126-27, 133
Chhinda 125-26
China 1, 98
Chullasuttasoma Jataka 43
Chulukisvara 126

Church of Monza 103
Coburn 79
Control of property 21
Cosmic creation 69
Couburn 78

Dabok Inscription 133
Daksha 73
Damara Kosthesvara 94
Danapati 128
Dancing girl 18, 94
Danda 118
Das Mutterrecht 7
Dasharatha 59-60
Davids, Rhys 29
Deambi 102, 129
Deva 102, 129, 131
Devagupta 125
Devaluation of women 88
Devanampriya 112
Devapatti 126
Devi 48, 65-72, 75, 77-82, 93, 94, 101-03, 112-13, 129-30
Devi Mahatmya 65-70, 72, 77-82
Devika Rangachari 103, 129
Dewal Prasati of Lalla 125
Dhammadina 34, 38
Dhammakathika 38
Dhammapada 29
Dhar, M.K. 97
Dharmanika 102, 129
Dharmasutras 22-23
Dharmashastras 11-12, 22-23, 111
Dhavalappadeva 133
Dhruvaswamini 122
Dhyani Buddha 97
Di-Kshema 92
Dialectics of sex 22
Didda 87, 90, 92-103, 129-30
Diddamatha 96
Discus 70
Divakarasena 123-24
Divyavadana 118
Domba woman 91, 102
Domestic chores 20
Dominance of patriarchy 39
Draupadi 62
Druvadevi 122
Durga Saptashati 66
Durga/Kali 65, 72-74, 77, 79-80, 82, 127, 133
Durga Mahishasurmardini 72
Durga Puja featival 80

Fanthom, E. 8
Egyptian Pharaohs 22
England 2
Engles model 21
Eran stone inscription 122
Erotic tendencies 20
Escape from an existence 35
Exegetical texts 51

Falk, Nancy 35, 47
Female donors 114-16
Female patronage 97
Female potency 81
Female principle 66, 78
Feminism 1, 4, 6, 22, 36, 42, 46
Feminist research 88
Feminist work on Buddhism 45
First wave of feminism 4
Foley, Helene P. 8
France 2, 16
French Annales school 3
French Revolution 2
Funeral rites 21

Gahapati Uggaha 44
Gandi or Gandi Patha 66
Ganguly, D.K. 113
Ganapati 93, 102, 129
Gandhari 62
Ganesra 114

Ganga-Yamuna Doab 120
Ganika(s) 45, 118
Gauri 82, 133
Gayakarnadeva 127
Gender inequality 6, 44
Gender justice 143, 167
Gender relations 2, 9-12, 30, 79-80, 119
Gender transgression 102
Germany 2
Ghatavasini 130, 133
Ghatotkachchha 123
Goddess pilgrimage 80
Goddess Worship 65-66, 68
Gosvaminidevi 128
Grahavarmana 125
Greece 1, 8
Gross, Rita M 37, 40, 51
Gujarat 122
Gupta 9, 58, 64, 77, 93, 119-20, 123-25, 131
Gupta Lichchhavi alliance 119
Guwahati 65

Haihaiyas 126
Hanuman 63, 95
Hara 73, 127, 132
Harems 97, 113
Hargaravarman 133
Harivamsa 73
Harshavardhan 124, 125
Heretical religions 117
Heroines 40
Himalaya(s) 70-71, 80, 90, 124
Himavat 73
Hindu religion 20
Hinayana 40
Hiuen Tsang 124
Horner, I.B. 9, 34
Horse sacrifice ceremony 64
Humes, Cynthia Ann 81
Hussnain 95
Huvishka 115
Huyuk 17

Image of women as passive victims 45
Images of Women in Anquity 8
Immoral woman 60
Indra 8, 33, 50, 58, 70-72, 118
Indraji, Bhagwanlal 118
Indrani 68
Indus Valley 22
Industrial Revolutions 3
Institution of marriage 19-20

Jaina sect 37
Jainism 111, 115
Jaipur 81
Jaisawal, Suvira 9
Jallandhara 125
Jammu 81
Jataka kathas 42
Jaunsar Bhawar 125
Jayadevi 102
Jayasimhadeva 127
Jhelum 95
Jivaka Komaravaccha 118
Jivaloka Mahadevi 129
Jodhpur 65, 81
Johanson, Donald C. 17

Kadamba ruler 125
Kaikeyi 59-60, 62
Kaitabha 68-69
Kaivartadevi 127
Kakatiya dynasty 101, 103, 130
Kakutsthavarma 125
Kalama 94
Kalhana 90-91, 94-96, 100-02
Kali 48-50, 65, 77
Kalika 72
Kama Sutra 11
Kamakhya 65, 81
Kampen, N. 8
Kankanapura 96
Kanyakubja (Kannauj) 126
Kapur, M.L. 99, 101
Kartikeya 102, 129

Karttika 123
Karuvaki 112-13
Kashmir 87, 90-92, 94, 96, 99-104, 129-30
Kasi 30
Kassapa 37
Kathahahari-Jataka 43
Kathotia 16
Katyayini 71, 82
Kaumari 68, 71
Kauravaki 28
Kausalya 59, 62
Kausiki 71
Kausiki Katyayini 71
Kautilya's *Arthashastra* 113
Kayasthas 91
Keyuravarsha 126
Khalama (Kumara) 114
Kharwai 16
Khema 31-32, 39
Khoh copper plate inscription 131-32
King Bimbisara 31, 39
King Chakravarman 91
King Kalasa 94
Kinsley, David 77, 81
Kiskindha 58
Kissa Gautami 38
Koliyans 45
Kolkota 81
Konanda copper plates 127
Kosala 30, 128
Kosambi, D.D. 5, 9
Kota 90
Kothi Tirtha Baramulla 95
Krishna 70, 102, 129
Krtya 82
Kshatridevi 127
Kshema 92-94, 97-98, 101, 103, 125, 129
Kshemagupta 92-94, 97-98, 101, 103, 129
Kshemasiva 125
Kubera 71
Kubernaga 121, 123
Kumaon-Garhwal 124
Kumaradevi 77, 93, 119-20, 122-23
Kumaragupta 93
Kumaras 114, 132
Kumaraswamin 132
Kundalakesha 37
Kunti 62
Kuntala 122, 125
Kusa 64, 119
Kushana 58, 64, 114
Kushana – Gupta period 64
Kusumahara 128

Lahimi 126
Lakha Mandal 125
Lakshmana 58-59, 63-64
Lakshmi 126, 133
Lalla 125-26
Lanka 58, 61, 63
Lata 96, 127
Laukika era 102, 129
Lava 64
Leakey, Richard E. 17
Lerner, Gerda 10, 18
Lichchhavi(s) 120
Lidder 97
Lion 70-71, 77, 114
Local gender prejudices 42
Lohara 92, 99-100
Lohitya Sindhu 133
Lombard 103
Lord of Gods 102, 129

Madgali 131
Madhu 68-69
Madhuban copper plate of Harshavardhana 124
Madhusudan 69
Madhyadesa 96
Madhyama Carita 68, 70, 72

Magadha 22, 30-31, 120, 124
Magadha-Maurya states 22
Mahabharata 24, 62, 66, 69, 79, 90, 101
Mahadevi 119, 122, 128-29
Mahamatras 112
Mahamatya 71, 72, 113
Mahamaya 69, 82, 127
Mahaprajapati 38
Maharaja Sarvanatha 132
Maharajadhiraja 119-20
Maharajadhuja-Paramesvari 128
Maharashtra 2
Mahasenagupta 124
Maheshwari 68
Mahiman 95
Mahisasurmardini 72
Mahisasura 70-71
Mahisha 68, 70, 72
Mahayana 40, 47, 50
Maja (Kanistha) 114
Malava king 124
Malaysimha 133
Malwa 122
Mangala 133
Manheim, R. 7
Manu 23-24, 117
Manusmriti 11, 22-24
Marana 102, 129
Markandeya Purana 65, 68, 70, 72
Marriage alliances 136
Masculine appellation 102, 129
Masculinity 11, 88-89
Mathura 13, 73, 114-18, 122, 130
    stone inscription 122
"Matriarchal" features 15
Matriarchy 5, 17
Matrimonial alliance 104, 119, 120-22, 124
Mauryan Inscriptions 112
Mauryan queens 113
Maya 69, 79
Mayuta of Ahushana 125
Mc Clure, Laura K. 8
Men's monasticism 46
Mesolithic period 16
Migaramata 45
Migaramatupasada 45
Mill, James 10
Misogynous literature 42
Misogyny 27, 39, 44
Modern feminism 1
Moggallana 31
Monasteries of Lo-Yang 98
Morality of women 44
Mother goddess 16, 18, 67-66, 72, 131-33
Mother Queens 122
Motichandra 9
Mukharis 124
Multiple marriage 60
Munda 68, 71
Mysogynist literature 50
Myth and Reality 9
Myth religion and Mother's Right 7

Nada 118
Nagadatta 125
Nanda 71
Nandagopa 71
Nandasi Akasa 114
Nandigupta 97
Nandutara 37-38
Narasimhi 71
Narasinhadeva 127
Naravahana 93-95
Narmada 127
Nettabhanja 127, 129
Neumann 29
Nibbana 29, 33
Nishumbha 68, 70-71
Nitya 82
Nohala 126

Orissa 103, 127-28, 130

Padmapani 97
Padmavati 112
Pala Period 126
Pali canon 34, 45
Pandit, R.S. 87
Paramabhattarika 128
Paramara Purnapala 126
Paramavaishnavi 128
Parameshwari 82
Parbatiya Plates of Uanamalavarmadeva 133
Parinirvana 51
Parvati 71, 82, 90, 125
Patacara 32, 33, 34, 38
Patañjali's *Yogasūtras* 24
Patliputra 113, 119-20
Patriarchal dominance 91
Patriarchal gender hierarchy 39
Patriarchal societies 42, 46, 48
Patriarchal value system vi, 27
Patrilineal ideology 104
Patrilineal orthodoxy 104
Physical aspect of womanhood 61
Pillar Edict VII 113
Pinchman 81
Pinkham 8
Pisan, Christine de 1
Plato's philosophy 39
Politico-religious milieus 58
Polyandry 90
Polygamy 43, 60, 113
Pomeroy, Sarah 8
Poona copper plate 123-24
Poonch 100
Post-Altekerian tradition v
Post-Mauryan Literature 64
Potter's wheel 17
Prabhakaravardhana 125
Prabhavati 122-24
Prabhavatigupta 123
Prakrit 78-79, 82, 91
Prakriti 78-79, 82
Prasenajit 43
Prataprudra Caritramu 93
Pre-Aryan cultures 81
Pre-gender society 16
Princess Isvara 125
Prisoners of gender 2
Prithvimahadevi 128
Prithvipala 99
Prithvisena 122
Property rights 6-7, 9
Pravarika 115
Punjab 125
Punna 30-31
Purana(s) 48, 65-68, 70-72, 79, 130
Purva Carita 68, 69, 72
Pushyabhutis 124

Queen Alhanadevi 127
Queen Dattadevi 122
Queen Didda 87, 94, 98, 101-02, 129
Queen Karuvaki 112-13
Queen's Pillar Edict 112

Rabani, G.M. 93, 101
Rajabhanjadeva 127
Rajagriha 118
Rajanaka 95
Rajapuri 99
Rajasthan 73, 132
Rajouri 96, 99
Rajtarangini 87, 90, 92, 95, 97-98, 100, 103-04, 129
Rajyasri 124-25
Raktabija 68, 77
Rama 58-65
Ramanujam, A.R. 77
Ramayana 57-59, 61-64, 66
Ravana 58, 61-63
Ray, H.C. 99
Razia Sultan 94, 103, 130
Reflections on Women in Antiquity 8
Regenerating ability 17

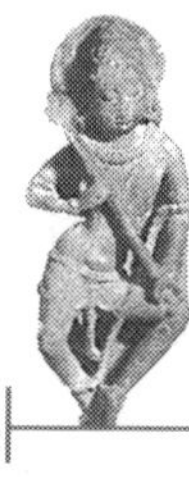

Religious donations 114-16
Rig Veda 19, 21, 77
Role of the State 22
Role of widows 4, 10
Roy, Kumkum 9, 13, 39, 98
Royal patronage 97, 115
Rishi Medhas 68
Rudrama Devi 93-94, 101, 103
Rudrasen II 122
Rudrasena II 122-23
Rules of Conduct 32
Russellkonda Plates of Nettabhanya 127

Sabdasiva 126
Sachia Mata temple 65, 81
sacred traditions 100
sage Isvarasiva 126
sage Vasistha 126
Shaiva 93
Shaivism 122
Saka-Kushana Period 114, 119
Saketa 120
Sakula 38
Sakyamuni 41
Samadhi 68
samgha of the almswomen 38
Samkhya philosophy 67
Samoli inscription 132
Samudragupta 93, 120-23
Sanchi 13, 47, 114
Sangramaraja 99-100, 102, 129
Sanika 131
Sankalia, H.D. 58
Sanskrit 20, 22, 57, 66-68, 77, 79, 87, 90-91, 127-28, 131
Saptashati 66, 68
Saravasti 126
Sarayū river 64
Sariputra 30
Sarnath 115
Sarthavahini(s) 114, 116
Sasaram 81
Satrap Rajula 114
Satyavrat 59
Saurashtra 96, 122
Savatthi 32
Savitri 59-60, 125
Sax, William 80
Schopen, Gregory 47-48
Scott, J.W. 89
Schreiner, Olive 2
Search for enlightenment 35
Sexual drive 50
Shakta Tantras 57
Shah, Kirit K. 12-13, 116
Shakti 66-67, 69, 71-72, 77, 79, 81-82, 131
Shapiro, H. 8
Shandhaka 131
Sharma, R.S. 9
Shrimali, K.M. 12
Shumbha 68, 70-71
Sidhesvara Caritramu 93
Silhana 101
Sindhu 96, 133
Singhapura rajya 125
Singh, Upinder 13
Sircar, D.C. 92, 124
Sirshagrama 123
Sita 57-65, 78
Sitabhanjadeva 127
Shiva 69-71, 73, 75, 78, 82, 90, 125-27, 132-33
Shivaduti 82
Skanda 70-71, 125
Smritis 23
Social prejudices 46
South East Asia 48
Sovanikara (goldsmith) 115
Sponberg, Allan 39
Shravasti 116
Sri Chanragupta 125
Srinagar 95-97, 99, 102
Srinivas, M.N. 6
Stein, M.A. 87
Stridhana 23

Strirajya 90
Stryadhyaska Mahamattas 113
Sugandha 90, 98, 101, 102
Sumangala 36, 127
Sumedha 35-36
Sundari 38
Sunder Kanda 60
Supratishtha 123
Suratha 68
Surya 71
Suryamati 90
Svetambara order 117

T'ang 98
Talbot, Cynthia 101, 103, 130
Tara 97, 133
Tarachandi 81
Testament of Shakta philosphy 67
Thapar, Romila 5, 28, 112
The canonical texts 27
The Case of Vanishing Nun 47
The City of the Ladies 1
the power of patriarchy 23
The Status of Women in Hindu India 8
Theodelinda 103
Theravadin literature 51
Therigatha 11, 27-30, 34-40
Tissarakkha 112
Tribhuvana 97, 128
Tribhuvanmahadevi 128
Trident 50, 70-71
Tripathi, L.K. 13
Tripathi, R.S. 119
Tripitaka 115
Tse-T'ien 98
Tunga 98-100, 102, 126-29
Turkey 17

Udayana 43
Udayaraja 99
Unmattasimha 128
Upanishads 66
Uppalavanna 31
Uttara Carita 68, 72
Uttara II 32
Uttara Kanda 63
Uttara-kula 135
Uttaradisa 98
Utthuka Khandakshetra 128

Vagambhrini Sukta 66
Vaisali 120
Vaishnavi 68, 71
Vaishno Devi 65, 81
Vajji 30
Vak 66, 130
Vakatakas 122-23
Vakdevi 130
Vani 130
Varahi 71
Varanasi 65
Vardhamana 116
Vardhana empire 125
Vardhana-Magadha alliance 124
Varahamihira 90
Varahi 68
Varna-Jati order 91
Varnas 113
Vasa 118
Vashistha 59
Vatayakshini 130
Vedas 22, 66
Verma, Chapla 41
Verses of the Elder Nuns 28, 33
Vibhishana 63
Vigraharaja 98, 126
Vijaya 10, 32, 133
Vilavanaka 123
Vimala 38
Vinaya 32, 38, 45-46, 48
Vinaya Vatthu 45
Vindhyachal 81
Vindhyavasini 70-71, 81
Virtuous woman 60
Vishakha 45

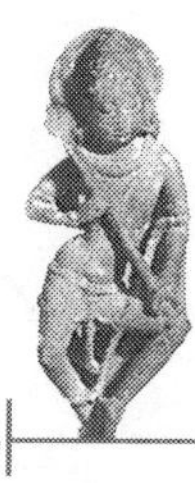

Vishnu 69-71, 73, 75, 78, 82, 91, 96-97, 126
Vishnuhasi 126
Vishnumaya 82
Vishakha 35
Vishwakarma 71
Vitasta 96
Volga 97

Walter, Jonathan 47
Welson, Liz 47
Witchcraft 97
Wolf, Margery 38
Woman-hater (anitthigandha) 42
Women slaves 19
Women's Life in Greece and Rome 8
Women's monasticism 46
Women's movement 2-3
Women's sexuality 18
Women's studies 3
World of Courtesans 9

Yadava, B.N.S. 102
Yasoda 71
Yasodhara 95
Yasovati 90
Yasovridddhi 128
Yijing, Chinese monk 47
Yoganidra 69, 82
Yuddha Kanda 62